12188527

W9-BCV-812

WITHDRAWN
NDSU

Collection Assessment Manual for College and University Libraries

Collection Assessment Manual for College and University Libraries

By Blaine H. Hall

ORYX PRESS
1985

The rare Arabian Oryx is believed to have inspired the myth of the unicorn. This desert antelope became virtually extinct in the early 1960s. At that time several groups of international conservationists arranged to have 9 animals sent to the Phoenix Zoo to be the nucleus of a captive breeding herd. Today the Oryx population is over 400 and herds have been returned to reserves in Israel, Jordan, and Oman.

Copyright © 1985 by
The Oryx Press
2214 North Central at Encanto
Phoenix, Arizona 85004-1483

Published simultaneously in Canada

Library of Congress Cataloging-in-Publication Data

Hall, Blaine H.
  Collection assessment manual for college and university libraries.

  Bibliography: p.
  Includes index.
    1. Libraries, University and college—Collection development.   2. Libraries, University and college—Evaluation.   I. Title.
  Z687.H35   1985   025.2'1877   85-13694
  ISBN 0-89774-148-X

Z
687
H35
1985

Contents

Preface

Regular, systematic collection assessments are essential to a well-managed collection development program. Assessments, when carefully planned and carried out, can tell you how well you are meeting your collection goals and the collection needs of your patrons. Assessing library collections, however, can be complex, requiring a variety of tools and a certain amount of expertise. This manual can help even the most inexperienced assessor plan an assessment, select and apply appropriate measurement techniques, analyze the results, and report the findings.

The principles and techniques recommended here have been drawn from the voluminous literature on collection evaluation. I have particularly relied on surveys of the literature by Bonn (1974), Lancaster (1977), Mosher (1984), and Wiemers et al. (1984) as well as the ALA "Guidelines for the Evaluation of the Effectiveness of Library Collections" (1979). I have also found the Association of Research Libraries (ARL) *Collection Analysis Project Manual* (1977) valuable for a number of useful measurement techniques.

Throughout this manual, in what can be only partial recognition of my indebtedness, are the names of those whose ideas and assessment techniques I have used. The bibliography in Appendix A lists all of these individuals as well as additional useful sources under one of 3 headings: Sources Cited, Surveys and Reviews of the Literature, and Supplementary Sources. Consult these works for more detailed information on the specific techniques or for information on techniques not included here.

The assessment techniques and measures in this manual were selected for their practicality. All of them can be used by any librarian willing to put forth the effort, time, and resources required to implement them. A few of the measures require data from previous years that may not be available in your library, but you can begin keeping such information for future assessments now. Collection evaluation should be a continuing process, not an occasional activity.

This is a training manual, not merely a procedures manual. It gives not only practical techniques and procedures for assessment, but also the broader rationale, explanation, and discussion necessary for professional librarians to develop tailor-made evaluation programs to meet a variety of specific assessment objectives. While the focus of this manual is on assessments in academic libraries, most of the principles and techniques can be used or adapted for almost any library. In fact, many of the measures recommended were originally developed, tested, and applied in nonacademic libraries.

This manual does not specifically deal with the assessment of nonbook materials such as microforms, computer software, realia, phonodiscs and tapes, films, slides, manuscripts, or archival material. For one reason, little or nothing has been published on such assessments. But most important, many of the measurement techniques used for print materials can be adapted to these other formats as well. It is not so much the format of the material that determines how these collections should be measured as it is the purposes and objectives for which they are being collected.

Blaine H. Hall

Collection Assessment Manual for College and University Libraries

Chapter 1
Planning the Assessment

Only through careful planning can your collection assessment be systematic and thorough enough to produce accurate and reliable data. In planning such an assessment, keep in mind

- Assessments should be conducted to obtain data for more effective collection development decisions.
- Assessments should consider how well collections are meeting the needs of users, both present and potential.
- Assessments must be based on a current, clearly stated collection development policy statement for the collection being assessed.
- Clear-cut, written objectives or outcomes to be achieved by the assessment must be stated.
- Subjectivity of judgment as to collection quality or adequacy can be reduced by a careful selection of both collection-centered and client-centered measurement techniques.

Libraries will vary considerably in their objectives for a collection assessment program, but, generally, they will want (1) to evaluate the success of their previous collection efforts, (2) to monitor their ongoing collection program, and (3) to provide empirical data for establishing priorities and allocating their resources to achieve collection goals and objectives. If your library has no overall assessment program, encourage library management to develop one or try to come up with your own long-range program. This is especially important in larger libraries where numerous collections may need to be assessed.

PROCEDURE

Select the collection or part of the collection to be assessed. In making your selection consider

- The size of the collection and the time and resources available to perform the assessment.

- Faculty or department interested in the collection.
- Accreditation requirements of a department or college.
- Growing, declining, or changing curricula and research programs.
- Complaints or suggestions about collections from users.
- An awareness of problems or concerns about a collection.
- Commitments to consortia.
- Your long-range assessment plan.
- Budgetary considerations.

Once this step is complete, review the collection policy statement for the collection you plan to assess. The review should ensure that policy statements reflect the current status of the following:

- The collecting level for the collection.
- Curricular and research programs served by the collection.
- Types and academic levels of materials to be acquired.
- Language, chronological periods, and geographical focus of materials to be acquired.
- Degree of overlap or cross-disciplinary use of the collection.
- Any cooperative agreements that might significantly affect the collecting level.

This policy review is important because the data obtained from collection measurements can only be interpreted in terms of the collection purposes. Keep in mind, also, that while one purpose of your assessment may be to provide data to help review the collection policy statement, this does not eliminate the need to begin the assessment with as clear and current a policy as possible.

Next, determine the objectives to be achieved by the assessment. The objectives for a collection assessment may vary considerably from librarian to librarian or collection to collection, depending on

- The time available.
- The size of the collection.
- The time elapsed since an earlier assessment.
- The purpose of the assessment (accreditation, changes in the curriculum or research needs, or justification of budget allocations).
- The kind of information needed about the collection or its use by patrons.

Always put your objectives in writing so you know what kinds of information you will need to obtain. Knowing this, you can more purposefully select the measurement techniques and plan their application to provide the needed data. Begin with a single general overall objective to give a broad focus to your project. Here are some examples:

- To learn more about the strengths and weaknesses of the library science collection.
- To provide information on which to build plans and specific recommendations to improve the library support for the Organic Chemistry Collection.
- To obtain data for revising the collection development policy statement for the Science Fiction Collection.

For an overall assessment of a collection, a general statement, such as those listed above, would be adequate. But such a statement should be analyzed into several specific subquestions to give more precise direction in planning and conducting the assessment. Extra time spent in clearly defining and stating exactly what specific questions you want your assessment to answer will make your work more purposeful and efficient and more likely to produce the desired results. Here is an example.

Overall Objective:

To determine the strengths and weaknesses of the Cinematic Arts Collection.

Specific Questions:

1. What is the gross size of the collection?
2. Is it growing at an acceptable rate?
3. How does the collection compare to standard bibliographies on the subject?
4. How adequate is the journal collection to meet patron demands?
5. Is the blanket order profile providing optimum coverage of appropriate current materials?
6. Is the collection sufficiently available and accessible to patrons?
7. Is the collection appropriate and adequate for the curriculum it supports?
8. Are any changes anticipated in the curriculum or research programs supported by the collection that would require changes in the collection development policy?
9. Are sufficient copies of heavily used titles available?
10. Is the reference collection adequate?

This example shows only a few of the possible questions that could be asked to provide a more precise statement of your assessment objectives. Obviously, a thorough assessment of a collection will require more questions than a limited assessment. You may only need or want to measure a few aspects of a collection: the adequacy or quality of the reference books, the use of journals, the adequacy of primary works of a literary author, the shelf accessibility, or the opinions of users about their needs and the library support of those needs. But whatever your purpose, state it precisely with the specific questions you want to answer about the collection. Next, select the best measurement technique(s) for gathering the information needed to answer each question. Since the remainder of this manual provides specific information about the various measurement techniques and the procedures to apply them, this discussion will only treat a few general considerations in selecting the most appropriate techniques.

Each measurement technique has been developed to obtain certain kinds of information, so your selection must be based on the specific questions you want to answer. A shelflist measurement, for instance, can help you determine the gross size of the collection, but it cannot show you how accessible the collection is to patrons or how current and up-to-date the collection is. Nor does it tell you how good the collection is, even though we often assume that bigger is better. If your purpose is to measure the quality of the collection, you will need to select other techniques, although gross size may be a good place to begin.

The important caution to remember in selecting measuring techniques is to be certain that they are reliable and valid for producing the kind of information required. When possible, try to use both collection-centered and client-centered methods that can provide a check against each other. A large gross size and a high percentage of items listed in standard bibliographies, for instance, may give the impression that the collection is in line with user demands. But client-centered measures, such as circulation data and availability studies, may show otherwise.

Conducting collection assessments can be time-consuming and may need to be carried out over an extended period of time to acquire reliable data. This will require a commitment of sufficient professional and clerical staff to perform the various measurement functions. For this reason, an important part of assessment planning is to estimate the resources required. In addition to staff, you may also need access to computer hardware and software, terminals for searching online databases, and the cooperation of other library staff and departments to provide required information. For this reason, you should try to estimate as accurately as possible the amount of staff, time, and equipment or other facilities you will need.

Table 1.1 is the beginning of an estimation table to help you do this. Your own experience or local circumstances may differ, however, and should take precedence. Your experience should also help you expand the table for other assessment functions.

TABLE 1.1. Estimation Table

Activity	Staff	Time
1. Card Catalog Checking	Clerical	50 items per hour
2. Compiling sample title list	Prof/Clerical	300 items, 15 hours
3. MAC-DEL Test	Prof/Clerical	15 minutes per day
4. MAC-SIM Test	Prof/Clerical	5 to 10 hours
5. Availability Test	Prof/Clerical	50 hours
6. Document Delivery Test	Prof/Clerical	4 to 10 hours
7.		
8.		
9.		
10.		

To help you implement the 6 planning suggestions mentioned above, complete the Assessment Planning Form (Figure 1.1). If your library requires you to submit a written proposal for approval before beginning an assessment, this form may suffice.

FIGURE 1.1. Assessment Planning Form

Name ——————————— Application date ————————————

Collection to be assessed ————————————————————————

Proposed start date ————— Proposed completion date —————————

A. Overall objective to be achieved by the assessment.

B. Specific questions to be answered about the collection.

FIGURE 1.1. Assessment Planning Form (continued)

C. Measurement techniques to be used. Include a statement as to what each will contribute to the objective.

1. Collection-Centered Techniques:

2. Client-Centered Techniques:

D. Estimate of resources needed.

1. Staff:

2. Time (specify in hours):

3. Equipment, Supplies, Facilities:

(Use additional pages if necessary.)

Chapter 2
Collection-Centered Measures

Numerous measuring techniques have been developed to conduct collection assessments. Some measure the collection against ideals or standards; others rely on counting or other mathematical and statistical computations; and still others focus on actual patron use of collections or their perceptions of how adequately collections serve their needs. All of these methods can furnish useful data for evaluation, but no one technique is sufficient in itself for conducting a thorough assessment, although a single method may be adequate for a limited assessment objective. Collection assessments can utilize either collection-centered or client-centered methods, but a thorough assessment will use some of both. This chapter examines the collection-centered techniques: compiling statistics, checking lists, direct observation, and applying standards.

COMPILING STATISTICS

The most frequently used assessment techniques have been those involving counting, presumably based on the premise that the size of a collection is correlated with its quality. But this is not always true. A carefully selected and weeded collection of 5,000 titles on a given subject, for instance, may be superior to a 10,000-volume collection not so carefully managed. In research libraries, however, the larger the collection, the more patron demands it will likely be able to meet. The mathematical and statistical measures usually used are

- Gross size.
- Volumes added per year.
- Unfilled requests.
- Formulas.
- Percent of growth.
- Interlibrary loans.
- Expenditures.
- Circulation.

Most formulas, however, have been developed for total libraries and not for individual subject collections. As a result, they are not included in this manual. Also, circulation statistics are client-oriented and are covered in Chapter 3, "Client-Centered Measures." Which of the others you can use depends on the existence of adequate records broken into sufficient detail to apply them to evaluating a specific subject collection. Libraries with automated systems that provide statistical data should be able to extract the necessary information relatively easily; almost all libraries will be able to obtain or calculate gross size, volumes added per year, and percent of growth data from manual counts and measures, from computer systems, or from combinations of both.

There are both advantages and disadvantages in using numerical and statistical data. Among the advantages are that they

- Are often readily available.
- Are easily kept or extracted from automated systems.
- Lend themselves to comparisons with other libraries or to internal comparisons over time.
- Can help eliminate subjectivity.

The disadvantages are that

- The counting may be inaccurate because of improper recording or inadequate definitions of the categories or units to be counted.
- The significance of the figures may be difficult to interpret in terms of judging collection quality.
- The data from one library may not be comparable with those from other libraries or even within the same library over time.

Gross Size

Gross size consists of obtaining title counts from an automated cataloging system or measuring the shelflist to determine the number of titles acquired by the library. Depending, of course, on your library's practice, counts may be made of the total holdings of the library, holdings in given subjects, holdings in specialized collections (Victorian Literature, Juvenile, etc.), or holdings of specific types of materials (periodicals, microforms, etc.) in total or by subject.

Measuring the shelflist is a relatively simple, straightforward process, but don't overlook some potential problems. In measuring the shelflist in libraries with materials classified in both Dewey and Library of Congress classification systems, it may be difficult to make comparable subject breakdowns since no satisfactory comparative schedules for the 2 systems are yet available.

Libraries with completely automated shelflists should be able to extract holdings information by subject classifications directly from the computer and won't need to measure the shelflist. But those libraries with only part of their collections on automated systems will have to combine automated and physical counts to obtain holdings information. It is important to remember that when you combine holdings data from more than one method of measuring, you must be certain that the units are comparable, i.e., volumes with volumes or titles with titles. You cannot combine counts of volumes and titles into one figure—this may cause a serious problem if you try to combine shelflist counts (titles) with cataloging counts (volumes) to obtain gross size or to calculate growth rate statistics. Also, the subject breakdown of cataloging counts may not be detailed enough to give data on narrow subjects.

But if you can avoid or overcome these potential problems, the shelflist measurement or the combination of the shelflist measurement and the automated shelflist statistics will give you an indication of the gross size of your collection, a useful beginning measure for the collection assessment.

Procedure

Since the assorted automated systems vary in the way statistical data can be extracted, you will need to use whatever method is required for your system. The shelflist measurement described here is for manually measuring a card-file shelflist.

1. Determine all shelflists applicable to the collection you are assessing.
2. With a retractable metal ruler, measure the total number of inches of tightly packed cards in each drawer of the shelflist(s) for the call numbers covering the collection being assessed. Do not measure the length of the drawer itself. Measure the cards from the sides rather than on the top to avoid having to contend with tabs or guide cards. Exert the same amount of pressure each time you measure to ensure the greatest accuracy.
3. Record the total number of inches and multiply that number by the number of cards per inch. Since card stock varies in thickness and since some shelflists, particularly for collections requiring extensive bibliographic description, may use more than one card per

title, determine the average number of cards per inch and the average number of cards per title for the files in your library. (See Appendix B, ''Statistical Aids,'' for instructions on how to do this.)
4. Try to obtain counts of any uncataloged collections related to the collection being assessed.

Analysis and Interpretation of Data

Probably the greatest value of gross size figures is that they can be used for comparisons with other libraries or with the same library for longitudinal studies over time. If your library uses the Library of Congress classification system, you can compare your counts with the latest edition of the *Titles Classified by the Library of Congress Classification: National Shelflist Count*. Future counts now planned by a number of libraries for every 3 years may provide comparative LC-to-Dewey conversion tables, but none are currently available. Such a comparison with a collection of known quality can give a rough quantitative indication of the quality of your collection.

Generally, there is a positive correlation between the size of a library collection and its ability to meet the needs of patrons, providing, of course, that the collection is appropriate for the patrons served and that it is continuing to grow. However, by itself, the number of titles in a collection is only a rough measure of quality, not a guarantee. Other measures must be used to ensure an accurate assessment of quality.

Another application of gross size data, when you can determine the number of possible users of a given collection, is to calculate the number of titles per capita if this is necessary or useful to your assessment objectives.

Once you have measured the shelflist, subsequent assessments will require only growth figures for the years since the initial count, if you can obtain data for comparable items (i.e., volumes or titles) from an automated system or other source. These figures can be added to the initial shelflist count figures. If your library shelflist is fully automated, it should be easy to obtain the latest cumulative data.

Volumes Added and Percent of Growth

It is generally agreed that the straight count of volumes or titles added per year is a more reliable indicator of collection quality than the percent of growth. The latter approach penalizes libraries with active weeding programs, yet their collections may be superior to those not carefully and consistently pruned of obsolete titles. If the subject breakdown of cataloging counts of volumes or titles cataloged annually fits the collection being assessed, this is a good source of data. But in figuring the percentage of growth, don't forget that a shelflist count by title cannot be compared with cataloging counts by volumes. The best source of items added would be an automated cataloging system, such as WLN, OCLC, RLIN, or a local automated cataloging system.

Procedure

To determine the volumes added per year, you merely obtain the figures cataloged or acquired. The cataloging figures will not include any uncataloged collections, and you may want to use acquisitions figures instead or combine counts of cataloged and uncataloged collections for an annual total.

To calculate the percent of growth, divide the number of titles or volumes added by the number of titles or volumes in the collection.

EXAMPLE

$$\frac{\text{Titles Added}}{\text{Titles in Collection}} = \frac{85}{2750} = .03\%$$

Analysis and Interpretation of Data

The rate of growth, like the shelflist count, can only be interpreted with a knowledge and understanding of local factors. And, as noted earlier, the actual number of volumes added may be more indicative of growth than the percentage, particularly if you have weeded the collection.

If it were possible to obtain exact figures on the number of titles published each year that should have been acquired by your library, you could calculate the percentage of titles acquired to show how well you are keeping up with new materials. Unfortunately, this information is difficult to find. Some very gross approximations could be made from Baker & Taylor's *Directions,* the *Cumulative Book Index, American Book Publishing Record, British National Bibliography, Deutsche Bibliographie, Le Livres de L'Annee-Biblio,* and similar publications if the subject categories in these sources are adequate.

However, the availability studies discussed in Chapter 3, "Client-Centered Measures," and the list-checking measure in this chapter can provide better indications of how well your library is doing in acquiring recent publications.

Expenditures

Expenditures data are important to collection assessments, but too often they are considered in isolation from other relevant data. Although some libraries have attempted to use cost-benefit analysis to evaluate library expenditures, more can be done by most libraries to use expenditures data in evaluating collections and collection support.

With automated acquisitions systems set up by subject account codes, expenditure data by subject can be correlated to holdings and circulation data to determine the appropriateness of budget allocations. You can also add other variables, such as average book prices and the number of potential patrons served by the collection, to arrive at an even finer-tuned picture of the relationship of expenditures to apparent needs. Figure 2.1 illustrates a graphic model of such a collection development profile comparing 3 variables—expenditures, holdings, and circulation by LC classification. You could also illustrate these same relationships with a bar graph. A computer graphics program can readily plot the data in either format, or it can be created manually. The important consideration is not the graphic representation but the correlation of the data as part of your assessment.

FIGURE 2.1. Collection Development Profile

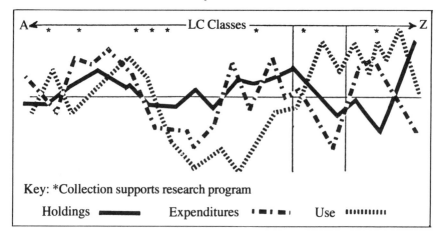

Key: *Collection supports research program

Holdings ━━━━ Expenditures ▪■▪■▪ Use ▮▮▮▮▮▮▮▮▮

This model covers the full spectrum of subject classifications. A similar profile can be developed for individual subjects over time to show trends in expenditures, growth rates, and use to obtain an ongoing picture of the relationship between expenditures for a collection and other relevant factors that would be useful in evaluating budget allocations.

Analysis and Interpretation of Data

By analyzing these graphic representations, you can identify areas of the collection where holdings and current-year acquisitions seem disproportionately high or low compared to the amount of use shown by the circulation statistics. Such apparent imbalances indicate possible problems that need to be investigated. Heavy research support, higher-than-average costs of materials, or one-time major purchases might require holdings or expenditures higher than the use figures would indicate. Only your knowledge of the collection and its purposes can tell you whether or not expenditures are out of line.

Unfilled and ILL Requests

If your library keeps records of patron requests for materials you are not able to supply or interlibrary loan requests, you can use that data in evaluating a subject collection. The information can be used along with other use data to measure the overall use a subject collection receives. It can also provide specific titles for creating lists of items you want to add to the collection.

Procedure

In using ILL and unfilled requests for evaluating a subject collection, you should do the following:

1. Categorize these records by subject and date.
2. Count the requests for desired time periods.
3. Total all of the requests.

Analysis and Interpretation of Data

These figures can be added to other use statistics to determine total use. Or, if you are creating want lists, you will need to look at specific titles and decide which of these you want to add to your collection. These decisions should, of course, be based on your collection development policies. Additionally, for journals, you may require a certain number of requests in a specified period of time before you decide to make the long-term financial commitment required for a periodical subscription.

CHECKING LISTS

List checking has long been used to measure the quality of library collections. In many research libraries, it has often been the major, if not the sole, measure used. List checking essentially assesses a collection in relation to what is published independent of immediate demand, availability, or use. So long as you can precisely delineate the curriculum and research support provided by the specific collection you are assessing and then select appropriate lists, this technique is one of the best for determining collection quality.

Advantages and Disadvantages

In making your decision to use this measure, consider the following advantages:

- A variety of published lists are available—comprehensive, specialized, popular, general, or research.
- Many such lists are backed by the authority and competence of expert librarians and specialists.
- Many lists are updated regularly to take into account the currently published materials.
- Lists can be compiled to fit the needs of an individual library or type of library.
- The procedure of searching lists is easy to apply, although the process can be time-consuming.

The disadvantages are these:

- Available lists may have been used previously as buying guides for the library being evaluated.
- Lists can be biased toward the viewpoint of the compiler or a group.
- Lists, even if appropriate for the subjects to be evaluated, may not reflect the interests, collection levels, or other purposes of your library.
- Many lists are not revised and become out of date.
- Lists may not be as representative of the library's subjects or purposes as its holdings are.
- Lists may be hard to find or compile for some subjects.

Types of Lists

Many types of lists of value in assessments are available, or you can develop lists for specific needs, albeit not without a great deal of time and effort. The following kinds of lists (with an example of each) have proven useful. Choose specific lists suitable for the collection you are assessing with care. The value of the results can be no better than the appropriateness of your choice.

- Standard bibliographies or basic lists (ALA. *Books for College Libraries*, 1975).
- Printed library catalogs (Eastman School of Music. Sibley *Music Library Catalog of Sound Recordings*, 1975).
- Specialized bibliographies: persons (Smith. *A Classified Shakespeare Bibliography*, 1963); subjects (Rehrauer. *The Macmillan Film Bibliography*, 1982); time periods (Cioranescu. *Bibliographie de la Litterature Francaise du Dix Septieme Siecle*, 1965).
- Current or retrospective publishers' lists (*American Book Publishing Record*, 1965–. Monthly with annual cumulations).
- Lists of reference works and bibliographic guides (Sheehy. *Guide to Reference Books*, 1976).
- Lists of periodicals (Modern Language Association. *MLA Directory of Periodicals*, 1984).
- Authorized lists from government or professional associations (UNESCO. *Bibliografia General de la Literatura Latinoamericana*, 1972).
- Published acquisitions lists from other libraries (Library of Congress. *Handbook of Latin American Studies*, 1935–. Annual).
- Literature surveys for various disciplines (Hoffmann. ''Survey of German Research Tool Needs.'' *Monatshefte* 70 [1978], 239–53).
- Citations from bibliographies and basic texts in a discipline (Dorson. *Folklore and Folklife*, 1972).
- Citation index lists (Garfield. *SCI Journal Citation Reports*, 1978–. Annual).

Procedure

1. Know the literature of the field you are assessing. An encyclopedia article, a review article, an annual review or year's work publication, or chapter(s) in basic texts can help you become knowledgeable if you have not had time to read the major subject journals regularly or to do constant reading in the field. For some subjects, specific manuals on how to develop a library collection for that discipline are available. These are often not only useful lists for checking but contain very

basic bibliographies of materials recommended for developing the librarian's expertise.

2. Select the best type of list(s) that will meet your assessment objectives.

3. Select the specific list(s) to check. You may want to discuss this with knowledgeable faculty members and obtain their suggestions. It is important that you search thoroughly to find the best possible lists against which to evaluate the collection. The quality of your assessment will be no higher than the appropriateness of the lists you choose.

4. Determine the extent of the checking required to give the desired results. For a given assessment objective, you may not need to check every section of a list or bibliography. Choose only those that are appropriate to the collection being assessed. (What you are doing is creating a weighted sample.) You can either check every title in your list or check only a sample.

   a. A complete check of the titles in the list(s) chosen may be desirable or necessary. If your list is a bibliographic essay in *Library Trends* or some other journal listing 80 items, you would not want to check fewer. But if your list contains 4,000 entries, you might want to do a sampling, depending on the amount of time and the thoroughness of the assessment intended. If you are checking to determine titles you should purchase, you would have to do a complete check. It takes a little over one minute to check a title in a card catalog from an alphabetized list, longer if the titles are arranged in some other way. Checking against an online list would be much faster.

   b. A random sample may be preferable if the bibliography is extensive and you are assessing to determine general adequacy rather than trying to develop a buying list. Sampling is suggested also if you want to determine which areas of a collection need more complete checking. Using a random number and sample size table (see Appendix B, ''Statistical Aids'') will help you obtain a statistically valid and reliable sample.

5. Check the list against holdings in the card catalog or in an online cataloging system. Use the most efficient method possible.

   a. An alphabetical method is the most efficient way to check a list against the card catalog since it avoids a lot of running back and forth. But if the effort to alphabetize the list takes too much time, then another method can be used.

   b. Each item can be checked in the order it appears in the list. If the list is short and not easily alphabetized, such as in a bibliographic essay, this is the best method.

c. If a lengthy bibliography contains several chapters or sections, items can be batched by checking all the A's in each chapter before going to the B's.

d. Search an online system with the most efficient approach, either by author or title, whichever is faster.

Whatever method you use, decide how the bibliography will be marked to indicate items in the collection. Will a check mark do, or do you need to write in the call number? Always write small but legibly and always in pencil. Ink cannot be erased easily and will sometimes smudge. If you are not doing the checking yourself, observe your assistants periodically to see that they are doing the checking efficiently. At best, list checking is a time-consuming process that you should make as efficient as possible.

Analysis and Interpretation of Data

The results of list checking can best be shown by using a tabular display similar to that illustrated in Table 2.1. The sections of the bibliography, the number of items in the bibliography, the number in the library, and a percentage column are typically used.

TABLE 2.1. Results of General Linguistics Survey

Section of Bibliography	Total Entries	Penrose Library	Percentage
Abbreviations	3	3	100
Directories	2	2	100
Bibliographies	27	15	56
Abstracts and Indexes	17	13	77
Dictionaries and Glossaries	32	25	78
Encyclopedia of Linguistics	1	1	100
Periodicals	27	14	52
Theory and Philosophy	68	57	84
History	4	3	75
TOTAL	181	133	73

Source: A. K. Wawrzysko, *Bibliography of General Linguistics.* (Archon Books, 1971).

The results of list checking are usually expressed as percentages. But neither the data nor the percentages say anything specific about the quality or adequacy of the collection. This requires an interpretation in terms of

• The objectives of the collection.

- The development level established for the collection.
- A breakdown of the collection into types of resources.

You might need such categories as

- Primary Sources
- Secondary Sources
- Reference Books
- Indexes
- Periodicals
- Others

You might also want an analysis by such subject areas as

- History of Chemistry
- Organic Chemistry
- Inorganic Chemistry
- Applied Chemistry
- Others

Generally, these areas should have been determined as you planned your assessment.

DIRECT OBSERVATION OF COLLECTIONS

This technique evaluates the collection through a visual inspection conducted by one or more experts—faculty subject specialists, scholars, librarians, or consultants. The examination may reveal size, scope, depth, and significance of the collection, recentness of material, physical condition (denoting level of use or nonuse), and the general atmosphere of the stack area.

Advantages and Disadvantages

There are certain advantages and disadvantages to using this technique:

- It can quickly reveal size, scope, and quality of the collection.
- It is impressionistic and not readily quantifiable.
- It will not usually result in a buying list of needed titles.

If you are contemplating using this technique, be certain of the qualifications of the evaluators, since the results depend entirely upon their experience and the quality of their perceptions. It is also important that they be knowledgeable about the academic and research programs supported by the collection in addition to their knowledge of the discipline and its publications. If the expertise is available, this method requires much less time than other methods and brings immediate results.

Faculty members in the various academic departments are probably the most likely sources of the required expertise. It may be possible, however, to obtain the services of a consultant or, in some instances, to have a librarian with sufficient expertise make such an evaluation.

Analysis and Interpretation of Data

The focus of an expert appraisal should be on the strengths and weaknesses of a collection, emphasizing what is needed to bring the collection to the desired level of quality or adequacy. Since the evaluator should be required to write a formal evaluation report, s/he will provide his/her own analysis. The report should address the specific questions and objectives established in the assessment planning. It is just as necessary to be clear about your objectives in expert appraisal as in any other assessment.

APPLYING STANDARDS

Applying standards to evaluate library collections has been a long-accepted practice. Regional accrediting associations have established standards for college and university libraries as have many professional associations or societies and the Association of College and Research Libraries (ACRL). While not everyone has been happy with the standards developed, nor with their application, they do offer direction and guidance to collection development and evaluation.

Accreditation Standards

Most postsecondary schools in the U.S. are members of one of 6 regional accrediting associations that accredit these schools every 10 years. Because of high public acceptance of accreditation, institutions voluntarily participate in the accreditation process. This process requires institutions to evaluate their resources and performance by identifying what they do well, determining the areas that need improvement, and developing plans for correcting weaknesses or deficiencies. Thus, accreditation can have a powerful impact in ensuring the quality and continuous improvement of educational institutions and programs.

Accreditation activities universally require the evaluation of libraries and learning resources as vital components of the educational process. These periodic reviews of library services and collections offer an excellent opportunity for libraries to make known their needs at a time when the institution is most likely to listen, particularly if the study team report recommends improvements or changes in libraries. The usual pattern for accreditation consists of self-study by the institution, an on-site visit by an evaluation team, and subsequent review by a central governing group of the association to arrive at a decision. The review considers the self-study report, the visiting team report and recommendations, and any responses the institution makes regarding the report.

To assist institutions in conducting the self-study and preparing for the accreditation team visit, most accrediting associations provide a self-study handbook and policy statements that give the criteria and guidelines or "standards" for library services and collections. In recent years, these standards have generally emphasized (1) quality rather than quantity and (2) judging the quality of the institution on the basis of how well it is fulfilling its stated purposes and objectives rather than on external expectations or predetermined levels of performance.

The accrediting associations do not use the standards and guidelines developed by professional associations but develop their own which, in many instances, are very brief. Virgo and Yuro (1981) provide summaries of the standards and guidelines of the 6 regional associations (see examples below). These statements often deal with housing, seating, lighting, and other noncollection matters, but many of the criteria not only relate to collection evaluation but may require assessment to obtain the necessary information.

This manual does not contain a complete list of standards statements for all accrediting associations, but copies of these standards can be obtained from the associations (see Appendix C, "Accrediting Groups Recognized by Council of Postsecondary Accreditation [COPA])," for addresses) or from your institution administration, academic departments, or professional schools. Since these standards undergo periodic revisions, try to obtain the most recent version.

Regional Association Standards

Following are standards statements from the Northwest Association of Schools and Colleges–Commission on Colleges (1984) and a self-study outline from the New England Association of Schools and Colleges–Commission on Vocational, Technical, Career Institutions (1982). As you can see, statements of standards are usually general and qualitative, but self-study outlines often specify the aspects of library operations to be examined.

Northwest Association Standard

IV. Library and Learning Resources

    A. Standard

        The purpose of a library and learning resources program is to support and improve instruction and learning in ways consistent with the philosophy and evolving curricular programs of the institution. Its goals and objectives must be compatible with and supportive of the institutional goals and objectives. It shall constitute a central support of the entire educational program and assist in the cultural development of students, faculty, and the community it serves. It shall be capable of supporting basic research in academic majors, to the level of degrees offered. It shall provide services, resources, and facilities which encourage and stimulate such activities as individualization of instruction, independent study, innovation, effective use of resources, and community development.

        Facilities, materials, and equipment shall be provided at a level of quality and quantity which will support and enhance the educational philosophy, goals, and objectives of the institution. Facilities shall be adequate to accommodate a satisfactory percentage of users in an inviting and efficient atmosphere. Materials shall have the depth and breadth appropriate for the achievement of the goals and objectives of the library and learning resources program. Equipment shall be available in sufficient variety and quantity to serve the needs of the users.

        Services include providing convenient and comprehensive access to library and learning resources, assisting in effective utilization of the library and learning resources, providing instructional and faculty development functions, such as design and production of instructional materials, and use of computer-based resources.

        Adequate and dependable support must be provided to assure sufficient resources and services. Development and management of the budgets are responsibilities of the administrator(s) of the library and learning resources program.

        The library and learning resources program shall be administered as part of the instructional program by qualified professional staff, with representatives of the faculty acting in an advisory capacity.

The number of library and learning resources personnel and their competencies must be based upon the specific objectives established for the program.

Wherever an institution provides programs, it must demonstrate that library and learning resources services, fully adequate to the programs, are conveniently available and used by students and faculty.

Occasionally an institution will make library and learning resources services available to students and faculty through specific arrangements with another institution or other agencies where the holdings and services are adequate to support the programs and capable of maintaining an adequate level of support. In such cases, it is incumbent upon the institution to demonstrate that these arrangements are fully effective, will continue to be so in the foreseeable future, and are capable of meeting the needs of prospective program changes and additions. (Reprinted by permission of the Northwest Association of Schools and Colleges—Commission on Colleges, pp. 44–45).

New England Association Self-Study Outline

Learning Centers

1. What are the institution's current figures with respect to library: (a) attendance, (b) circulation, (c) holdings and acquisitions (by books and periodicals . . .), (d) inter-library loans, and (e) other information relating to library use?

2. What were the institution's expenditures during each of the past three years for (a) books, periodicals, bindings, and supplies and equipment, and (b) library salaries (professional, clerical)? (c) In what areas are the institution's present library holdings most satisfactory? (d) If the library holdings are believed to be inadequate or weak, estimate the cost of remedying deficiencies in each area and within the total collection. (e) What are the institution's plans for remedying the deficiencies?

3. (a) Does the library (or other facility) serve as a learning center for other audio and visual media? (b) What learning resources of these types are currently available?

4. Describe the library staff organization and record the training and experience of each member. (a) Is each professional staff member accorded the rank and status appropriate to qualifications and position? (b) Is the library adequately staffed with qualified professional, semi-professional, technical, and clerical personnel to pro-

vide appropriate services in resources as identified by the goals and objectives of the library?

5. (a) To what extent and how are faculty and students involved in the formulation and implementation of library policies and procedures? (b) Who selects and who approves library purchases? (c) What is the faculty and student evaluation of the library, including its strengths, needs, and holdings?

6. (a) How adequate are library facilities in reading space, equipment, hours available, and reference help? (b) What improvements are planned during the next five years?

7. On the basis of the self-study analysis and the Commission's Standard on Library identify the following: (a) strengths, (b) weaknesses, and (c) if appropriate, recommendations for improvement. (Reprinted by permission of the Northwest Association of Schools and Colleges–Commission on Vocational, Technical, Career Institutions, p. 8).

Professional Association Standards

In addition to the regional accrediting bodies, a number of professional associations also accredit specific educational programs in these institutions or in single-program schools that prepare students for professions or occupations. The standards published by the National Council for Accreditation of Teacher Education (*Standards for the Accreditation of Teacher Education.* Washington, DC, 1982) illustrate the kinds of library standards statements typically formulated by professional associations:

5.1 Library

The library is viewed as the principal educational materials resource and information storage and retrieval center of an institution. As a principal resource for teaching and learning, the library holdings in teacher education are sufficient in number and quality for the students served and pertinent to the types and levels of programs offered. The acquisition policies should reflect a commitment to multicultural education. The recommendations of faculty members and national professional organizations are seriously considered in maintaining and building the collection. Library service assures both students and faculty members access to the holdings.

Standard: The library quantitatively and qualitatively supports the instruction, research, and services pertinent to the needs of each teacher education program.

5.2 Materials and Instructional Media Center

Modern media and materials are essential elements in the communications system of contemporary society. For this reason, teachers need to understand the technologies that make such media and materials usable in their teaching and need to possess skills in using them. As a means to assist prospective teachers in developing these understandings and skills, the institution makes available and accessible to students and faculty members appropriate teaching-learning materials and instructional media that reflect cultural diversity in American society. A program for the preparation of teachers includes the use of teaching-learning materials and instructional media in two important ways: prospective teachers are instructed in how to devise and use modern technologies in their teaching, and modern technologies are utilized by the faculty in teaching students.

In maintaining and developing the collection of such materials and media, the institution gives serious consideration to the recommendations of faculty members and appropriate national professional organizations.

Standard: A materials and instructional media center for teacher education is maintained either as a part of the library, or as one or more separate units, and supports the teacher education program. (Reprinted by permission of the National Council for Accreditation of Teacher Education, pp. 25–26).

The standards for graduate programs are similar to those for the basic programs with an emphasis on the need to meet greater demands.

G-5.1 Library

The adequacy of library holdings is a major factor in establishing the quality of advanced programs. As the principal educational materials resource and the information storage retrieval center of an institution, library holdings are adequate for the numbers of students and faculty to be served, and pertinent to the kind and level of graduate programs offered. The operation of advanced programs requires library resources substantially larger than those required for basic programs. The library resources required for doctoral programs vary widely but, in any case, are substantial, and exceed considerably those for master's programs.

The recommendations of faculty members and professional organizations are given serious consideration in maintaining and building the collection. Adequate library service is provided to ensure that students and faculty members have access to the holdings.

Standard: The library provides resources that quantitatively and qualitatively support instruction, independent study, and research required for each advanced program.

G-5.2 Materials and Instructional Media Center

Advanced programs call for a greater number and variety of instructional materials and media than basic programs. In maintaining and developing the collection of such materials and media, the institution considers seriously the recommendations of faculty members, students, and appropriate national professional organizations.

A program for graduate students includes the development of advanced knowledge of skills in the use, research, and the evaluation of present and emerging technological aids for instruction. Students incorporate learning theories and are innovative in devising instructional strategies. Graduate faculty and students are provided numerous opportunities to share their findings.

Standard: A materials and instructional media center is maintained either as a part of the library, or as one or more separate units, and supports the advanced programs. (Reprinted by permission of the National Council for Accreditation of Teacher Education, pp. 41–42).

Library Association Standards

In addition to the library standards set up by accrediting and professional associations, the Association of College and Research Libraries (ACRL) has established standards for all types of college and university libraries. Like the standards from other organizations, these are usually general and qualitative. Though they don't spell out specific numbers of volumes or dollars or study stations, they do, nonetheless, provide information on building and managing adequate library collections and providing effective patron services. Copies of these standards are reprinted in Appendix E. You should become familiar with the statement for your kind of library and use it as appropriate for your collection assessments.

Advantages and Disadvantages

In deciding whether to consider standards as an appropriate measure in your assessments, keep in mind their advantages:

- They are generally widely accepted, authoritative, and persuasive in getting support from administrators.
- They can (and should) be related to the goals and objectives of your library and institution.
- They are especially effective when issued and required by accrediting agencies.

But their disadvantages should not be overlooked:

- They are sometimes difficult to evaluate objectively and quantitatively.
- Interpreting the standards may be difficult.
- Experts may disagree about their validity since they are often highly subjective.

Procedure

1. For subject collections, check with academic departments to see if they have accredited programs or if they intend to apply for accreditation; if so, find out the date of the next accreditation. This will not only help you plan well in advance to avoid the too-frequent problem of the library finding out about anticipated accreditation involvement at the last minute, but it will also show your willingness to support the academic department.
2. Obtain a copy of the applicable standards and guidelines to be used in the assessment. The department should be able to supply this, but if they cannot, write to the relevant accrediting organization. Those recognized by the Council on Postsecondary Accreditation (COPA) are listed in Appendix C of this book.
3. If the purpose of the evaluation is for an accreditation self-study, consult with the academic department to find out exactly what kind of information you will be expected to supply about the library.
4. Having determined what information is needed, select and implement the measurement techniques that will provide the required data.
5. Consider what noncollection-related data are needed and obtain these from the relevant sources. (Information about library use instruction, reference services, expenditures, seating, circulation, etc., will probably be available from the library administration or other library departments.)
6. Prepare a written report of your findings for the academic department and/or the accreditation visiting team.

Analysis and Interpretation of Data

While some standards statements may be general and offer little help as to the kinds of information required to show compliance, they are important for collection assessments. Accreditation standards generally require study and evaluation of library resources and services and collection assessments to obtain the required information. The data obtained will vary, of course, depending on the particular standards required of your institution. And the measurement will often require several of the techniques presented in this manual. Consequently, no description of the analysis and interpretation can be given here.

However, all librarians should become familiar with the standards developed by accrediting and professional associations for specific subjects and types of libraries applicable to their responsibilities and use them in collection assessments whenever possible.

Chapter 3
Client-Centered Measures

As pointed out in Chapter 2 of this book, collection-centered assessments enable a library to measure its holdings primarily against external standards. However, librarians are well aware that the collections themselves do not necessarily create satisfied patrons. Books, even if acquired and included in the catalog, are not always immediately available on the shelf. Even when they are, users don't always find them without difficulty and delay. Since we acquire library materials primarily to make them available and accessible to patrons, the ultimate success of a collection development program cannot be determined solely by collection-centered measurements. Only by measuring the actual and perceived use can the utility of a collection development program to present and future patrons be determined.

To measure the utility of collections, you can choose measures from 2 basic approaches—user studies and use studies. You can survey users to determine their needs and your success in meeting those needs. And you can measure the use your collections are receiving or how readily they can accommodate patron requests.

This chapter discusses a variety of techniques for measuring utility: user surveys, availability and accessibility studies, circulation studies, and citation analysis. Other use measures applied to assessing specific types of materials and for some other specific purposes are included in Chapter 4, "Assessments for Special Purposes."

USER SURVEYS

Public service agencies such as libraries need continuous feedback from their users to avoid losing touch with the needs of the people they serve. One good way to obtain this feedback is the user survey. Users may be surveyed on a number of concerns—their needs for various types of materials and services; their perceptions of how well the library is meeting their needs; and their ideas on how the library can improve its collections, services, and policies.

Before deciding what and how to survey, you should first answer the question—why? Do you really need a formal survey to know what your patrons think? What specifically do you want your users to tell you about? Designing a brief, unambiguous survey instrument is not easy. Nor is the validation, the administration, the tabulation, or analysis of the results always a simple matter. And since too-frequent surveys may become a nuisance to patrons, creating antagonism rather than eliciting useful information, your decision on surveying should be considered carefully.

A user survey for assessing individual subject collections is usually more limited in scope than a general user survey for an entire library and its services and is less likely to require the major effort of the general survey. However, if your library is planning to conduct a general survey, it may be possible for you to include questions about specific collections as part of that survey. It may also be possible for the collection development department to conduct a collection assessment survey of a number of collections rather than having each individual subject specialist conduct a separate one. A combined effort can spread the work over more people and call on the expertise of more librarians in the process.

Advantages and Disadvantages

Surveys, like other measures, have some disadvantages:

- Too frequent or too many patron surveys can cause users to grow weary and refuse to cooperate in your study.
- Library users are sometimes passive, inconsistent, and uncooperative.
- The poorly based opinions of ill-informed users may count just as much as those of well-informed and knowledgeable users.
- Some collections or parts of collections may be ignored for lack of subject expertise among users surveyed.
- Good surveys can be difficult to plan, execute, and interpret.
- The results may be misinterpreted or used to support faulty conclusions and recommendations because respondent opinions may not be accurate perceptions.

In spite of these weaknesses, however, carefully planned, executed, and interpreted surveys can help you

- Identify levels and kinds of user needs for materials and services.
- Reflect changing interests and trends that might affect collection development policies and practices.
- Determine satisfaction and dissatisfaction of patrons.
- Benefit from the knowledge and expertise of faculty and researchers familiar with the collection.
- Suggest areas of weaknesses and strengths in collections and services.
- Measure your success in correcting problems or strengthening weaknesses discovered in earlier studies or surveys.
- Provide information as to the ability and willingness of patrons to use certain kinds and formats of materials, i.e., foreign language publications and microforms.

However, because survey data are based on opinions and perceptions, they should generally be supplemented with or corroborated by other more objective measures before final decisions on library policies and practices are made.

Developing a Questionnaire

Developing a statistically valid and reliable survey instrument and methodology requires a certain amount of expertise. However, knowing a few basic principles of good survey instrument development will help. In addition, before you design one of your own, consult a good text on the subject. Several are listed in Appendix A, "Bibliography."

As you plan a survey, consider the whole process before beginning, from understanding exactly why you want certain information to knowing what decisions you hope to make based upon it. Begin with a written objective before you start to formulate the questionnaire.

Objective

Your objective should be written as specifically as possible showing that you understand exactly what you hope to achieve.

Example: To gather information about (a) the kind of patrons who use the linguistics collection, (b) their needs, (c) the way they use the collection, and (d) their opinions and attitudes about the adequacy and availability of the collection.

The stated objectives will help you determine

1. *The methods to be used to gather the data.* Basically, you can use questionnaires, checklists, interviews, or a combination of these. The principles discussed here apply to all methods.
2. *The time period in which to conduct the survey.* You should choose a time when the people you plan to survey will be available and likely to respond. Avoid semester breaks and holiday and test periods when people may be too busy or preoccupied with other matters to respond.
3. *The universe or population you need to survey.* If you want to know something about the use of a collection, don't leave out important user groups in your survey, unless you have some legitimate reason for doing so. A survey of undergraduates about a research collection would not likely elicit useful information about research use.
4. *The kinds of questions to be asked.* Most surveys involve the gathering of 3 types of data: demographic, preferential, and behavioral. You can write questions or checklists to gather this information.

   Demographic data include age, sex, race, education, rank, or status, socioeconomic level, etc. Avoid asking for personal information that is not directly relevant to your objective. If age and sex are not likely to be useful as variables in interpreting the results, don't ask for either of them.

   Preferential data include information about what times respondents like to use the library, what formats of materials they prefer, what locations they like to work in, what subjects they are interested in.

   Behaviorial data reveal what respondents actually do. What times of the day, week, semester they use the library; how long they stay each visit; what materials they use. Since people's preferences and behavior may differ, using both types of questions approaches the problem from 2 different points of view that create a check on the other.

Writing Questions

The following suggestions will help you develop the questions for your survey instrument:

1. *Avoid vague or ambiguous wording (often based on vague thinking).*

Example: List the periodical titles you read regularly.

Do you really want to know every title or just those in linguistics? And would *journal* be a better word than *periodical?* Remember the stated objective of your survey as you write your questions.

Example: List the linguistics journals you read regularly.

2. *Avoid library jargon that your respondents may not understand clearly.*

   Example: serial, pamphlet, stacks, range, circulation.

   If necessary, work a brief definition into the question or use a note.

3. *Provide ranges and categories for responses rather than asking open-ended questions.*

   Open-ended questions may seem easier to write, but structured responses are much easier to tabulate and analyze. Also, most respondents find structured responses easier and quicker to answer.

4. *Provide response categories sufficient to cover all possibilities.*

   Example: In your last visit to the library did you come to (a) borrow, (b) consult, (c) return materials?

   How does the respondent answer if 2 or more apply? Be sure to provide sufficient categories for all possible responses or add an "other" category.

5. *Use some questions that can be corroborated by some other measure.*

   Example: How many linguistics books have you checked out this month?

   If circulation records are available, you can compare the survey responses against actual circulation figures as a check against the accuracy of the survey data. People are not likely to remember accurately the kind of specific information you may be requesting.

6. *Order the questions logically so respondents can keep related things together.*

   Avoid, for instance, intermingling questions about use with those about collection strengths so respondents don't have to jump from one unrelated topic to another.

7. *Keep the number of questions limited and uncomplicated.* The shorter the questionnaire, the more people will be inclined to respond.

Testing

Having completed your survey instrument, try it out in a pilot study to work out any problems with the questions. It may be possible to test the questionnaire in one class or section of a class before you use it for all classes or with one or 2 faculty members before using it with all faculty. Even having a few colleagues review the questions may help if a formal pilot study is not possible.

Interviews

What has been said above about survey instruments, of course, applies to interview schedules. Consider the following advantages and disadvantages of doing interviews before deciding on this method.

Advantages and Disadvantages

Interviews have some distinct advantages when the number of people to be included is not so large that time and location constraints become a problem, especially since

- The response rate is generally higher.
- You have the opportunity to clarify meaning.
- There is less danger of respondents giving careless or hasty answers.
- You may be able to develop goodwill and improve relations with library users.

On the minus side, besides often being too time-consuming, the personal interaction between interviewer and respondent may affect the reliability of the results because

- Interviewers may have difficulty in reacting the same way to all respondents.
- Respondents may be less than honest without anonymity.
- Your explanations or clarifications of questions may bias the responses.
- It may be difficult to get all of the information recorded, particularly if you are using open-ended questions.

Procedure

If you have had little or no experience in planning and conducting surveys, study a basic text on the subject. You can also profitably follow Line's suggestion (1967, p. 45) to "find out whether any questionnaires previously used for a survey can be repeated or used in part." In fact, this is probably the best way to proceed. Appendix D, "Sample Survey Instruments," contains a number of questionnaires that can be adopted or adapted to survey library users about typical collection development issues. Most of them were developed as part of the successful ARL Collection Analysis Project (CAP) conducted at Brigham Young University (BYU), Massachusetts Institute of Technology (MIT), and other libraries. You should be able to find at least one survey to meet most of your assessment needs. You can also combine the best elements of several and add additional questions of your own, if necessary, to create an instrument tailored to your specific objectives. You may also have used some previously in your own library, and others can be found in the library literature. Appendix D contains the following 9 instruments:

1. *BYU Faculty Survey of English Collection.* The questions cover a broad range of behavioral and preferential information about collection adequacy and user needs. This questionnaire can be easily adapted to other subject disciplines and user groups.
2. *CAP Faculty Research Survey.* This tool is used with faculty to obtain information about their areas of specialization, their current and anticipated research projects, and how adequate they consider library collections to be to support that research. A similar questionnaire could be created to determine curriculum support needs.
3. *CAP Graduate Student Library Research Survey.* Similar to the faculty survey, this form obtains data on graduate student research needs.
4. *CAP Needs Survey of Major Academic Units.* This survey is sent to academic department and college heads to obtain information about anticipated changes in instructional and research programs and the adequacy of library support for these programs.
5. *CAP Importance/Success Survey.* This useful instrument, developed by the Association of Research Libraries (ARL) for their collection analysis project, asks respondents to indicate what types of materials are useful for their work and how well the library presently meets those needs.
6. *The M.I.T. Libraries Seek Your Help.* This questionnaire was used by MIT in their ARL CAP study.
7. *BYU Faculty Periodicals Survey.* A simple, brief way to help evaluate periodical holdings of a collection that also produces a want list.
8. *CAP Faculty Interview.* This questionnaire shows how a fairly lengthy list of topics can be covered systematically and uniformly

FIGURE 3.1. Document Delivery Data Sheet

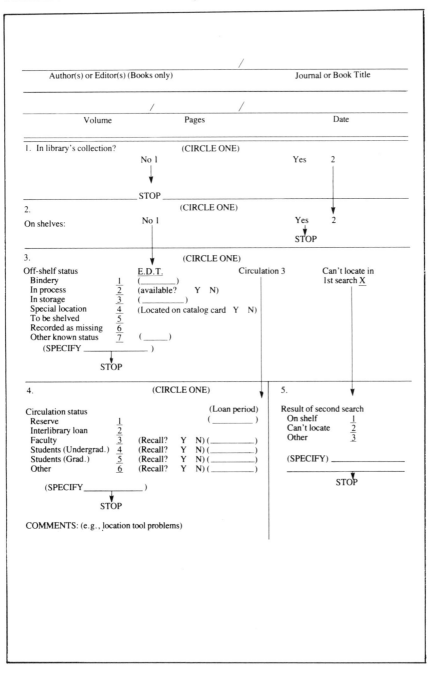

FIGURE 3.2. Document Delivery Test Analysis Form

	Number of Sample Items by Category	Time Category	Composite Time Total
1. Not in collection		5	
2. On shelf		1	
3. Checked out–reserve		2	
4. Checked out–faculty		*ORT	
5. Checked out–grad.		*ORT	
6. Checked out–undergrad.		*ORT	
7. Checked out–ILL		*ORT	
8. Checked out–other		*ORT	
9. In bindery		5	
10. In process		4	
11. In special location		*EDT	
12. Reshelving process		3	
13. Recorded as "missing"		5	
14. Other known locations		2	
15. On shelf - 2nd search		3	
16. Can't locate -2nd search		5	
17. Other outcome - 2nd search		*EDT	
TOTALS			

Mean speed–Total of column 3 divided by the total of column 1

$$CI = \frac{5 - \text{mean speed} \times 100}{4}$$

*Estimated Delivery Time (1–5)
This could be 1–5, depending on the whereabouts of a given title, and will have to be determined on a title-by-title basis.

*Optimum Return Time (1–5)
This could be 1–5, depending on the actual due date of a given title in circulation. It should be determined on a title-by-title basis.

by one or more interviewers. This example covers a number of library issues, many that you may not need for assessing a specific collection. But it illustrates the idea that you can cover a number of topics in one interview rather than using a number of separate questionnaires.

9. *CAP Student User Survey*. This brief survey could be used during exit interviews or passed out in the library for return at the exits. It can also be modified to fit specific subjects rather than the library as a whole. If you decide to conduct such a survey, use the following steps:

  a. Write your survey objective.

  b. Determine the kind of survey to be conducted—sampling, complete population study; the groups to be included—faculty, undergraduates, graduates; the method(s) to be used to gather the data—interviews, mailed questionnaires, questionnaires distributed to users in the library. In selecting the population to be surveyed, don't overlook any multidisciplinary interests in the collection being assessed. Include people from all departments interested in the collection. Organic chemistry, for example, would be used by many life science disciplines as well as chemistry.

  c. Develop and test your questionnaire or interview schedule. See the sample survey instruments in Appendix D to see if you can use or adapt one of them to your needs. You might also want to consult a good text on surveys and questionnaires for additional help to develop your own.

  d. Obtain names, addresses, and phone numbers (if needed to make appointments for interviews) of the people you plan to survey (see Appendix B for help with sampling).

  e. Distribute questionnaires or schedule appointments for interviews. It is a good idea to prepare a brief cover letter to send with the questionnaire explaining the reason for the survey, the value of user input in library efforts to improve the collection and patron services, and the date by which the questionnaire should be returned. Be sure to include a self-addressed envelope (stamped if it is to be mailed). If you are distributing this in a class, you can explain the purpose and collect the questionnaires directly.

  f. Follow up, if necessary, with calls or an additional letter if the questionnaires have not been returned by the due date. This will require some form of coding each questionnaire and recipient.

But do not violate anonymity of responses in anonymous surveys.

g. For questionnaires being handed out in the library or for exit interviews, select the dates and times to be used for the study and train the necessary staff to conduct the interviews and cover all exits.

h. Tabulate and analyze the results. A blank copy of the form can often be used for the tally. Chapter 5, ''Reporting Assessment Results,'' discusses the use of tables and charts for presenting survey data.

Analysis and Interpretation of Data

Because of the wide variety of possible surveys librarians might conduct as part of a collection assessment, it is impossible to provide any but the most general principles for analyzing the data obtained. As with all the other assessment measures, survey data, too, can only be interpreted in terms of your library's objectives and collection development policies. Remember, also, that you are generally dealing with opinions, not facts, with survey data, and you must avoid equating what people perceive with what actually exists. This is particularly important if some of the respondents are not knowledgeable about the issues or situations you are asking about. It is always desirable to try to obtain objective data that can be used to corroborate the survey information. This does not mean that you ignore user perceptions. If they believe something about your library, it will obviously affect their reaction, regardless of what the real situation may be. User opinions can be a valuable way of becoming aware of possible problems or weaknesses that you can pursue in further or subsequent assessments.

AVAILABILITY AND ACCESSIBILITY MEASURES

Availability and accessibility measures, using either simulated or actual data, help you determine the capability of your library to make its materials available with as little delay and difficulty for the user as possible. Since the availability and accessibility of materials are affected by various library policies and procedures, these measures also provide useful data for changing those that may be interfering with patron access to materials.

Availability refers to the likelihood that patrons will find desired materials on the shelf when they need them. Accessibility refers to the difficulties (usually measured in time delays) that patrons encounter in actually obtaining the materials. Using availability and accessibility studies, you can measure your library's ability to provide materials to patrons. The availability and accessibility measures recommended here have been selected from a number in the literature because they are effective, relatively simple, and not too time-consuming to employ.

Since most of these measures require sampling techniques and other statistical considerations to ensure validity and reliability, refer to Appendix B, "Statistical Aids," for help on these important matters. The statistical formulas peculiar to a given technique, however, are given with the discussion of the technique.

Document Delivery Capability

The document delivery capability measurement outlined here was developed by Orr and others (1968) for the National Library of Medicine but has been shown to be applicable to other types of libraries as well. The Document Delivery Test (DDT) combines both availability and accessibility into one numerical index number by measuring both the *adequacy* of the collection and the *speed* with which the library can meet patron demands, either from its own stock or from interlibrary loan. Test results are computed into a Capability Index (CI) showing the relative ability of the library to serve patron demands. If all items are immediately available on the shelf, the index is 100.

Since the samples are not derived from actual demands by patrons, this test is best considered a measure of the *potential* document delivery capability rather than the *actual* capability. Other techniques are available to measure the capability of the library to meet actual patron demands. Both kinds of measures can help us assess collection utility.

This test requires a random sample of 300 bibliographic citations obtained from a much larger pool and checking them against the card catalog and the shelf. If they are not on the shelf (immediately available), they are searched further to determine their status in the library and how long it would take to make them available or, if not acquired, to see how long it would take to obtain them through interlibrary loan.

The test takes about 4 hours to complete, depending on the number of items in the sample, and not including the time required to develop the 300 citations. It is 95% reliable. Its value and validity depend upon how representative the citation sample is and on how well that sample represents the actual needs of your library users.

Since the sample items are not derived from actual patron requests for materials, if you wish to approximate actual users at the catalog, you can use untrained students or clerical staff to do the initial search of the catalog and shelves. Trained staff members, however, should be used to do the follow-up searches for ''not on the shelf'' and ''not acquired'' items.

Procedure

1. *Select the citation pool to be sampled.* The major problem here is deciding which library files or published sources to use. A number are possible, depending on the specific objectives of your assessment.
   a. Shelflist. This can be sampled for the entire library or for a particular subject collection. It reveals the shelf availability of items acquired by your library but not what was not acquired. Appendix B, ''Statistical Aids,'' provides instructions on selecting a shelflist sample from a card file or an online database.
   b. Citations from published lists and bibliographies. These may be the same lists used in the list-checking measurement. This source will avoid the bias of leaving out items not acquired by your library.
   c. Citations from a selected group of journals or books identified as reflecting your clients' interests in the collection.
   d. Baker & Taylor, Blackwell, or other approval plan or blanket order jobber invoices for a given period. These would measure the capability of the library to furnish documents obtained for a certain time period and could provide a list of recently published items. They would also help to remove the bias of the shelflist sample, which contains a high percentage of older items less likely to be in demand. These might also more closely approximate actual demands. They would, of course, leave out nonstanding order or blanket order materials.
   e. *American Book Publishing Record* or its equivalent for other countries for recent years for a given subject. This would measure your library's ability to provide recently published materials. However, this sample would be biased by including materials that the library did not and should not acquire.
   f. Bibliographies on appropriate subjects obtained from computer searches of various online bibliographic databases, such as WLN, RLIN, OCLC, BRS, DIALOG, and SDC. These will

reveal your library's capability to support with documents its online bibliographic search services.

g. Recent acquisitions lists, if your library produces such lists. These are useful for checking on items recently cataloged and added to the collection. When selecting the citation pool from which to derive the sample, try to make it as representative of user demands as possible. This will ensure that the test results will be as useful as possible, even though the sample is not based on actual user requests. The pool should also be quite extensive—Orr recommends about 4,000 items—to achieve statistical validity at the ± 95% level. If the pool is smaller, a larger percentage of items would need to be selected for your sample (see Appendix B for sample size table).

2. *Select a 300-item sample.* Use the sampling techniques and random number tables in Appendix B. Enter each item on a Document Delivery Data Sheet. (See Figure 3.1, "Document Delivery Data Sheet," which can be reproduced.) You will need a separate sheet for each item.

3. *Check each item in the library catalog.* If you wish to approximate actual users more closely, have this step done by an untrained employee.

4. *Search for items not found.* A trained employee or professional should take all the slips for items not found in the catalog or on the shelves, recheck the catalog, and try to find in the library the acquired items, noting the results according to the categories on the Document Delivery Data Sheet. Some items may require a second search the following day.

5. *Tabulate the results.* When all sheets have been searched, tabulate the results into column 1 of the Document Delivery Test Analysis Form. (See Figure 3.2, "Document Delivery Test Analysis Form," which can be reproduced.)

6. *Compute the Capability Index.* Multiply the number in each of the 17 categories by the time code from Table 3.1 and enter the amount in column 3. The time codes indicate delivery times.

7. *Using the following formula, complete the data analysis to determine the Capability Index (CI).*

$$CI = \frac{5 - \text{mean speed}}{4} \times 100$$

To determine the mean speed, total columns 1 and 3 and divide column 3 by column 1. For example, if column 1 (total sample items) is 300 and column 3 (composite time total) is 855, the mean speed would be 2.85. Applying this to the above formula, you obtain:

$$CI = \frac{5 - 2.85}{4} \times 100 = CI = \frac{2.15}{4} \times 100 =$$

$$CI = .5374 \times 100 = 53.75 = 54$$

TABLE 3.1 Accessibility Time Codes

Code	Time
1	Not more than 10 minutes
2	More than 10 minutes, but not more than 2 hours
3	2 hours to 24 hours
4	Over 24 hours to 1 week
5	Over 1 week
*EDT	
**ORT	

*EDT = Estimated delivery time. This could be 1–5, depending on the whereabouts of a given item, and will have to be determined item by item.

**ORT = Optimum return time. This could be 1–5, depending on the actual due dates of a given item in circulation and will have to be determined item by item.

Analysis and Interpretation of Data

The Document Delivery Capability Index determined by this measure combines both delivery time and the adequacy of the collection into a single number indicator of library services. But the meaning of the number can only be interpreted in terms of your individual library or collection. The higher the index, the less time the patron must wait to obtain the desired material. Roughly, each of the 5 delivery time categories would be equivalent to 20 points on the index scale. An index of 80–100 would tend to indicate that the majority of the materials would be available within 10 minutes. An index of 0–20 would mean that a majority of the items would be deliverable in over a week. Most libraries would undoubtedly consider such a collection inadequate.

However, if the curriculum and research program supported by the collection is small, a lower capability index may not be as serious as it would for a collection supporting a more extensive and heavily used academic program. As you analyze the meaning of the index keep in mind that this test is not a measure of actual demands on the collection but only a simulation. Its adequacy as a measure of actual demands depends on how well your sample respresents the actual needs of your users.

The Document Delivery Analysis Form can also give you additional information about the collection and its management. For instance, you can determine the percentage of the sample in various categories, i.e., items in or not in the collection, items immediately available on the shelf, total items in circulation or circulating to the various categories of users, items classed as missing, etc.

You can also tabulate the data obtained from the DDT on the Availability Analysis Form to arrive at a different indicator of availability (see p. 48). Since collection measurements require considerable time and effort, try to use the data obtained from each technique used to tell you as much about the collection being assessed as possible.

Availability Measure

An availability test developed by Paul Kantor (1977) for the Association of Research Libraries' Collection Analysis Project obtains data from users of the library catalog. As patrons approach the catalog, they are given an Availability Study Form (see Figure 3.3, ''Availability Study Form,'' which can be reproduced) and asked to use it as scratch paper on which to write the author, title, and call number of books they want to find during this visit to the library. Then they are asked, as they search for the desired titles, to mark those they can't find and to deposit the study form in a collection box located near the library exits. About every 15 minutes, a library searcher takes the forms from the box and tries to locate the checked titles and determine why they are not available on the shelf. The data are then analyzed on the Availability Analysis Form to determine both the overall percentage of availability and the percentage of dissatisfaction caused by each of the 5 causes of patron failure to find materials. The process is simple, but it does require sufficient help on the day of the study to hand out the sheets to patrons and to do the follow-up searches every 15 minutes.

This measure can also be based on a sample from the shelflist or other citation sources, such as those discussed earlier for use in the DDT. In fact, if you cannot conveniently obtain information directly from catalog users, you can use the data obtained from the DDT to make this measure without having to gather additional data. A shelflist sample, however, tends to overestimate availability since many of the items in the sample may be little-used titles and more likely to be in their proper place on the shelf.

Kantor's Measure of Availability determines the level of immediate patron satisfaction and the causes for patron dissatisfaction or failure to find desired titles. It postulates that patron failure to find desired titles is a factor of several ordered determinants:

1. Failure of the library to acquire the desired book (DACQ).
2. Failure of the patron to copy call number correctly from the card catalog (DCAT).
3. Failure to find the book because it is in circulation to another patron (DCIRC).
4. Failure of library procedures, such as slow shelving, putting items in special locations other than the stacks, etc. (DLIB).
5. Failure of the user to find the book when it is correctly shelved (DUSER).

These determinants must be arranged in this order because if number one is true (the library failed to acquire a title), nothing else applies; if number 2 is true (the patron misread the catalog), then that is a sufficient cause for failure, and so on.

Procedure

1. *Select an appropriate time for conducting the study.* Do not choose an atypical time of the year, such as the beginning or end of a semester or during summer terms unless you have a specific reason for measuring the availability of materials during slack periods. You will need to run your study long enough to obtain a sample of about 400 titles. This may be done on one day or several days, either consecutively or scattered.

2. *Prepare materials and train staff.* You will need about 500 Availability Study Forms initially, since some will not be returned, and sufficient staff trained to hand out the forms and do the follow-up searches at 15-minute intervals. The follow-up must be done promptly to minimize the effect of other patrons who might be looking for the same titles or shelvers replacing books. The searching takes about 10 minutes per item.

   Searchers should be given the Availability Study Searcher Checklist (see Figure 3.4, "Availability Study Searcher Checklist," which can be reproduced) to guide them in the searching process. Instruct them not to spend a lot of time trying to locate

books that might be in use in the building or to assume that all books not circulating or not on the shelves are in use. Books not found should be put in category 10 and coded DLIB.
3. *Search all items marked "Can't Find."* As the Availability Study Forms are dropped off at the exits, they should be separated into those with items marked "Can't Find" and those not marked. The latter are assumed to be items that were promptly available to the patron and will be tabulated as "satisfactions" later in the analysis of the study data. Those with titles marked "Can't Find" should be searched, preferably within 15 minutes after being dropped in the box, using the following ordered steps:

a. Is the item readable?   If No (indecipherable), tally as
                             DX. If Yes, continue.

b. Is it in the catalog?   If No, tally as DACQ. If Yes,
                             continue.

c. Is call number correct?   If No, tally as DCAT. If Yes,
                             continue.

Note: Complete these first 3 steps for all items in the batch before going to step d. These 3 steps are all done at the card catalog or OPAC terminal.

d. Is book on the shelf?   If Yes, tally as DUSER.
                             If No, continue.
e. Is book checked out?   If Yes, tally as DCIRC.
f. If none of the above,   tally as DLIB.

You may want to subdivide any of these categories and pursue the matter further. This will enable you to pinpoint more exactly the causes of failure within the category. The Availability Analysis Form used for the final tabulation of the results allows for up to 3 subdivisions in each category (Figure 3.5). These subdivisions should be decided as you plan your study, not when you are tabulating the data. In this way, the specific cause for failure can be recorded directly on the Availability Study Form as the searcher is determining the failure category. If adding the subdivisions changes the searching procedure outlined above, be sure to modify the procedure and train searchers so they know exactly what to look for and where to find it.

FIGURE 3.3. Availability Study Form

We are studying the availability of books in our library. Please use this form as scratch paper and write the author, title, and call number for each book you are looking for. If you cannot locate a title in the library, check the "Can't Find" column. Please drop this form at the Exit Control Desk when you leave the library. Thank you.

Author	Title	Call Number	Can't Find	DX	DACQ	DCAT	DUSER	DCIRC	DLIB	Number of Copies
						Library Use Only				
1.										
2.										
3.										
4.										
5.										
6.										
7.										
8.										
9.										
10.										
11.										
12.										

FIGURE 3.4. Availability Study Searcher Checklist

What to Look For	Where to Look	Failure Category
1. Acquired by library	Card Catalog/OPAC	DACQ
2. Incorrect call number on patron sheet	Card Catalog/OPAC	DCAT
3. Book in special area identified on catalog card/OPAC	Card Catalog/OPAC	DUSER
4. Book properly shelved	Stacks	DUSER
5. Book misshelved	Stacks near proper place for call number	DLIB
6. Book in reshelving	Sorting shelves, loaded book trucks, circulation staging area	DLIB
7. Book circulating	Circulation records or system	DCIRC
8. Book found in area not identified on catalog card/OPAC	Ask at reference desks on all floors to see if they know whereabouts	DLIB
9. Book in use in-house	Drop shelves near call number area, tables.	DLIB
Other:		

Note: Do not spend a lot of time trying to locate books in the building. But don't assume that books that can't be found are in use. If no trace can be found, put it in category 10 and code it DLIB.

FIGURE 3.5.   Availability Analysis Form

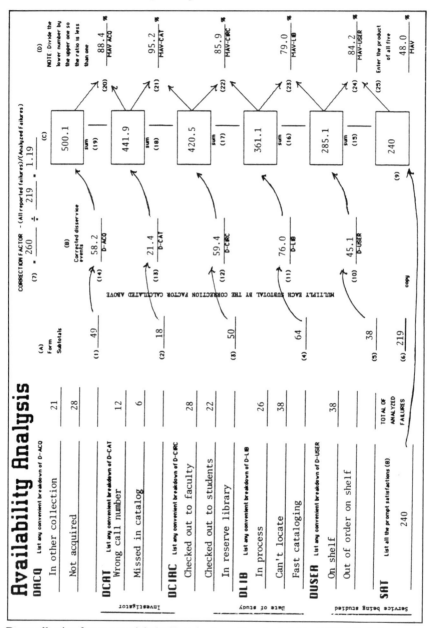

Data collection forms copyright by Tantalus Inc., Cleveland, Ohio 44118. Blank forms are contained in the ARL publication "Objective Performance Measures for Academic and Research Libraries." Data Analysis Software is available from Tantalus Inc.

4. *Tabulate and analyze the data from each of the Availability Study Forms on the Availability Analysis Form.* The following procedure for tabulating and analyzing the data may seem complicated, but you can easily do it by carefully following the steps here. As you read through the example, you can follow the process step by step on the worked example form (Figure 3.5).

EXAMPLE:

After completing the user sampling, we determine that there are 500 items listed on the Availability Study Forms. Of these, 240 were not marked "Can't Find" and were apparently immediately available on the shelf and presumably found by patrons. Of the remaining 260 marked "Can't Find," 41 are undecipherable (DX) and not analyzed, 49 are DACQ, 18 are DCAT, 50 are DCIRC, 64 are DLIB, and 38 are DUSER. This is a total of 260 failures or patron dissatisfactions, of which 219 are analyzed.

We begin by entering the 260 and 219 on the analysis form at point (7) in the upper right-hand corner on the lines "Total Failures" and "Analyzed Failures" respectively. Next, we divide the total failures by the analyzed failures to get the correction factor (1.187 or 1.19).

Now we enter the analyzed dissatisfactions down column A, "Form Subtotals," lines 1–5, and the "Total of Analyzed Failures," on line 6. This total should be the same as the number of analyzed failures in the upper right-hand corner.

On the bottom left-hand corner, line 8, we enter the total number of satisfactions (240) and also enter it at the bottom of column C, line 9.

Next, we multiply each of the form subtotals in column A, lines 1–5, by the correction factor (1.19) and enter the product in column B, "Corrected Disservice Events," lines 10–14. This distributes the unanalyzed (DX) items proportionally among the 5 dissatisfaction categories.

Now, in column C, we add items 9 and 10 and place the sum in box 15 (240 + 45.1 = 285.1), add items 15 and 11 (285.1 + 76.0 = 361.1) and put in box 16, add and put items 16 and 12 into box 17, items 17 and 13 into box 18, items 18 and 14 into box 19. The sum in box 19 should equal the total items in the study (500).

Finally, we work down column D, lines 20–24, dividing the number in box 18 by the number in box 19 and putting the quotient in box 20 (441.0 divided by 500.1 = 88.4%), dividing the number in box 17 by the number in box 18 and putting the quotient in box 21, dividing box 16 by box 18 and putting the quotient in box 22, box 15 by box 16 and putting quotient in box 24. This gives the Measure of Availability (MAV) for each of the performance categories; or, in other words, states as a percentage of 100 the probability that each of the 5 determinants of availability will provide immediate satisfaction or availability of desired titles to patrons. Line 20, for instance, shows that 88.4% of the items sought by a patron in this library will have been acquired; line 22 shows that for every item sought, 85.9% will not be circulating.

To determine the overall MAV, we multiply all 5 measures together ($88.4 \times 95.2 \times 85.9 \times 79.0 \times 84.2 = 48\%$). As a check, this should be the same as dividing the number of prompt satisfactions by the total number of items sought (240 divided by 500 = 48%).

You can prepare a similar form to analyze your own data or obtain a blank form from Paul Kantor's *Objective Performance Measures for Academic Research Libraries* (ARL, 1984); Data Analysis Software to perform these calculations is available from Tantalus Inc., Cleveland, OH.

Analysis and Interpretation of Data

As with all measures, the Measure of Availability percentage can only be interpreted in terms of the individual library or collection. An MAV of 48% means that 48 times in a 100 a patron will be able to find a desired item immediately available on the shelf. For a service organization, such a low probability of satisfaction seems too low, yet national studies show that the average MAV is only between 40 and 60% for academic libraries.

One of the greatest values of this availability measure is that it provides data from which to evaluate the causes for the library's failure to satisfy user demands. By determining the failure rates of the specific performance categories measured—acquisitions, catalog use, circulation, library procedures, and user errors—the library has available the necessary information to take corrective measures.

To determine the impact of each of the performance categories on the total number of dissatisfactions, we divide the number of dissatisfactions in each category by the total number of dissatisfactions. In our worked example, for instance, the DACQ (acquisitions failures) accounts for 22% of the total dissatisfactions (58.2 divided by 260 = 22.38%); DCAT, 3%; DCIRC, 23%; DLIB, 29%; and DUSER, 17%.

To correct deficiencies discovered through this study, the best approach is to try to improve the factor accounting for the greatest percentage of dissatisfactions, in this instance, the DLIB (library procedures or policies), until it is no longer the lowest, and then work on the next lowest factor. If you have subdivided any of the categories, these subdivisions may help you see more specific reasons for failures.

Using the results of the study, you can recommend changes in policies, work procedures, facilities, personnel, etc., to correct possible inconsistencies or bottlenecks that may be creating barriers to your users finding materials they need.

Further collection evaluation may also be necessary to see whether or not your library is allocating sufficient funds for the collection. A careful analysis and interpretation of the results of an availability study can produce significant insights into library policies and procedures and result in more effective management decisions.

Accessibility Measures

The accessibility of library materials and services to patrons is contingent on the amount of time required for patrons to obtain what they need. Library services involve both *effort* time (the time required for the patron or librarian to perform a task, such as finding a call number in the catalog, locating the book on the shelf, and checking it out at circulation) and *delay* time (the waiting time required for a task to be performed, such as sending off an ILL request, waiting for mail delivery, notifying the patron, and waiting for him/her to pick up the item). Since these times may range from a few minutes to months, a gross average, such as that determined through the Document Delivery Test Capability Index above, does not provide sufficient specific data on which to take corrective action to improve the accessibility.

Kantor (1977) suggests some techniques that can give the evaluator more specific information on the time required for a library to provide specific services or perform specific functions that may be slowing down the access of patrons to library materials.

Measurement of Effort by Simulation (MAC-SIM)

Studying the effort required in some access activity can be done through simulation, duplicating the activity a few dozen times and averaging the time required. For example, you can study catalog use by simulating the activities of patrons in using the catalog, finding the desired items on the shelf, and checking them out at circulation.

Procedure

The procedure for such a simulation is simple, requiring a simulator and a method for recording time. A stopwatch is also helpful in measuring the steps accurately. Using an untrained student assistant can more nearly approximate the typical library patron, although in some instances an experienced professional may be able to detect unnecessary steps in the procedure that are increasing the time required and reducing the accessibility. The time can be recorded on a sheet with headings similar to those below:

Trial No.	· Step 1	Step 2	Step 3	Step 4

A card catalog use simulation would be recorded in minutes and seconds and analyzed as follows:

Trial No.	At Catalog	To Get Book	To Check Out
1	1:30	4:15	2:20
2	:55	2:30	1:30
Total 2	2:25	6:45	3:50
Average	1:13	3:23	1:75

After a sufficient number of trials, total each column and average it.

Similar studies can be done of the effort required to obtain items through ILL or circulation recall, or to evaluate the time required for technical processes, weeding, reclassifying, etc. The items used for simulation studies can be taken from the dissatisfactions obtained from the availability study explained earlier, from the shelflist, from requests for specific services, from items received in the acquisitions process, and from other sources.

Analysis and Interpretation of Data

Simulation studies show how much *effort* time is required to perform various library tasks and can help the library detect bottlenecks or unnecessarily long procedures that may be slowing down or frustrating user access to materials and services. When used with other utilization studies they can often provide the basis for making needed changes in library policies, procedures, and physical arrangements.

Measurement of Access Delay (MAC-DEL)

To measure the access delay time in providing patron services or in performing other library processes, Kantor suggests using flow analysis, which postulates that the events in the processes used by a library to deliver patron services are like the flow in a pipeline. The delay time from request to delivery (Measurement of Accessibility determined by ability to deliver services, MAC-DEL) can be measured by determining the number of requests in process and dividing this by the rate of handling the requests:

MAC-DEL = Number of requests pending
Handling rate (requests per day)

For practical purposes, the handling rate is the average between the number of requests received per day and the number of items delivered to patrons per day.

This technique, with some modifications, can be used to estimate the delays associated with any library process with a fairly steady level of use, not only in public services but in processing procedures as well.

The worked example (Figure 3.6) shows this technique applied in a 10-day study of a hypothetical ILL service. On each day of the study, the number of requests received is entered in column 2, and the number of items picked up by patrons is entered into the last column. At the end of each day, the number of items still pending in each of the 4 steps of the process is determined and entered into the appropriate pending column. At the end of the 10 days, the data are analyzed as follows:

1. Total each column.
2. Calculate the average of each column.
3. Transfer the averages of the "Requests Received," column E, and the "Delivered," column L, to the rate factor calculation boxes in the upper right-hand corner.
4. Add these 2 numbers (E + L) and divide 2 by this sum.
5. Put the rate factor thus calculated into the rate factor box. This factor is used to convert the pending column averages to "working days of delay."
6. At the bottom of the sheet, multiply each column average by the rate factor and then total. This computes to 9.2 working days of delay. By looking at the average delay times for each of the pending categories, you can determine the greatest causes for the delay. In this example, more than half the delay is beyond the library's control (5.2 days in transit and 1.5 days waiting to be picked up).

Procedure

1. Determine the library service or process to be studied, the specific objective to be achieved by the study, and how long the study will run.

FIGURE 3.6. Delay Analysis Form

DELAY ANALYSIS

TIME PERIOD	NUMBER OF REQUESTS RECEIVED	Pending in To Send	Pending in Mails	Pending in Notify	Pending in Pickups	Pending in	Total Pending	NUMBER OF ITEMS DELIVERED
7/31/82	18	20	80	20	20		140	12
8/1	16	16	85	19	26		146	10
8/2	9	23	91	18	22		154	1
8/3	14	14	88	23	30		155	13
8/4	17	21	81	28	33		163	9
8/7	23	15	83	31	25		154	32
8/8	16	18	76	20	23		137	33
8/9	15	22	78	15	24		139	13
8/10	12	22	85	18	21		146	5
8/11	16	16	72	20	19		127	35
COLUMN TOTALS (1)	156	187	819	212	243		1461	163
COLUMN AVERAGES (2) (E)	15.6	18.7	81.9	21.2	24.3		146.1	16.3 (1)

MULTIPLY EACH COLUMN AVERAGE BY THE RATE FACTOR

(6) AVERAGE DELAY PER PHASE		1.2	5.2	1.3	1.5		9.2 days

TOTAL DEL.

(Sample)

Service Studied _____

Dates of Study _____

Investigator _____

(3) RATE FACTOR CALCULATION

15.6 (E)   16.3 (1)

(4) Sum

2 ÷ 31.9 = 0.063 days (5)

RATE FACTOR

The rate factor is the delay per item pending.

Data collection forms copyright by Tatalus Inc., Cleveland, Ohio 44118. Blank forms are contained in the ARL publication "Objective Performance Measures for Academic and Research Libraries." Data Analysis Software is available from Tantalus Inc.

2. Prepare a DelayAnalysis Form similar to the one shown in Figure 3.6. Write in the dates for the study in the first column and the steps in the pending columns. (Blank forms for this can be found in Paul Kantor's, *Objective Measures for Academic Research Libraries,* ARL, 1984.)

3. Provide tally sheets or counters on which to count each day's requests or transactions and train all personnel in the purposes and procedures for the study.

4. At the end of each day, fill out the appropriate information on the Data Analysis Form and, at the end of the study, analyze the results using the process explained above.

Analysis and Interpretation of Data

The interpretation of the data depends on the purpose of the study, but the general purpose of this accessibility measurement is to discover the length of delay time in providing or delivering services. If the delays seem too long for satisfactory service, you may be able to recommend changes to the library administration that would improve the service. If you find the delays to be largely beyond the control of the library, you will at least understand the causes.

CITATION ANALYSIS

Citation analysis is a quantitative method of identifying the important literature in a subject discipline. It is used to predict, from works authors have used previously, materials likely to be used by researchers in the future. The method studies the number of references researchers have made to the published works of other researchers and the number of citations these works have received. While most citation analyses have been based on journals, books can be used as sources of citations. But the patron use of books would be better measured by circulation studies.

The principle underlying citation studies is Bradford's law of scattering (1948), which postulates that a small core of journals will publish the great majority of articles in a discipline and the remainder will be scattered in a large number of journals. Those journals less directly related to the specific discipline will publish fewer of the relevant articles. Thus if you can determine the core journals for a discipline, you can likely satisfy a majority of the demands of researchers in that subject by collecting the core journals.

Two approaches to citation analysis can be of value in collection assessments. The first uses an *ad hoc* corpus of basic texts, research reports, annual reviews, dissertations, or journal articles as sources of references to the cited literature. These references are then compared to library holdings to find out if the work could have been written with the resources available at that library. This manual, however, covers this as a list-checking measurement in Chapter 2, "Collection-Centered Measures."

The other approach uses the citation analysis studies now available from the Institute for Scientific Information (ISI), the publishers of *Science Citation Index (SCI), Social Science Citation Index (SSCI),* and *Arts and Humanities Citation Index (A&HCI).* The latter index, however, has received little study of citation patterns, and citation reports are not available for the disciplines covered by that index. These will likely appear in the future. Preliminary work, however, has shown that the citations in the arts and humanities journals more often cite books, reviews, and literary and artistic works than they cite other journal articles.

For journal citation studies in the sciences and social sciences, however, the most reliable tools for citation analyses are the annual *SCI Journal Citation Reports (JCR)* and *SSCI Journal Citation Reports (JCR).* These are recommended for the following reasons:

- They are based on a broad corpus of the journal literature in the disciplines covered by these indexes.
- They include data from the previous 10 years or more, allowing some longitudinal measurement.
- They make adjustments for frequency of publication and the number of articles published, since the more articles published each year, the more likely a journal will be cited by researchers.
- They reflect the changes in citation patterns as they develop in a discipline.
- They provide cautions and discussions of library applications of the data to help users interpret the results and make adjustments for local applications.

Assumptions

Before deciding to use citation studies in your assessment, review the following assumptions implicit in the method (some suggested by Subramanyam, 1980, p. 356).

1. *Citation frequency is a valid measure of the significance of the literature of a discipline.* User surveys bear out the fact that, at least among scientists and social scientists, references in other articles and books do serve as leads to information for their own research and publication.

2. *All publications cited by an author have actually been used and have provided significant information.* While this may not always be true, most researchers are responsible in citing only those sources that have contributed to their research.

3. *All publications used have actually been cited.* This assumption is probably more likely to be questioned than #2. Writers rarely cite, though often use, textbooks, encyclopedias, handbooks, and other reference tools. They also read many journals to keep up with their subjects that they do not cite in their publications.

4. *The subject content of the cited documents is related to that of the citing document.* Without the time-consuming process of checking every source article, it is impossible to determine the accuracy of this assumption, but its impact will most likely be related to cross-disciplinary subjects.

5. *The source journals covered by the* JCR *adequately represent the entire subject field and reflect the objectives and purposes of the library collection being evaluated and the research program it supports.* A number of factors influence the citation frequency and accuracy with which this method represents the use of journals in a discipline:

   a. Age—the longer a journal has been published, the more it is likely to be cited.
   b. Frequency—weeklies and monthlies will generally be cited more often than quarterlies or annuals.
   c. Size—the more articles published, the greater likelihood of a journal being cited.
   d. Circulation and cost.
   e. Language.
   f. Controversiality of subject matter.
   g. Reputation of the authors published in the journal.
   h. Coverage by indexing and abstracting services.
   i. Availability and extensiveness of library holdings.
   j. Reprint availability.

And, of course, your collection may not need to represent the full extent of the subject represented in the citation studies available.

Remember, too, that these studies are based only on research use and publication and may ignore other uses relevant to your library.

6. *The number of times a journal is cited is directly proportional to its value or intrinsic worth.* Alerting services, review journals, trade magazines, house organs, and similar publications are often important sources of information to researchers but are rarely cited. And a low citation frequency does not necessarily mean that the journal quality is intrinsically low. Also, classic articles may often be cited for ''cosmetic'' reasons rather than for their intrinsic worth. Some journals may also be cited heavily for only a few articles, giving them a prominence undeserved overall.

Obviously, you may not be able to accept all of these assumptions in a given assessment. But if you are aware of them, make allowances, and use other measures to corroborate the results as necessary, *JCR* data can provide objective information to help you make informed collection development decisions.

Advantages and Disadvantages

Citation analysis has a number of advantages and disadvantages as predictors of future use:

1. *Citation lists are readily available for the sciences and social sciences through ISI* Journal Citation Reports.
2. *The method relates directly to the interests and practices of users.* But often researchers use and cite only materials *readily* available to them and many useful items may be ignored. In fact, the availability of journals and other materials to researchers has a strong bearing on what gets cited. Those items less likely to be available, such as foreign journals, will be underrepresented.
3. *The lists include items from peripheral areas of the subject or from related subjects, but some peripheral or related areas may be overlooked or underrepresented.* The *JCR* for both the sciences and social sciences include all the journals from all 3 databases, including the *A&HCI*, that cite or are cited by journals in each discipline. This ensures coverage of cross-disciplinary subjects.
4. *The method is generally easy to apply if you have the* JCR *for the subjects you want to evaluate.*
5. *This method will show you only what journals are being cited by researchers in published works.* The needs of graduate and undergraduate students and nonpublishing users of the collection may be

overlooked except as far as their use parallels that of your publishing users.

Journal Citation Reports

Since both the *SCI Journal Citation Reports* and the *SSCI Journal Citation Reports* are extensive documents and have excellent introductions to explain what they contain, how the data were obtained, and how to read and interpret the various "packages" of information, this description will only list the various parts and explain briefly the information they provide.

This description is based on the 1982 *SCI JCR,* but the *SSCI JCR* has an identical format. Both *JCRs* come as part of their respective citation indexes, but if your library does not subscribe to the indexes, both *JCRs* are available for purchase separately. The *SCI JCR* consists of 5 data "packages": (1) Journal Ranking Package, (2) Source Data Listing, (3) Journal Half-Life Package, (4) Citing Journal Package, and (5) Cited Journal Package.

Journal Ranking Package

This part consists of 8 sections that rank the science journals in a number of ways:

Section 1: Alphabetic list of science journals cited in references of *SCI, SSCI,* and *A&HCI* source journals (over 4,000 in 1982 report). This report shows the number of citations each journal received in 1982, the number of source items or articles it published, and the impact factor (derived by dividing the number of citations by the number of source items published). This factor adjusts citations received to the number of citable articles published rather than merely showing the raw number of citations per journal, which favors journals publishing more articles. This section also shows the immediacy index, the measure of how quickly the average cited article in a given journal is cited.

Section 2–6: These sections rank the science journals according to several indicators:

Section 2: By total citations for all years.
Section 3: By impact factor.
Section 4: By immediacy index.
Section 5: By source items published in year of report.

Section 6: By number of citations to previous 2 years in articles published during year of report (i.e., in 1980–81 for 1982 report).

Section 7: An alphabetic list of social sciences journals indexed by *SSCI* and giving the same information as that given for science journals in Section 1. (The *SSCI JCR* gives in this section a list of the science journals indexed by *SCI*.)

Section 8: A breakdown of *SCI* source journals arranged by subject category and ranked by impact factor. This section enables users to analyze citation data within specific disciplines. This section also gives the cited half-life for each journal. The half-life is the number of years going backward from the present which account for 50% of the total citations received by the cited journal in the current year.

Source Data Listing

This data package lists each *SCI* source journal alphabetically and gives information about the number of nonreview articles (i.e., those publishing research results), the total number of references contained in those articles, and the average number of references per nonreview article. It also gives the same information for review articles. Finally, it gives the same information for the combined articles. This enables you to determine the average number of citations in a given field, since the number of references vary considerably among disciplines. You need this information to avoid drawing unwarranted conclusions about the importance of a journal based only on the data in section 2 of the Journal Ranking Package.

Journal Half-Life Package

As a partial measure of obsolescence, this package shows the use an *SCI* source journal receives over a period of time. The half-life is the number of years it takes to account for half the citations in the current year. It is divided into 3 sections:

Section 1: Cumulative Chronological Distribution of Citations from Citing Journals. It shows the cumulative percentage of citations in current year for articles published in each year, back 9 years, and a cumulative figure for earlier years.

Section 2: Cumulative Chronological Distribution of Citations to Cited Journals. This shows the cumulative percentage of citations *received* by the cited journal in current year for articles published in each year, back 9 years, and a cumulative figure for earlier years.

Section 3: Journals Ranked by Cited Half-Life. This ranking is in ascending order of half-life, but its significance has not yet been fully analyzed.

Journal Citing Package

This package shows what journals each source journal has cited by publication dates for the previous 10 years. This does not list every journal cited by that source journal but has a limit of 100 or, if less than 100, the number of titles that account for 85% of the total citations. Any references beyond these limits are included in an ''all other'' subentry. The minimum is 6 titles if the source journal can supply that many.

Journal Cited Package

This package gives the same information for *cited* journals as the previous package gives for *citing* journals.

Procedure

1. Obtain the appropriate ISI *Journal Citation Report* for the collection you are assessing.
2. Read the introduction, which explains the nature and purpose of the *JCR*, the descriptions of each of the data packages, and the use or value in collection management.
3. Select those portions of the report appropriate for your specific assessment objectives.
4. Extract the information you need and interpret the results in terms of your library and collection objectives.

Analysis and Interpretation of Data

Since each assessment may use different parts of the *JCR*, no detailed explanation of how to interpret the data is possible. However, the following values of these reports have been extracted from the introduction to the 1982 *SCI JCR:*

• They can help avoid *ad hoc* decisions on journal selection.
• The chronological spread of citation counts should be invaluable in optimizing retention schedules.
• They can provide objective evidence for the optimum makeup of general and special journal collections.
• Yearly reports will, over time, show or imply the changes taking place in citation patterns and use of journals.

- They can form the basis for cost-benefits analysis in allocating acquisitions funds.
- They can show multidisciplinary linkings of journals to help evaluate cross-disciplinary uses of journals.
- They can suggest the need for more thorough evaluation of an area using other measures.

CIRCULATION STATISTICS

Another important, though not unchallenged, measure of collection utility is circulation. Use studies have been questioned, particularly in research libraries, when their purpose is to determine by past use what would most likely be used in the future. Certainly conditions change, research interests and curricula change, faculty and students change, and libraries and the interests they serve vary widely. Yet, libraries must manage their resources wisely to serve the needs of their patrons not only now but in the future. To do this, knowing what materials to purchase, what items to house in prime space, what to relegate to less accessible locations, what to preserve, and what to discard is essential and becoming increasingly more important as prices rise and buying power and budgets fall. And one of the few statistical indicators of future needs is a careful and judicious evaluation of past use.

Where adequate and consistent circulation records of past use of library materials exist, these statistics can help provide data for a number of collection management and assessment decisions:

1. Weeding.
2. Storing.
3. Preserving.
4. Buying multiple copies.
5. Records conversion.
6. Reclassification.

Circulation statistics can also be combined with expenditures, acquisitions rates, holdings, and research and curriculum support information by subject to monitor materials allocation budgets more objectively (see Chapter 2, ''Collection-Centered Measures''). They may also alert you to collections that are under- or overdeveloped.

Circulation statistics can be obtained from either manual or automated circulation systems, although manual records do not offer the number of possible uses that automated systems do. But even manual records can supply information about user classes, use by call number or subject ranges, and use of individual titles, provided that obtaining this information from paper records is not too cumbersome or time-consuming.

Automated systems, however, offer greatly improved access to a much wider variety of data. From them, you can usually find:

- User class—faculty, graduate, undergraduate.
- The use of various subject areas by Dewey or LC classification and by whom.
- The age or publication date of circulating materials.
- The types and formats of circulating materials.
- The language of the circulating items.
- The last circulation date of specific items.
- The library or branch circulating the item.
- Circulation for given time periods.

Procedure

Since circulation systems vary in the amount and kind of information extractable and the method used to obtain it, no specific procedure can be set. You will undoubtedly have trained staff able to help you get some or all of the above information from your system.

Analysis and Interpretation of Data

The circulation data available to you will vary with your system, but some general principles will help you interpret it.

It is important to remember that past use should be considered only one of a number of factors that govern the utility of a collection. It is vital to know the curriculum, research, or other use the collection is being built to serve. Otherwise, you may hastily assume that heavy use indicates a "good" collection or that a low use indicates that the collection is being overbuilt or can be discarded. Remember also that circulation statistics will understate the use of a collection where in-library use may exceed external use. Studies show that, in some disciplines, this may be 4 to 5 times higher than circulation. You may need to study the in-library use of materials before you use circulation statistics as the basis for collection decisions (see below). Also study carefully the user class information to see which academic departments are using the materials.

Chapter 4, "Assessment for Special Purposes," explains a technique for using circulation statistics to help make weeding decisions, a common application for use studies, and gives additional explanations on the use and analysis of circulation statistics. You can also use that same technique for the other collection management functions noted above.

MEASURING IN-LIBRARY USE

When employed as the sole indicator of use, circulation studies have raised some serious questions concerning validity. Yet as automated circulation systems are refined and become more widely used, the use data they can provide should not be ignored. Studies have shown, however, that for some subjects, in-library use may be significantly higher than external circulation. And for noncirculating materials or collections, circulation systems provide no use data. What is needed is a procedure for measuring in-library use.

The ease or difficulty in measuring this function will vary from library to library, depending to a great extent on the volume of reshelving and the arrangements for patrons to deposit materials for counting.

The measure involves counting the number of individual items replaced on the shelves or in files, excluding items returned from outside circulation. The major problems in ensuring the accuracy of these counts are the number of items patrons return to the shelves themselves rather than placing on drop shelves and the length of time required to obtain a reasonably accurate estimate of use.

If you can work around these difficulties, the following method should help you get the job done.

Procedure

1. Determine what kind of information you need to obtain. If all you need is to find the number of items used in the library and not which specific items have been used, you should be able to simply count the items in the call numbers appropriate to the collection you are assessing. If you need to know the use of specific volumes, you can use the periodical use study technique described below.
2. Decide on some reasonable time limits for the study. You may want to do the count for a typical week, month, semester, or other time period. If you are using this in conjunction with out-of-library circulation statistics, you would want to try to obtain a reasonable estimate of in-library use for the same period. But you may want to

do a sampling study and project the data to the full period. See Appendix B, "Statistical Aids," for help in sampling.
3. If possible, post signs in the area where the study is taking place asking patrons not to reshelve any materials but to place them in designated spots.
4. Prepare a log for shelvers to use in tallying the number of items reshelved. These can be placed on the ends of book trucks or on the shelves in the staging or sorting areas. This sheet can be arranged by types of materials (monographs, periodicals, tapes, recordings, microfiche, etc.) to fit various areas where materials relevant to the collection being assessed are being counted. Don't forget to include reserve or other noncirculating areas of the library in your study.
5. Obtain the support and cooperation of the shelving supervisors and train shelvers in the details of marking and preserving the logs.
6. Collect the logs as often as necessary to avoid losses and tabulate and analyze the results at the end of the study period.

Analysis and Interpretation of Data

The meaning and significance of the data obtained from this measure can only be determined by the purpose for the study. There are 2 basic reasons for measuring in-library use: to determine the ratio between in-library use and outside circulation and to obtain actual in-library use counts by subjects and/or types of materials.

The first reason offers substantial long-term benefits in assessing collections. If you discover from this study that in-library use and outside circulation are virtually equal or that they are related by a specific ratio, then you can either rely with reasonable confidence on circulation statistics being an accurate indicator of collection use, or you can use the ratio established by the study to increase or decrease the circulation figures in determining use. However, you would probably need to determine the ratio for each subject collection unless the subjects were similar in their use patterns. Many science subjects, for instance, might be similar as might many literature or history subjects, but possibly not in comparison with each other.

The second reason would be more applicable to noncirculating collections such as periodicals, phonodiscs, microforms, or reserve materials if no circulation records are kept. And, of course, you can use the technique to obtain actual use figures to be added to your assessment rather than merely to establish a ratio.

PERIODICAL USE STUDY

The literature contains numerous reports of journal use studies using a variety of sources of data: citation analysis, ILL requests, photocopy requests, user questionnaires, loan slip count, shelving statistics, etc. Many of these may not be appropriate in some libraries for lack of available data. Also, most of these were short-term studies conducted in special libraries or in science libraries with limited collections. These traditional methods also have several inherent disadvantages:

- Short-term studies may not adequately reflect long-term use and thus cannot be used reliably for decision making about storage, discarding, or cancelling subscriptions.
- Some of the traditional studies do not give title-by-title evaluation.
- Most of these studies are applicable to one library, and the results cannot be generalized.

The following simple technique provides reliable title-by-title data on periodical use in libraries where periodicals do not circulate and must be used in-house. It is easily conducted and monitored over an extended period to produce data that can be used to make continuation, retention, and weeding decisions. This method, developed by Shaw (1978) at Case Western Reserve University and used there successfully for several years, is easily adapted to individual subject collections or to the entire holdings. It can also be used for both bound volumes and current unbound issues.

The technique is based on the premise that a small number of titles accounts for a large percentage of the use of library collections and, thus, the important concern is to distinguish the used portion of the collection from the unused portion. If conducted over a long enough period, this study technique eventually reaches a "constant fraction," the point where the percentage of the journal collection used no longer increases. When this condition is reached, Shaw says, "There is a high probability that those volumes or titles that have not been used will not experience significant use in the foreseeable future."

The result of the study, then, is to show which titles are used and which are not thus providing reliable data for making decisions about retaining or disposing of individual titles or volumes.

The study procedure is simple. As journals are reshelved after use, the shelver places a gummed dot label on the spine of each bound volume or on the shelf front if the study involves current unbound journals in slotted shelves. Each used volume receives only one dot, regardless of the number of uses, since we are only trying to distinguish the used titles from the unused ones. (An alternative study methodology to be discussed later can be used if you need to know the number of uses an issue or volume receives.)

To monitor the results, you or a staff member walks along the shelves about once a quarter and records on a tally sheet the volumes with the dot labels on them. After each count, you determine the percentage of the titles and volumes used. This continues until no additional uses are observed. The longer the study proceeds, the fewer dots that are applied, which means that the long-term study takes little more effort and time than a short-term study and produces significantly more reliable results.

Procedure

The procedure to use when attempting a periodical study is as follows:

1. *Select the area or subject to be studied and obtain a list of the journal titles for the subject being studied.* (Computerized serials systems make this quick and simple.)
2. *Determine the number of volumes in each title to obtain the total number of both titles and volumes.* Count incomplete volumes as a full volume. If there is room on your list, you can use the list as a tally sheet. If not, prepare a tally sheet by title and volume.
3. *Instruct shelvers in applying the gummed dot label on the spine of each periodical volume as it is reshelved, or for current periodicals, on the shelf rather than to the individual issues.* This enables the study to continue even if individual issues are picked up for binding, which may occur if the study continues over a binding period or more.
4. *Collect data every 4 months by examining the shelves and noting which titles and volumes are marked.* Use the same tally sheets throughout the study to avoid the need to replicate data recorded in an earlier tally.
5. *Continue the study until you reach the "constant fraction" state, that is, until the percent of the volumes and titles used does not increase.* This will probably take at least 2 years or more. Less conclusive results could be obtained in a shorter time.

Alternative Method

Another method is affixing to the spine or the shelf a one-inch-square, blank, gummed label the first time a title or volume is reshelved. Thereafter, for each subsequent use, the shelver makes a hash mark on the label.

This will enable you to determine how often a given title is used, which might be useful in determining whether or not a given journal should be allowed to circulate or should be kept, cancelled, or weeded out of the collection.

If you use this technique, you can tally the results every 4 months (or more often if necessary) by removing the labels from the books and replacing them with clean labels. The used labels can then be pressed onto the tally sheet for later counting. The shelvers must also be informed as to how to handle the labels should they become filled before the regular tally time.

In determining whether or not to use this alternate method, be sure you have a specific objective to be achieved, since it takes more time and effort to conduct this kind of a study. Remember, too, that for most decisions about the disposition of a journal title, just knowing that it has been used will usually be adequate, since a small number of titles will account for a large majority of the use of the journal collection. Still, this alternate technique may be helpful in studying the value of marginal titles rather than for use in evaluating entire subject journal collections.

Analysis and Interpretation of Data

The data are best interpreted in terms of the percentage of the titles and volumes used. This requires knowing the number of journal titles and volumes in the collection being studied. From this, you can then compute the percentage of both titles and volumes used each time you make a tally.

Zero use would obviously be a significant indicator, but it cannot serve as the exclusive justification for cancellation of a subscription or other decision. You would need to consult with faculty and collection development staff to be sure that the intellectual content of the collection would not be subverted. Other considerations might be the existence of internal or external indexing or abstracting or commitments to consortia.

Chapter 4
Assessments for Special Purposes

In a sense, all assessments are made for special purposes since each is performed to achieve some specific objective. But this chapter focuses on assessment techniques for making specific decisions or for evaluating several specific collection development functions.

ASSESSMENTS FOR WEEDING DECISIONS

An important reason for assessing a collection is to determine what materials should be discarded, stored, preserved, or replaced by alternative formats—i.e., weeding. Most libraries, sooner or later, face the problem of making room for newer acquisitions. For many public and college libraries, this should be standard practice. But even research libraries may find it necessary to discard or store little-used materials to make room for newer acquisitions or to try to increase accessibility to more recent information. More books don't necessarily mean more satisfied users if the older materials keep them from readily finding current information. For many libraries, use or nonuse may provide the best criterion for weeding. For others, particularly research libraries or those supporting publication programs, use studies should be used with other methods.

Mosher's 4 observations for a collection review and weeding program (1980, p. 173) make good sense:

1. Use methods appropriate to the library's goal and to the disciplines or subjects under consideration.
2. Be practical. If pruning obsolete multiple copies, noncurrent texts, or superseded editions from the collection is the objective, it can best be done by a simple and rapid shelf reading; no complex methodology is required.
3. Use more than one method; be sure to use subject expertise and knowledge to supplement and correct the results of more mechani-

cal techniques. The time saved by inappropriate shortcutting will probably have to be repaid many times over in dealing with user dissatisfaction and other problems.

4. Do not hesitate to use faculty to help provide subject expertise missing in the library staff and to check proposed candidates for pruning. Librarians and faculty are colleagues working toward common goals, and interchange is usually mutually beneficial.

Mosher also reminds us that ''the process is simpler and more straightforward in science and technology collections (which is why nearly all of the more quantitative and mechanical techniques have been devised for or tested on them), and more complex and problematic in humanities collections, and is also more straightforward in public library, undergraduate or college collections than in research collections.''

Use Study Method

The most widely recommended objective and quantitative technique for making weeding decisions is past use. Line and Sandison in their review of measurements based on publication dates, last date of circulation, and citation studies concluded that these are often based on questionable assumptions or do not reflect all the issues that need to be considered in making weeding decisions. We should not conclude, however, that use studies are not worthwhile. The key is to match the measurement with the library's collection objectives and to make allowances for the assumptions and reservations associated with a given measurement technique.

Date of publication has sometimes been recommended as a basis for weeding decisions, but actual use is less arbitrary and more directly related to user demands on a given library. In many libraries where research is not a significant factor in patron use of collections, discarding materials that have not circulated for a certain period of time has proven quite satisfactory. Even in larger research libraries, use measurements help make preliminary decisions for both storage in less accessible locations and discarding. A final decision about most items, however, should be made only after review by a competent subject specialist and perhaps a check of the items in a standard bibliography of the subject.

For noncirculating serials, citation analysis and in-library use measures can provide useful information (see Chapter 3, ''Client-Centered Measures''). For circulating materials, Schwarz and Olson have found the methodology used by Trueswell (1968) based on last circulation date a good indicator for making weeding decisions. Their technique uses (1) the previous circulation date obtained from a sample of circulation records and (2) the last circulation date stamped in the books on the shelves to establish a core collection of items that will likely meet a predetermined percentage of future demands on the collection. Any item that has not circulated within the time period is in the noncore collection and a candidate for weeding.

The measurement technique described here is used to determine the cutoff point, the exact date to be used to decide what goes into the core collection. Once that date is determined by this measure, weeding is done by checking the last circulation date stamped in the books on the shelves. Those that have not circulated since the cutoff point are weeded and either discarded, stored, or replaced in some other format, such as microform. The technique can be used for a complete library or for specific subject collections.

Assumptions

This measurement is simple and can be done by clerical staff or student assistants once the sampling procedure has been set. However, you must have the required circulation records available, and you must have the due date of circulating materials stamped in them. In addition, you must be able to accept or make allowances for the following assumptions that underlie the measure:

- The best method for predicting use is immediate past use.
- In-house use is similar to external use.
- Use patterns do not change radically over time.

Obviously, if circulation records do not exist or if date due slips are not placed in circulating materials, this measurement is not possible. But growing automation of libraries will make these data almost universally available to libraries in the near future.

Past use, of course, does not always predict future use, but past experience, when tempered by an awareness of changing circumstances or trends, is one of the few indicators of future experience; it is probably the only quantifiable measure available to try to anticipate future demands on a library collection. If your collection policy statements are kept current with curriculum and research needs served by the collection, the margin of error can be minimized.

Also, for a given collection, in-house use may not be similar to external circulation. Wide variations have been reported among various disciplines. If you suspect that external circulation does not reflect in-house

use in your library, you will want to measure in-house use (see Chapter 3, "Client-Centered Measures") to see how it compares to external use and make adjustments before using this technique to make weeding decisions.

Procedure

Use the following procedure to attempt a use study:

1. Select the collection to be measured and the number of items to be checked. You may want to check every item in the circulation record if the number is not too large. For shelf checks of most collections, you would want to select a random sample large enough to ensure reliability and validity (see Appendix B, "Statistical Aids"). The circulation and collection samples need not be the same number of items.

2. From the circulation record (card or computer files), record the *previous* due date on a slip of paper or 3 × 5 card, one item per slip to aid sorting later. For items that have circulated for the first time, write the call number on the slip, check the shelflist, and use the acquisitions date in lieu of previous due date.

3. On the shelves, check the date due slips and record the *last* due date on a slip of paper or 3 × 5 card, one item per slip to aid sorting later. For items that have not circulated, write the call number, check the shelflist, and use the acquisitions date in lieu of last circulation date.

4. Sort the circulation data slips or cards into groups by 6-month periods.

5. Prepare a Circulation Sample Data Table (see Table 4.1) and tabulate the results from the data slips or cards. Carry the Circulation Cells column out in 6-month increments until you have accounted for the total number of items in the sample (see Table 4.5).

6. Calculate the Cumulative Circulation and % of Cumulative Circulation columns on the Circulation Sample Data Table. (Divide the number in the Cumulative Circulation column by the total number of items in the sample to obtain the % of Cumulative Circulation. This column should show 100% if you have correctly accounted for every item in the sample.)

7. Sort the collection data slips or cards into groups by 6-month periods.

8. Prepare a Collection Sample Data Table (see Table 4.2) and tabulate the results from the data slips or cards. Carry the Cells in

Months column out in 6-month increments until you have accounted for the total number of items in the sample (see Table
4.6).

TABLE 4.1. Circulation Sample Data Table

Circulation Cells in Months	Circulation per Cell	Cumulative Circulation	% Cumulative Circulation
6			
12			
18			
	(After 60 or 72 months, 12-month increments		
–	may be sufficient.)		
–			
–			

TABLE 4.2. Collection Sample Data Table

Cells in Months	No. of Items in Cell	Cumulative No. in Sample	% of Collection
6			
12			
18	(After 60 or 72 months, 12-month increments		
–	may be sufficient.)		
–			
–			

TABLE 4.3. Circulation vs. Collection Sample Table

Cells in Months	% of Circulation	% of Collection
6		
12		
18		
–		
–	(Use the same increments as on the 2 previous tables.)	
–		
Etc.		

9. Calculate the Cumulative No. in Sample and % of Collection
   columns on the Collection Sample Data Table (see Table 4.2).
   (Divide the number in the Cumulative No. in Sample column by
   the total number of items in the sample to obtain the % of

Collection. This column should show 100% if you have correctly accounted for every item in the sample.)

10. To more easily define the cutoff point, prepare a Circulation vs. Collection Sample Table (see Table 4.3) and transfer the % of Circulation information and the % of Collection data from the Circulation Sample Data Table and the Collection Sample Data Table (see Table 4.7).

11. If you know the number of titles in the collection, you can prepare an Estimated Weeding Table using the following format.

TABLE 4.4. Estimated Weeding Table (Collection Size: _____)

Cells in Months	% of Future Use to be Satisfied	% of Collection to be Weeded	No. of Items to be Weeded
6			
12			
18	(Use the same increments as on the previous tables.)		
–			
–			
–			

Complete the weeding table by (1) transferring from Table 4.3 the % of Circulation column to the % of Future Use to be Satisfied column, (2) calculating the % of Collection to be Weeded by subtracting the % of Collection on each line of Table 4.3 from 100, and (3) calculating the No. of Items to be Weeded by multiplying the total items in the collection by the % of Collection to be Weeded (see Table 4.8).

Analysis and Interpretation of Data

The information obtained from this measure shows the use of the collection from the present to a point in the past. If you have determined that the assumptions underlying the measure are appropriate to your library, you can now set the cutoff point for determining the core collection. You do this by looking at what percentage of the circulation is accounted for by what percentage of the collection and deciding what percentage of user satisfaction you are willing to accept. The last circulation date corresponding to that percentage of circulation becomes the cutoff point. All items that have circulated from the present to the cutoff point are in the core collection. All items that have not circulated within that time period are in the noncore collection and candidates for weeding. The following completed example should make the process clear.

TABLE 4.5. Circulation Sample (N=1,944)

Circ. Cells in months	Circ./Cell	Cum. Circ.	% Cum. Circ.
6	1160	1160	59.67
12	290	1450	74.58
18	183	1633	84.00
24	74	1707	87.80
30	56	1763	90.68
36	21	1784	91.76
42	30	1814	93.31
48	15	1829	94.08
54	20	1849	95.11
60	11	1860	95.67
66	12	1872	96.29
72	12	1884	96.91
84	13	1897	97.58
96	9	1906	98.04
108	15	1921	98.81
120	5	1926	99.07
132	8	1934	99.48
144	4	1938	99.69
156	2	1940	99.79
168	1	1941	99.84
169+	3	1944	100.00

Table 4.5 shows the result of the measurement of a circulation sample of 1,944 items in a library of 141,000 items. As the table shows, almost 60% of the items circulating had circulated previously within the past 6 months and over 90% within the past 36 months. This pattern follows that of most academic libraries.

Table 4.6 shows the impact of circulation on the collection itself. Here only about 27% of the collection accounts for the circulation for the past 12 months (a relatively small percentage), and only 64% of the collection had circulated during the past 5 years.

But by combining the data from the 2 tables (see Table 4.7), you can clearly see what percent of the circulation is being met by what percent of the collection.

At 6 months, about 17% of the collection provides almost 60% of the circulation. At 36 months, about 50% of the collection accounts for over 91% of the circulation. And at 60 months (5 years), 64% of the collection accounts for almost 96% of the circulation. To achieve a small 4% increase in the circulation satisfaction rate would require retaining and housing 36%

TABLE 4.6. Collection Sample (N=1,580)

Cells in Months	No. of Items per Cell	Cumulative No. in Sample	% in Cell
6	274	274	17.34
12	153	427	27.02
18	103	530	33.54
24	105	635	40.18
30	86	721	45.63
36	57	778	49.24
42	72	850	53.79
48	56	906	57.34
54	61	967	61.20
60	46	1013	64.11
66	65	1078	68.22
72	35	1113	70.44
84	62	1175	74.36
96	65	1240	78.84
108	122	1362	86.20
120	49	1411	89.30
132	83	1494	94.55
144	39	1533	97.02
156	24	1557	98.54
168	14	1571	99.43
169+	9	1580	100.00

of the collection. Or stated another way, weeding 36% of the collection would only result in a 4% decline in meeting circulation demand in this library.

Of course, this sampling study does not do the weeding. It only helps you determine what items should be weeded. The actual weeding, however, can be performed by clerical or student assistants without agonizing over each title. The last circulation date on the checkout slip in each title on the shelf is all that needs to be examined. Those titles falling outside the cutoff point are removed for discarding or storing.

Before actually discarding books removed by nonprofessionals, however, it is advisable to check these titles against standard bibliographies and have subject specialists and faculty review the selected items to avoid costly mistakes in discarding valuable titles that might not be replaceable. Professional evaluation, of course, is essential to determining whether to discard or to store. This decision should be made on the basis of a number of local criteria discussed below.

In addition to studying use based on last circulation to obtain information for making weeding decisions, you may want to try to study in-library use or use citation analysis studies. These 2 methods can be important in

TABLE 4.7. Circulation vs. Collection Sample

Cells in months	% of Circ.	% of Coll.
6	59.67	17.34
12	74.58	27.02
18	84.00	33.54
24	87.00	40.18
30	90.68	45.63
36	91.76	49.24
42	93.31	53.79
48	94.08	57.34
54	95.11	61.20
60	95.67	64.11
66	96.29	68.22
72	96.91	70.44
84	97.58	74.36
96	98.04	78.84
108	98.81	86.20
120	99.07	89.30
132	99.48	94.55
144	99.69	97.02
156	99.79	98.54
168	99.84	99.43
169+	100.00	100.00

libraries that do not circulate periodicals or where extensive in-library research occurs. These techniques are discussed in Chapter 3, "Client-Centered Measures," as are other uses for circulation studies.

Table 4.7, then, provides the information you need to set the cutoff point. Just decide what percent of future circulation demands you will realistically be satisfied filling from your present collection. If you decide that 98% would be satisfactory, the cutoff point would be 96 months or 8 years. Column 3 shows that the core collection at that point would consist of about 79% of the total collection. The remaining 21% could be weeded.

However, Table 4.8 shows the impact of various cutoff points on the number of titles in the collection and the number of titles that would need to be weeded. If, for instance, the cutoff point is 96 months (8 years), you would be able to weed about 21% of the collection or 29,835 volumes.

Title-by-Title Method

To supplement use studies or when the use study methods of making weeding decisions are not appropriate for your library, you will generally

TABLE 4.8. Estimated Weeding (Collection Size: 141,000)

Cells in Months	% of Future Use to be Satisfied	% of Collection to be Weeded	# of Titles to be Weeded
6	59.67	82.66	116,550
12	74.58	72.98	102,901
18	84.00	66.46	93,708
24	87.80	59.82	84,346
30	90.68	54.37	76,661
36	91.76	50.76	71,571
42	93.31	46.21	65,156
48	94.08	42.66	60,150
54	95.11	38.80	54,708
60	95.67	35.89	50,604
66	96.29	31.78	44,809
72	96.91	29.56	41,679
84	97.58	25.64	36,152
96	98.04	21.16	29,835
108	98.81	13.80	19,458
120	99.07	10.70	15,087
132	99.48	5.45	7,684
144	99.69	2.98	4,201
156	99.79	1.46	2,058
169+	100.00	100.00	803

have to make a title-by-title evaluation. Ideally, this should be based on a comprehensive weeding plan. Such a plan should be founded on criteria derived from collection development policies that reflect the nature and use of publications in the various disciplines, the needs of users, and the resources available to house and manage collections.

General Guidelines

In making a title-by-title evaluation, consider the following general guidelines to ensure a responsible result from what is obviously a highly subjective activity:

- Use sound judgment and common sense.
- Become familiar with the literature of the subject before attempting to weed and consider the historical importance of the work to its discipline.
- Become aware of any cross-disciplinary use of the materials being evaluated.

- Do not discard solely on the basis of physical condition. Valuable materials can be repaired, preserved, or microfilmed.
- Consult with faculty to take advantage of their expertise and to keep them informed of what you are doing. In many instances, faculty members will be willing to assist in the evaluation. But be aware of their specialized interests that may result in weeding some other faculty members' essential titles.
- Weigh the value of the information content of the work. Consider also the availability of the information in other, perhaps more current, works on the subject.
- Consider the apparent use the item has received as evidenced by its physical condition or circulation dates stamped inside.

Guidelines for Selecting Items for Storage

In selecting items for storage, look for the following kinds of titles:

- Out-of-date scientific and technological material. Determine the definition of ''out-of-date'' in consultation with faculty.
- Older editions of works for which new editions exist, especially when the new editions have been revised and updated.
- Books on highly specialized topics that are covered or duplicated in more extensive studies.
- Books in uncommon languages on very specific topics.
- Books by noncontemporary minor authors.
- Early imprints that are not wanted in special collections.
- Biographies of obscure people.
- Books in any discipline in which the information is now considered dated.
- Translations of works when your library has the work in the original language. But in some instances, it may be preferable to keep the English translation of a foreign language work in the stacks.
- Older books obviously unused, uncut, etc.
- Books not needed on a given academic level, i.e., too advanced or too elementary.
- Books covering periods of time not useful for the discipline.
- Potential replacement copies, i.e., duplicates of heavily used titles not needed presently.
- Sets of an author's complete works when other editions fill the present need.
- All titles over a certain age or items that have not circulated in the past 5 (or some other predetermined) years.

Guidelines for Selecting Items for Discard

When discarding items, exercise more caution than when storing them, since they will no longer be available to your patrons. Look for the following as you make your selection:

- Second and additional copies of titles with no demand.
- Practical duplicates, i.e., exact reprints, second or subsequent printings, etc., with identical collation except for date of publication or place of publication.
- Student course outlines, lab manuals, textbooks, etc., no longer currently used and having little or no current reference value.
- Older editions not needed in a storage collection.
- Multiple copies of noncontemporary minor authors, particularly when unused.

Special Considerations for Weeding Serials

Line and Sandison suggest some specific things to look for when trying to decide what serials require weeding:

- Consider "dead" titles, both those that have ceased publication and those your library no longer subscribes to.
- Examine journals for which current issues receive little use to see if they can be cancelled and back issues discarded.
- Determine whether some titles fall off in use so completely after a certain length of time that they can be discarded rather than bound and retained.

The best way to determine these considerations is through a periodical use study or citation analysis to determine more exactly (1) the use of current issues, (2) the use of older volumes, and (3) the use of "dead" titles (see Chapter 3 for a discussion of citation and use study techniques). Since serial runs often occupy significant amounts of stack space even in storage areas, these use studies can be helpful in making the decision to purchase back runs of little-used but still important journals in microforms as an alternative to discarding or storing.

Citation analyses have shown that there may be more interdisciplinary use of serials than librarians have supposed. So if you plan to consult faculty on weeding decisions for serials, consult those from all areas that might conceivably use a particular title, not just those most obviously likely to use it.

ASSESSING APPROVAL PROGRAMS

Since many libraries maintain one or more approval programs, an important assessment activity is to evaluate these programs. The literature contains a number of studies designed to determine how successful these programs are in comparison with other methods of obtaining materials, but this manual will deal only with assessing the suitability of the subject profiles periodically to ensure that the library is receiving materials appropriate to its needs. If the profile is too narrow, you may not be receiving sufficient materials or may be ordering too many titles from notification slips. If the profile is too broad, you may be returning more books than would be necessary or filling the stacks and expending funds on items not really appropriate to your collection.

Like collection development policies, approval program profiles need periodic revision. Fortunately, many of the approval dealers, such as Baker & Taylor, provide management reports that can help you review the approval profiles. The specific procedures discussed here apply to Baker & Taylor only, but other dealers provide similar reports to help you evaluate their programs as well.

Reports are available from approval dealers quarterly and annually. In some instances, cumulative reports for 3 or more years may also be produced. But for evaluating a specific subject collection, the annual report and cumulative reports should be sufficient, since the quarterly activity is likely to be too small to be useful in isolating problems. In fact, you may want to examine reports for several years to avoid overreacting to what may be one-time or atypical aberrations.

Baker & Taylor furnishes several useful management reports, including an Approval Program Subject Report (not shown) that gives the number of titles available in each of the 131 subject area categories and a 2-part *Management Report* (see Figure 4.1). Part I reports the plan activity by subject—the number of books supplied, returned, and several cost factors, and Part II analyzes the returned book activity. This report is supplied for each of the 131 subject areas showing the activity of each of the 5,516 specific subjects appropriate to each of the subject areas. A summary report showing only the 131 subject areas is also included. The example here refers to the subject area report used for evaluating the profile for an individual subject collection.

Baker & Taylor Management Reports (Part I—Plan Activity)

This part of the report is arranged in 11 columns giving the following information:

Column	Information Given
1	LC subject class designator
2	Subject descriptor (based on curricular and publishing patterns, not LC subject heading terms)
3	Number of books shipped
4	Total list price for books shipped in each category
5	Net price for books shipped in each category
6	Average net price per book shipped in each category
7	Number of books ordered from notification slips
8	Percentage of books ordered from notification slips
9	Number of books returned to Baker & Taylor
10	Percentage of books returned to Baker & Taylor
11	Comments

Analysis and Interpretation of Data

The information on this report can alert you to potential problems with the approval profile or with the review procedures for books and notification slips. For example, if the percentage of books ordered from notification slips (see column 8) exceeds 10% in any category, the profile may be too narrow to obtain all the titles you desire, resulting in delay and unnecessary paper work in ordering. It might also indicate a lack of discrimination in reviewing and ordering from notification slips, resulting in acquisitions inappropriate for the collection.

If the percentage of books returned (see column 10) exceeds 5 to 10%, the profile may be too broad. In fact, Baker & Taylor allows a 10 to 15% return rate, but when the rate exceeds 10%, the company will do a return analysis to help the library determine the appropriateness of its profile.

Thus you should carefully analyze the management report to detect potential problems that may be decreasing the effectiveness of your program.

The number of books shipped (see column 3) tells you the number of titles actually supplied you in the 5,516 subjects covered by the approval program arranged by the 131 subject areas. By comparing this number with the total acquisitions or cataloging count in these subjects (assuming that you have this information available), you can determine the impact the approval program is having on your total acquisitions in the various subjects.

Baker & Taylor does not provide a report of books available for each of the 5,516 subjects, but the Approval Program Subject Report (not shown) does give the number available, the average list price of titles, and the total list price of all titles on the system for each of the 131 subject area categories. This enables you to compare your receipts with the total available in the broader subject areas. And since Baker & Taylor supplies materials from over 14,000 publishers, this information should help you compare your expenditures and acquisitions rates against an extensive record of current publications. In addition, the average list price may be useful in determining whether budget allocations to specific subject areas realistically reflect the marketplace. Over time, this information can help you assess the effects of inflation and price increases on your materials budgets.

Allowances have to be made, of course, for the fact that Baker & Taylor may not adequately represent foreign publications, juvenile treatments, or certain formats. As with all assessment measures, your library's policies and practices determine the meaning and significance of the data obtained from approval plan evaluations.

Baker & Taylor Management Reports (Part II–Returned Books)

Since returned books represent an expense to both the library and the vendor, reducing the number of returned books by refining the profile is an important assessment activity. This part of the *Management Report* is particularly well-suited for such an evaluation because it shows specifically why books were returned. (This assumes that when your library returns a title, you indicate the reason for the return, since this report is based on individual library responses.) The ''Return Reason'' part of the report uses alphabetic codes A–T that correspond to the numeric codes printed on the reverse of the green copy of the bibliographic data form supplied with each book shipped, a copy of which is included with each book returned (see

Figure 4.2). This section of the report shows the number of books returned for each reason. However, since more than one reason may be given for a return, the total in this section may be higher than the total number of books returned.

The "Return Code Distribution" section of the report shows the number of books returned arranged by Baker and Taylor's modifier codes listed on the back of the yellow notification slips (see Figure 4.3). If more than one modifier is used to describe the book (e.g., publishers, physical format, and academic level), the total number shown here will be higher than the total number of books returned. The one book returned in Figure 4.1, Part II, for example, has 7 modifiers to describe it, but it is one book returned, not 7.

Analysis and Interpretation of Data

Since both sections of Part II of this report show each book under as many categories as apply (i.e., under each reason given for its return and under all applicable modifier codes), the data can only be analyzed by considering the numbers in each category. For instance, if a large number of returned books were coded 105 (academic level, extracurricular), it might be a sign that the profile should be adjusted to supply slips instead of books for that academic level or to exclude them entirely. Any time the return rate in any of the return code distribution categories exceeds 5% of those supplied, the profile should be reviewed to see if adjustments need to be made. This will alleviate the unnecessary review and return of so many unwanted titles. The return percentage appears in the upper right-hand corner of Part II.

In addition to using the reports for assessing the approval program itself, you can also compare the information with other acquisitions information available in your library. You might, for instance, want to compare expenditures by subject on the approval programs with expenditures for the same subjects for materials obtained from other sources to determine the impact of the approval purchases on your collection development activity.

OVERLAP STUDIES

Chapter 2, "Collection-Centered Measures," discusses the technique of measuring a library's collections against standardized or *ad hoc* lists and the national shelflist counts as a comparative measure of quality. Some of these lists may have been based on the holdings of specific libraries. However, other kinds of comparative evaluations are possible. One method

FIGURE 4.1. Baker & Taylor Management Report

AP240 — APPPOVAL PROGRAM — THE BAKER & TAYLOR CO. — 09/08/84

ACCT U800235 BRIGHAM YOUNG UNIVERSITY — ATTN. ANTONY FERGUSON

RPT-CNTRL LISTING BY SUBJECT DESCRIPTOR — RPT-PERIOD SEP-83 THRU AUG-84

STATION	SUBJECT-------DESCRIPTOR	SHP-QTY	LST-PRC	NET-PRC	AVG-NET	SLP-ORD	PCTG	RTRND	PCTG	COMMENT
PE	ENGLISH LANGUAGE (GENERAL)	2	18.70	15.52	7.76					
PE	ENGLISH LANGUAGE (SPECIFIC	2	49.90	41.42	20.71					
PE	ENGLISH LANGUAGE DICTIONAR	8	105.03	86.30	10.78					
-PE	ENGLISH LANGUAGE HISTORY	1	6.40	5.31	5.31					
PE	OLD AND MIDDLE ENGLISH	2	42.00	34.85	17.42			1	50.0	
PE	ENGLISH GRAMMAR	2	56.57	46.74	23.37					
PE	ENGLISH SEMANTICS	2	26.45	21.95	10.97					
PE	ENGLISH ETYMOLOGY	2	59.13	49.08	24.54					
PE	ENGLISH DIALECTOLOGY	2	34.70	28.80	14.40					
PE	BLACK AMERICAN ENGLISH	1	15.95	13.24	13.24					
PE	ENGLISH LANGUAGE FOR FOREI	22	215.40	181.62	8.25					
BF	LISTENING	1	8.25	6.85	6.85					
LB	READING AND READING IMPROV	3	70.90	58.85	19.61					
PE	ENGLISH COMPOSITION	20	279.56	229.81	11.49					
PE	RESEARCH AND REPORT WRITIN	2	23.90	20.74	10.37					
	NONRETURNABLE SUMMARY		.00	.00						
	NOTIFICATION SLIP SUMMARY		.00	.00						
	TOTAL PE ENGLISH LANGUAGE	72	1,012.84	841.08	11.68			1	1.3	

AP240 — APPROVAL PROGRAM — THE BAKER & TAYLOR CO. — 09/08/84

ACCT U800235 BRIGHAM YOUNG UNIVERSITY — *** MANAGEMENT REPORT *** — RPT-PERIOD SEP-83 THRU AUG-84

PE ENGLISH LANGUAGE — SHPD 72 — R-N-SLIP-ORDS — PCT-R-N .0 — RTRN-QTY 1 — RTRN-PC

*** RETURN REASON ***

A	1	E	I	M	Q
B		F	J	N	R
C		G	K	O	S
D		H	L	P	T

*** RETURN CODE DISTRIBUTION ***

A01	C01	1 E01	1 F03	G05	H07	I06	J06
A02	1 C02	E02	F04	G06	H08	I07	J07
A03	C03	E03	F05		H09	I08	J08
A04	C04	E04	F06	H01			J09
		E05		H02	I01	J01	J10
B01	D01	1 E06	G01	H03	I02	1 J02	J11
B02	1 D02		G02	H04	I03	J03	J12
B03	D03	F01	G03	H05	I04	J04	J13
B04	D04	F02	1 G04	H06	I05	J05	

Used with permission of Baker & Taylor.

is to plan and conduct joint assessments of collections with consortia or other nearby libraries with whom you have cooperative collection development or other reciprocal programs. These assessments can use the standard measuring techniques covered in this manual.

ARL National Collections Inventory Project

Another method is to participate in or use the results of the Association of Research Libraries (ARL) National Collections Inventory Project. Unlike list checking, this approach does not compare titles with your holdings but compares instead existing collection strengths and current collecting levels. Each participating library defines its collecting level in various subject collections by preparing a conspectus showing existing collection strengths and current collecting levels. The conspectuses are entered into a national online database. Libraries can then compare their collection strengths and collecting levels with those of other libraries to help in collection evaluations and other collection development functions. The information can also be used for locating libraries with significant collections in specific subjects for ILL or reference services.

The preface to the draft manual (Reed-Scott, 1984) for the project indicates that the purpose of this project is to coordinate the management of national research collections and to determine responsibilities for maintaining and preserving them. Encouraging systematic collection assessments is an important goal of the project as libraries develop the conspectuses for their collections. The resulting database will prove useful for future comparative assessments among academic libraries.

The National Collections Inventory Project is based on the conspectus program developed by the Research Libraries Group (RLG). A conspectus outline has been or is being developed for each of the Library of Congress broad subject divisions or major disciplines such as linguistics, physics, art and architecture, sociology, etc. These divisions are further broken down into subject categories and the subject categories into subject descriptors. The subject division Art and Architecture, for example, is divided into Visual Arts, Decorative Arts, etc. And Decorative Arts is further subdivided into History, Interior Decoration, Industrial Design, etc. These descriptors are derived from Library of Congress classification schedules or, in some instances, added from another source when no LC category exists. Figure 4.4 shows part of the Brigham Young University Library conspectus for "Decorative Arts," a subject category of the Art and Architecture division.

FIGURE 4.2. "Return Reason" Section of Baker & Taylor Management Report

	Code	Reason for Return
Group A Duplicates	1	Title is already in our collection
	2	Title is on order
	3	Title is received/on order from a foreign source
	4	Title is on standing order by series
	5	Title is on standing order with publisher or received by organization membership
Group B Collection Development Decisions	6	Material is too highly specialized
	7	Geographic areas of limited interest
	8	Specific topic is of limited interest
	9	Treatment is too popular
	10	Treatment is too low level
	11	Scholarship is poor
	12	Treatment by this publisher is unsatisfactory
	13	Textbook: not wanted
	14	Readings/reprinted articles not wanted
	15	Unacceptable format
	16	Library already has adequate material in this subject
Group C Shipping	17	Volume is defective/damaged
	18	Wrong volume has been sent

Used with permission of Baker & Taylor.

FIGURE 4.3. "Return Code Distribution" Section of Baker & Taylor Management Report

Modifier Codes

A Publishers	**G Subject Development**
Commercial	History Bibliography
Univesity Press	Biography Legal Aspects
University Affiliated	Studies & Teachings
Societies & Associations	Techniques
B Country of Publication	**H Textual Format**
United States	Lab Manual
Canada	Readings
Great Britain	Pictorial Treatment
Foreign	Directories
	Anthologies
C Language of Publication	Text, Lower
	Text, Upper
English	Programmed Material
French	
Spanish	**I Academic Level**
Other Foreign Lang.	
	Undergraduate
D Edition	Graduate
	Professional
First	General Supplementary
Subsequent	Extra Curricular
Translation	Selected Graduate
Reprint	
	J Geographic Designators
E Physical Format	
	United States
Hard	Canada
Paper	Latin America
Spiral	Great Britain
Loose Leaf	West Europe
Multi-Media	East Europe, USSR
	Near East, N. Africa
F Continuations	South-SE Asia
	Africa
Series, Vol 1	Far East
Series, Any No	Oceania
Serials, Vol 1	
Serials, Any No	
Sets, Vol 1	

Used with permission of Baker & Taylor.

FIGURE 4.4.   Subject Category Conspectus

```
ARTCAT7   NK


ID          LC CLASS      PCR     SUBJECT                                              ECS/CCI    NOTES
---------------------------------------------------------------------------------------------------------
ART192      NK600-1133            History                                               2/2E

ART193      NK1135-1149           Arts and Crafts Movement                              2/2E

ART194      NK1151-1158   CTYG    Industrial Design                                     3/3E

ART195      NK1160-1678           Decoration and Ornament, Design                       3/3E

ART196      NK1700-3505           Interior Decoration                                   3/3E

ART197      NK2200-2750           Interior Decoration - Furniture                       3/3E

ART198      NK2775                Interior Decoration - Rugs and                        2/2E
                                  Carpets

ART199      NK2975-3096           Interior Decoration - Tapestries                      2/2E

ART200      NK3700-4695           Ceramics                                              3/3F

ART201      NK4700-4890   NYPG    Costume                                               3/3F

ART202      NK5000-5015           Enamel                                                2/2E

ART203      NK5100-5440           Glass                                                 2/2E

ART204      NK5300-5399           Stained Glass                                         2/2E

ART205      NK5800-5998           Ivory and Ivory Carving                               1/1E

ART206      NK5800-5998           Metalwork                                             2/2E

ART207      NK8800-9505           Textiles                                              2/2

ART208      NK9600-9955           Woodwork                                              2/2E

ART209                            Other Decorative Arts                                 2/2E

ART210      TR                    Photography: History and Technique                    3/3E


Brigham Young University Collection Data - January 1985
```

Reproduced by permission of the Research Libraries Group, Inc.

Participating libraries analyze their collections and current collection policies by subjects and indicate (1) existing collection strengths (ECS) and (2) current collecting intensity (CCI), using one of the collecting level and language codes given.

Collecting Level Codes

0–Out of Scope. Not collected.

1–Minimal Level. Very basic works only.

2–Basic Information Level. Up-to-date general materials that introduce and define a subject; basic reference works.

3–Instruction Support Level. Supports undergraduate and most graduate instruction or sustained independent study.

4–Research Level. Major published sources, including journals, required for dissertations and independent research.

5–Comprehensive Level. All significant works of recorded knowledge in all applicable languages; a "special collection" aiming at exhaustiveness.

Language Codes

E–English with little or no foreign language material.

F–Mostly an English language collection with some foreign language materials included, primarily in Western European languages.

W–Wide selection of materials in all applicable languages, no language predominating the selection.

Y–Primarily in one foreign language or in the vernacular languages of a particular non-English-speaking geographic area.

It is assumed that the higher the level of the collection, the more foreign language material it will contain.

The conspectus also allows for scope and comment notes to help define more exactly the scope of the collection or to show a further breakdown of a subject not provided by the conspectus.

Assigning level and language codes requires judgment based on a universal perspective and knowledge of the subject, the bibliography of the subject, existing publications and publishing patterns, and the ability to relate these to the materials in the collection being evaluated. To assist those making these judgments, ARL has prepared expanded guidelines for some conspectus divisions (and is in the process of preparing guidelines for all divisions). In addition, validation studies will provide a checklist of publications in various subject disciplines against which a library can measure its local collections to ensure more uniformity in interpreting and assigning the collecting level codes.

Some subjects, such as cross-disciplinary and area studies, are not covered as well by the conspectuses as needed. But separate conspectuses are being developed for some of these subjects. For others, the RLG Conspectus On-Line can bring together appropriate subjects.

RLG Conspectus On-Line

As libraries complete their conspectuses, they will be entered into the RLG Conspectus On-Line, a part of the Research Libraries Information Network (RLIN). Any library with an RLIN search account and any RLG member will have dial-up access to the database. Libraries without dial-up access can purchase printouts for individual subjects or the complete inventory from the ARL Office of Management Studies.

As of January 1985, the national inventory project is available to all research libraries in the U.S. and Canada. Over the next few years, many research libraries will participate in the program and enter their conspectuses on the system.

Presently, the online conspectus can be searched interactively by subject divisions, subject category words and phrases, specific subject words and phrases, Library of Congress classification numbers, existing collection strength codes, current collecting intensity codes, and scope notes.

Figure 4.5 reproduces the printout obtained from the online conspectus by searching the subject descriptor, "Industrial Design." The first column shows the individual libraries by their RLG code. The second column shows the existing collecting strength (ECS)/current collecting intensity (CCI). The + sign next to the code CTYG (Yale University Sterling Library) indicates that Yale has assumed primary responsibility for developing a major collection in industrial design.

Procedure

Libraries that participate in the national inventory program or who have online access to the Conspectus On-Line will be able to obtain a users manual for the system that fully explains its use. No explanation is given here.

Analysis and Interpretation of Data

The information on existing collection strengths and collecting levels from the conspectuses can be used for a number of comparative purposes:

FIGURE 4.5. Online Conspectus for Industrial Design

```
PROD      Conspectus LON      ART194            Search          UTBG-COL
FIN SP INDUSTRIAL DESIGN# - 1 record
+
(ART194) ART AND ARCHITECTURE - DECORATIVE ARTS                 PCR:CTYG
   Industrial Design                                            NK1151-1158
_____
         CJPA   0/0
         COSG   3/3
         CSUG   2/2
       +CTYG    4/4F
         CUBG   1/1
         CUDG   1/1E
    # DCLC      4/4    Techniques at level 3.
         IAUG   2/2
         ILNG   2/2
         INDG   0/0
    # INIG      0/0
         INPG   3E/3E
    # MAAR      4/4
         MABA   2/2
         MACA   0/0
         MDJG   1/2F
         MIUG   2/2
         MNUG   2E/2E
```

Reproduced by permission of the Research Libraries Group, Inc.

- It can provide information about libraries you may want to compare your collection strengths with.
- It can help you find information about libraries you may want to cooperate with in collection development.
- It can provide information about collection strengths for making ILL requests.
- It can give you information about research collections to provide reference service to researchers in your institution.
- It can give you information to help set objectives and priorities for budget allocations, collection evaluation, and other collection management decisions.

- Since the conspectus categories establish national norms for collection descriptions based on LC classification numbers, you may be able to improve your collection descriptions in collection development policy statements, budget categories, etc., to make future comparative evaluations easier.

To obtain the greatest benefit from the inventory, however, you must evaluate your own library collection objectives and know the kinds of curricular and research programs your collections support in the various subject disciplines covered by the conspectuses. But with that knowledge and understanding, the comparative data can help you make important collection development decisions.

Chapter 5
Reporting Assessment Results

The collection assessment is not complete until the results have been reported clearly and concisely. The length of the report and the kind and amount of data to be included will vary depending on the scope and purpose of the assessment, but it should be complete enough to support any collection development decisions based on it. In planning your report you must not only decide what to include in the report, you also need to consider how best to present it for the greatest clarity and economy. The suggestions here are not cast in stone, but they can help you make some basic decisions. For detailed instructions on report writing, you can refer to any number of technical and report writing manuals as well as style manuals, such as Campbell or Turabian.

CONTENTS

Generally, your report should include the following elements, some of which are suggested by Mosher (1980, p. 542):

- A general overview of the collection, its purpose, and its function in the library's overall collection program.
- The purpose and objectives the assessment was to achieve.
- The methods and measurement techniques used.
- Any problems encountered in using the measurement techniques, particularly problems that may have affected the results or that required adaptations of the techniques.
- The measurement data with sufficient discussion, analysis, and explanation for a clear understanding of its meaning and significance.
- A discussion of specific strengths and weaknesses of the collection.

- Peripheral discoveries or observations of use to the library.
- Recommendations for specific actions to remove *undesirable* weaknesses in the collection, including want lists, weeding or storage needs, etc.
- Suggestions for further analysis or assessment of the collection, including recommended methods.
- Any specific information required by accrediting organizations or your library.

ORGANIZATION

A long-established principle of organization requires that reports should have a beginning, middle, and end, or, in other words, an introduction, body, and conclusion. The elements listed above fit into various parts of this pattern. Obviously, you may vary the suggestions that follow to fit your specific needs, but they are based on sound practice and should work well for most assessment reports.

Beginning

The introduction need not be long, but it should help your readers orient themselves to what is to follow. Include, as appropriate, the following elements:

1. General comments about the collection.
   - Purpose
   - Size
   - Curriculum use
   - Clientele served
   - Collecting level
   - Research use
2. The reason why you made the assessment, including the purpose and objectives you hoped to achieve, the scope and limits of the assessment, the relationship of this assessment to earlier assessments, and (when appropriate) its relationship to a larger plan of assessments for the collection or for your library.
3. The methods or measurement techniques you used in the assessment. (You should not discuss them in detail here but only give a list of them or a general statement about them. You only want to give an overview of your methodology in the introduction.)

4. A brief explanation of any problems you encountered in using the techniques or in making your assessment, particularly if these difficulties affected the results or required adapting your methodology or the techniques.

Middle

This is the body of your report, the place where you fulfill the expectations set up by the introduction. This section of your report should be carefully organized and flow logically. One way to achieve this is to use a topic outline. It need not be too detailed, but it should be done. Then, as you write your report, these outline headings can be inserted into your paper as headings and subheadings to help readers follow the logical structure of your report or to locate more easily a specific topic within it. (Headings are discussed later.)

Organization

Since the body of your report presents, analyzes, and interprets the results obtained from using various measurement techniques, you can logically structure your report around these measures. An assessment using both collection-centered and client-centered measures could be organized and outlined using the 3-level structure illustrated in Figure 5.1.

Note that each level of the outline does not need to be developed in exactly the same way or in the same detail. The outline should be derived from the material to be organized, not forced upon it.

The headings from the outline should be used as headings in your report, using the hierarchical structure detailed in Figure 5.2 and illustrated in Figure 5.3. This enables your readers to see clearly the organizational structure of your report.

Content

As you plan and write your report, keep these principles of content and presentation in mind:

- Present the raw data in sufficient detail to enable readers to see how you arrived at your conclusions and recommendations based on those data.
- When your data are extensive, use tables and graphs to present them and then extract pertinent details to provide meaningful support to the necessary textual discussions and explanations. Remember that

the reader may ignore the tables and charts and read only your commentary.

FIGURE 5.1. Three-Level Outline Format

Introduction

I. Collection-Centered Measures
  A. Shelflist Measurement
  B. List Checking
    1. Methodology
    2. Presentation of Data
    3. Analysis of Results
    4. Conclusions
II. Client-Centered Measures
  A. User Survey
    1. Methodology
    2. Survey Results
    3. Conclusions
  B. Circulation Study
    1. Procedure Used
    2. Results
III. Conclusion
  A. Summary of Conclusions
  B. Recommendations
  C. Suggestions for Further Assessments

- Discuss the significance of the data presented in your tables and graphs. Do *not* expect readers to be able to see the same meaning or significance in the raw data that you do.
- In discussing the data, lead your reader through the reasoning necessary to understand your conclusions and to see that they are sound.
- Discuss specific problems, qualifications, or cautions in the use of the measure or in the interpretation of the data you obtained from its use.

End

At this point, wrap up the report and leave your readers with a clear understanding of the results obtained from the measurements and the conclusions and recommendations you have arrived at. A short report may require only a paragraph or 2 preceded by the heading "Conclusion." A longer report may need to be more elaborate, depending, of course, on the scope of the assessment and the results obtained. For longer reports, use headings that show clearly your conclusions and recommendations:

- If you drew conclusions point by point as you presented and analyzed the data from each measuring technique and if your summary will be fairly lengthy, use "Summary" or "Summary of Conclusions," "Recommendations," and, when appropriate, "Suggestions for Further Assessments" as centered main headings (see Figure 5.1).

- If your summary is only going to be one paragraph or so under each heading, use "Conclusion" as a centered heading and "Summary" or "Summary of Conclusions," "Recommendations," and, if needed, "Suggestions for Further Assessments" as side headings.

Note: In longer reports or when you have extensive detailed data that would interrupt the flow of ideas and make your report less readable, put the material in appendices. This is a good place to include copies of survey instruments and long or multipage tables. If you use appendices, follow these guidelines:

- Generally, include only material that might help readers understand your process more clearly or obtain more detailed measurement data.

- If you put your detailed data in an appendix, condense or select from those data sufficient detail to support your conclusions and include them in the body of your report. The report must be complete and sufficient in itself without the appended material.

- Each different item should be included as a separate appendix and labeled separately, usually with capital letters (Appendix A, B, etc.). If you have only one appendix, just label it "Appendix."

- Don't forget to refer in the body of your report to the appended material. This will ensure that what you are appending is directly related to points in your report. It will also direct your reader to it at the most appropriate time.

HEADINGS

To help both you and your reader, use headings to label the parts of your report. These headings help you organize your material much like an outline. In fact, the different levels of headings should correspond to the parts of your topic outline. Headings also help readers quickly see the component parts of your report and help them read it more easily or find specific parts quickly.

The various levels of headings are distinguished by placement on the page and by typing style. Choose the form of your headings to create a hierarchical pattern based on emphasis. Centered headings, for instance, receive greater attention than side headings and underlined headings more emphasis than those not underlined. Generally, avoid caps since readability studies show that all caps are harder to read than upper and lower case letters. Follow the principles in Figure 5.2 for setting up a heading system suitable for most assessment reports.

FIGURE 5.2. Principles of Heading Format

Title: Use upper/lower case, centered, underlined.

1st Level
   Main heads:
      Upper/lower case, centered, not underlined or bold. Triple-space before and double-space after (corresponds to Roman numeral level of outline).
2nd Level
   Side heads:
      Upper/lower case, flush left on separate line, underlined. Triple-space before and double-space after. This could be bold instead of underlined (corresponds to capital letter level of outline).
3rd Level
   Side heads:
      Upper/lower case, flush left on separate line, not underlined. Double-space before and after (corresponds to Arabic numeral level of outline).
4th Level
   Paragraph heads:
      Upper/lower case, indented 5 spaces, underlined, followed by a period. Begin text of paragraph on same line (corresponds to lower-case letters of outline).

If you have access to a word processor that can print bold or other forms of display lettering, you have greater possibilities for headings. However, choose a type style that harmonizes well with the type used for the rest of the report and follow a hierarchical arrangement.

The 4-level heading system presented in Figure 5.3 can be done on a printer with a bold-type capability. If your typewriter does not have that capability, underline the title instead.

For a 3-level arrangement, you could drop the paragraph heads or one of the third-level side heads. Nothing is sacred about the order as long as you consistently follow the hierarchical concept in whatever method you select.

FIGURE 5.3. Four-Level Heading Illustration

Title

(Type the title on the twelfth line from the top of the page. If your typewriter does not have a bold capability, underline the title instead. Begin the text of the report 15 lines from top of the page.)

First-Level Head (Centered)

(This is centered without underlining on a line by itself 3 lines below end of previous paragraph. It could be bold instead of underlined.)

Second-Level Head (Side)

(This is placed flush left and underlined on a line by itself 3 lines below end of previous paragraph. This could be bold instead of underlined.)

Third-Level Head (Side)

(This is placed flush left and not underlined on a line by itself 3 lines below end of previous paragraph.)

Fourth-Level Head (Paragraph). (This is indented and begun on the same line as the text, underlined, and followed by a period.)

TABLES AND GRAPHICS

In writing assessment reports, using tabular and graphic presentations of data can reduce the length and complexity of the text. Graphics can also dramatize the magnitude of ranges and trends and give data a visual dimension impossible with words. The increasing availability of word processors and computers with graphics and spreadsheet capabilities makes the use of tables and graphics in assessment reports relatively simple. In fact, with programs such as Lotus 1,2,3, Supercalc, and numerous others, the graphic representation can be created at the same time the computer is computing and analyzing the raw data.

Computers can produce all kinds of tables, called spreadsheets, as well as a wide variety of charts or graphs. This manual, however, will not attempt to explain the use of computers to create graphics. If you have computer graphics programs available, you should also have manuals and training programs to help you learn how to use them. Here we will deal only with principles and practices for using tables and graphics effectively in assessment reports.

Principles of Using Tables and Graphics

1. Use them to reduce lengthy and sometimes wordy or confusing prose presentations.
2. Use them to dramatize concepts visually.
3. Make them as self-explanatory as possible.
4. Plan and organize each one carefully, keeping them simple, clear, and uncluttered.
5. Establish the proper relationship between the graphic aid and the text.
   a. If the graphic aid relates to a conclusion to be drawn, refer to it in the text. But avoid such misleading or obvious references as "Table 1 proves," "Figure 2 shows," or "Table 3 is a list of. . . ."
   b. Comment only on significant data or information in the chart or table, not everything. Both text and graphic aid should be understandable without the other.
   c. Give directions for reading and interpreting the graphic aid when it is complex.
6. Place the table or graphic aid in the most effective and accessible location in relation to the textual commentary.
   a. Place it as close to the text it relates to as possible. If it is small enough, put it on the same page as the text. Try to begin the page with text, if possible.
   b. If you can, put a full-page table or chart on a facing page.
   c. If it is long or relates to a number of parts of your report, put it near the beginning or at the end of the report.
   d. If it is long and complex, consider putting it in an appendix and creating condensed versions for inclusion at appropriate places in the text.
   e. If the data you want to present are too extensive for a single page, use an oversized sheet and fold it; prepare them on an

oversized sheet and have them photographically reduced; or try to break up the data into several tables.

    f. If a table is too wide to fit on the length of the paper, put it broadside with the heading against the spine or left edge.

    g. Triple-space before and after the table or chart.

7. Use a clear and consistent labeling system.

    a. Tables and charts should be numbered and labeled separately.

    b. Tables should be designated "Table" if you have only one or "Table 1," "Table 2," etc.

    c. Charts or graphs should be designated "Figure," if you have only one, or "Figure 1," "Figure 2," etc.

    d. Each table or figure should also be given a title. This can be centered 2 spaces above or below the table number. Use an inverted pyramid form if it is more than one line. Or place the table number at the left corner of the table, one line above or below the top line, followed by a period and double-space. Use upper- and lower-case letters, not all caps. Here is an example:

(Above the table line)

Table 1
Combined LC and Dewey Collection
Availability Measurement

or

Figure 1. Combined LC and Dewey Collection
Availability Measurement

(Below the table line)

Figure 1
Comparative LC and Dewey Holdings

or

Table 1. Comparative LC and Dewey Holdings

8. Select the chart or graph form best suited to the data to be represented. The 3 forms listed here should prove sufficient for representing most assessment data.

FIGURE 5.4. Computer-Produced Line Chart

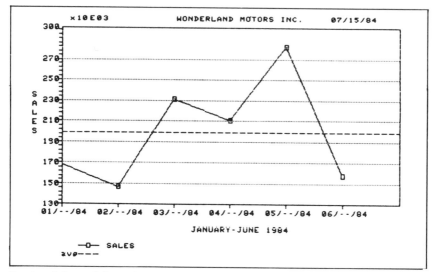

Reprinted from *Information Management,* November 1984, with permission of the publisher.

FIGURE 5.5. Computer-Produced Bar Graph

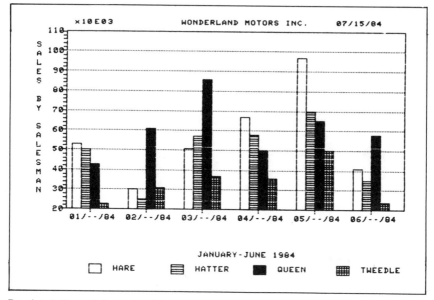

Reprinted from *Information Management,* November 1984, with permission of the publisher.

a. Line charts (the most commonly used) are good for representing and dramatizing trends, continuous processes, or changes over time (see Figure 5.4). Multiple-line graphs can show a number of variables at the same time.

b. Bar graphs, both vertical and horizontal, dramatically represent sizes, amounts, or quantities of things and relative sizes of parts of a whole (see Figure 5.5). They also depict relative amounts

FIGURE 5.6. Computer-Produced Pie Chart

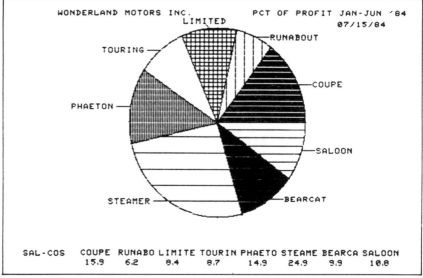

Reprinted from *Information Management*, November 1984, with permission of the publisher.

of several things at the same time or of the same things at different times.

c. Pie charts show divisions of a quantity, area, or population. Labels and percentages must be placed on or alongside each segment, since it would be impossible to estimate relative size accurately (see Figure 5.6). The segments may also be filled in with different colors or lines and cross hatching to dramatize the contrasts.

SAMPLE ASSESSMENT REPORT

The following report is an edited version of a longer report of an actual collection assessment. It is included here, not because it is particularly exemplary, but because it attempts to illustrate most of the principles outlined in this chapter. The original version contained longer explanations of procedures and more tabular material, but this version should give you an idea of what an acceptable report should look like.

Assessment Report
Lee Library Cinematic Arts Collection
Brigham Young University
October 31, 1983

The Harold B. Lee Library is building a research-level collection in Cinematic Arts to support B.A., M.A., and Ph.D programs. The emphasis of both the curriculum and the library collection is on film history, criticism, and production. An important part of the library support of the Theatre and Cinematic Arts programs is the Arts and Communications Archive. However, this assessment does not include that manuscript and memorabilia collection.

The objective of this assessment was to determine the size of the collection, some indication of its quality, and the availability to and use by patrons. To obtain data to measure these qualities, the assessment used the following collection-centered and client-centered measures: (1) shelflist measurement, (2) checking holdings against a film book bibliography and journals lists, (3) a document delivery test, (4) an availability study, and (5) a periodical use study. A circulation study would have been desirable, but reliable data were not available from the computerized circulation system.

Collection-Centered Measures

The collection-centered measures attempted to determine the gross size and indication of the quality of the collection by a shelflist measurement and comparison of holdings against a film literature bibliography.

Shelflist Measurement

Since the Lee Library has collections in both DDC and LC classifications, it was impossible to make a detailed comparative subject breakdown of the shelflist measurement. No satisfactory conversion table is yet available although it would be desirable to have an indication of the number of titles in the collection in the subdisciplines of film studies.

The comparison of the counts of the 2 collections revealed, surprisingly, that the LC collection was larger than the DDC collection even though the LC classification has only been used since 1977. As Table 1 indicates, almost 60% of the cinematic arts materials have been acquired in the past 6 years, an indication that we are building the collection at a faster rate than in earlier years in keeping with the increased emphasis on cinematic arts in the curriculum. Yet the collection is still relatively small, only 2,375 titles. In comparison with film studies bibliographies, this number is low. However, many of the bibliographies list numerous popular treatments of the subject, an area that the curriculum does not currently emphasize.

TABLE 1. Shelflist Measurement Results

Classification	No. Titles	%
DDC 791.43–.438	990	.42
LC PN 1993–1999	1,385	.58
Totals	2,375	100

Bibliography Check

The collection was checked against a film bibliography—Jack Ellis, *The Film Book Bibliography, 1940–1975*—using a random sample of 356 titles covering all aspects of film studies. However, I made no attempt to create a stratified sample. Instead, the sample was selected by taking every fifteenth entry from the numbered list of 5,352 titles, resulting in the subject breakdown shown in Table 2.

TABLE 2. Library Holdings by Film Subject

Subject	No. in Sample	No. in Library	%
Reference Books	27	8	.30
Film Technique and Technology	42	22	.52
Film Industry	13	3	.23
Film History	27	12	.44
Film Classification (Genres)	22	14	.64
Biography	117	51	.44
Individual Films	40	20	.50
Film Theory and Criticism	20	14	.70
Film and Society	25	13	.52
Film and Education	22	11	.50
Totals	355	168	.47

The 47% makes the collection appear relatively weak; particularly weak are reference works and works on film as an industry. However, because the bibliography covered only works published through 1975, the results cannot be considered conclusive. It measures only the DDC collection, which accounts for only 42% of the collection. In addition, many of the titles listed in the bibliography are popular rather than scholarly works and are purchased on a highly selective basis for the collection. Obviously, a further evaluation of the LC collection is needed, but at the time of the assessment, no recent bibliography was available. The recently published *Macmillan Film Bibliography* will now make a subsequent assessment possible.

Even so, for the size of the cinematic arts program and recognizing the scholarly focus of our collection, the 47% figure represents a collection adequate for current demands. Should the number of students or the research demands increase, particularly for pre-1975 titles, the collection would not be adequate.

Client-Centered Measures

To determine how well the collection seemed to be able to serve current users, 2 client-centered measures were used: document delivery capability test and an availability analysis. Both used the same data.

Document Delivery Capability Test

A sample of 400 titles, 220 taken from *The Film Book Bibliography* used in the card catalog check and 180 from the computerized shelflist of titles cataloged in the LC classification 1977–1981, was used to conduct Orr's Document Delivery Capability Test (DDCT) to determine how readily the library could deliver a hypothetical list of titles. The measurement was made on March 9–10, 1983, with a follow-up check on March 22. Each sample title was checked on the shelf. If it was not on the shelf, the sorting shelves were checked; and if not there, the computerized circulation files were checked. Since the DDC items represented published items rather than just items acquired by the library, these titles were also checked against the card catalog.

Of the 323 items acquired by the library (see Table 3), 76% were immediately available on the shelves or sorting shelves, 8% were circulating, and 15% were missing. These data were further analyzed on the Document Delivery Test Analysis Form (see Figure 1). This test combines

TABLE 3. Document Delivery and Availability Sample

	Number	% of Total	% of Acquired
Total Sample	400	100	n/a
Acquired by Library	323	81	100
On Shelf	232	58	72
Not on Shelf	91	23	28
On Sorting Shelves	12	03	04
Checked Out	26	07	08
Return Time—24 hours +	5	01	02
Return Time—1 week+	14	04	04
On Reserve	7	02	02
In Other Known Shelving	5	01	02
Missing After Tracing	48	12	15

both shelf availability and accessibility into one index number by measuring the adequacy of the collection and the time required to furnish requested items. The delivery times are coded as follows:

Code	Time
1	Not more than 10 minutes

2	More than 10 minutes but not
	more than 2 hours
3	2 hours to 24 hours
4	Over 24 hours but not over one week
5	Over one week

The analysis of the data on the Document Delivery Test Analysis Form (see Figure 1) resulted in a Capability Index of 64. Since each time category corresponds roughly to 20 points on the index scale, the CI of 64 suggests that most items could be furnished on the average in less than 2 hours.

Availability Analysis

However, to further pinpoint the causes for patron failure to find materials, the same data were tabulated on the Availability Analysis Form. This methodology postulates that patron failure to find desired titles is a function of 5 causes: (1) failure of the library to acquire a title (DACQ), (2) failure of the patron to use the catalog correctly (DCAT), (3) failure to find title because it is circulating, (4) failure of library procedures (shelving, special locations, etc.) (DLIB), and (5) failure of patron to find properly shelved titles (DUSER).

As Figure 2 shows, the library will have acquired a desired item (MAV ACQ) 81% of the time. However, this figure is skewed because the LC sample was based on acquired items only. Further, the data show that the major determinant of patron dissatisfaction is the library procedures and operations (MAV LIB)—reshelving, reserve, and missing items. Together, these account for 40% of the failures to locate desired items. The overall availability (MAV) is only 58%, which means that 42% of the time, patrons will fail to find what they want immediately available. However, most academic libraries score only between 40 and 60% on availability, so we are on the higher end of the range. Still, some action needs to be taken to improve library procedures for keeping track of acquired titles.

Periodical Holdings Studies

List Checking

Because of a known lack of cinematic arts journals in the library, I compared current subscriptions to *Ulrich's International Periodical Directory* and the list of journals indexed in the *Film Literature Index* and discovered that we subscribed to only 16 out of the 125 indexed or 13%. Of course, many of these journals are not appropriate for our collection because of language, geographical interest, or popularized treatment, but some basic journals are missing, creating problems for patrons. A careful review of Katz, *Magazines for Libraries,* and the annual review of film journals published in *International Film Guide,* was made to create a want list of 15 additional titles, the total subscription cost for which would be $167.50. In addition, an attempt should be made to acquire back issues of each title to have a complete run.

Periodical Use Study

A use study of film periodicals was conducted from November 1, 1982, to May 1, 1983, for bound periodicals in the stacks and from November 1,

1982, to August 31, 1983, for unbound issues in the Current Periodicals Reading Room (CPRR), using Shaw's periodical use study method of marking spines with a stick-on dot when a volume was reshelved (for stack journals) and a hash mark on a label placed on each issue of the unbound (CPRR issues).

Six of the 15 currently active titles received no use. But of these, 2 are not subscription titles and 2 were used as bound volumes for earlier years. Of the bound titles, only 3 of the 35 titles received no use. Of course, this study did not attempt to count the number of uses. It was sufficient to know only that they received some use. It is evident that film journals are being used. Our experience at the reference desk also shows that the lack of sufficient titles indexed in the *Film Literature Index* hampers patron research.

Summary and Conclusions

The Cinematic Arts Collection consists of over 2,300 monographic and journal titles. Compared to a bibliography of over 5,000 titles and *Ulrich's International Periodical Directory*, listing over 280 film journals, and the *Film Literature Index* of 125 journals, our collection appears to be relatively small and inadequate. However, these figures are misleading. The literature of film is characterized by a high percentage of popular treatments geared to the film buff rather than the film scholar or practitioner. Many of these are excluded by our collection development policy. Also, the LC collection, which represents well over half of the total collection, is not adequately represented in the study. In only 6 years, this collection has exceeded the DDC collection, indicating a healthy growth rate. Further study of the LC collection is necessary.

It is obvious that the journal collection, however, is extremely inadequate by any measure used. Our holdings do not meet current demands and are far below what a research level collection requires. In addition, some areas of film studies are not covered by the standard or basic journals available.

Recommendations

To improve the Cinematic Arts Collection in line with the research support level specified in the collection development policy, we should do the following as soon as possible:

1. Immediately subscribe to the 15 journals in the want list. (Not included here.)
2. Conduct further in-depth assessments of specific areas of the film collection shown to be below needs—reference collection, film production, film scripts.
3. Compare holdings of books acquired since 1975 by using the *Macmillan Film Bibliography* to see if recent acquisitions are keeping up with the literature being published.
4. Attempt to acquire important retrospective titles, probably in microform.

APPENDIX

FIGURE 1. Document Delivery Test Analysis Form

DOCUMENT DELIVERY TEST ANALYSIS FORM

	Number of Sample Items by Category	Time Category	Composite Time Total
1. Not in collection	77	5	385
2. On shelf	232	1	232
3. Checked out - reserve	7	2	14
4. Checked out - faculty	14	*ORT −5	70
5. Checked out - grad.	5	*ORT −4	20
6. Checked out - undergrad.		*ORT	
7. Checked out - ILL	—	*ORT	
8. Checked out - other	—	*ORT	
9. In bindery		5	
10. In process		4	
11. In special location	4	*EDT −1	4
12. Reshelving process	11	3	33
13. Recorded as "missing"		5	
14. Other known locations	1	2	2
15. On shelf - 2nd search	11	3	33
16. Can't locate - 2nd search	38	5	190
17. Other outcome - 2nd search		*EDT	
TOTALS	400		983

Mean speed - Total of column 3 divided by the total of column 1

$$CI = \frac{5 - \text{mean speed} \times 100}{4} \qquad CI = \frac{5 - 2.46 \times 100}{4} = 63.5 = 64$$

*Estimated Delivery Time (1-5)   This could be 1-5, depending on the whereabouts of a given title, and will have to be determined on a title by title basis.

*Optimum Return Time (1-5)   This could be 1-5, depending on the actual due date of a given title in circulation. It should be determined on a title by title basis.

FIGURE 2.   Availability Analysis Form

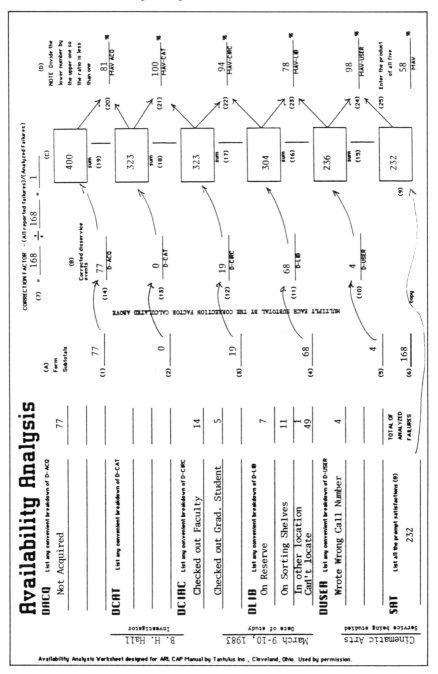

Availability Analysis Worksheet designed for ARL CAP Manual by Tantulus Inc., Cleveland, Ohio. Used by permission.

Appendix A
Bibliography

SOURCES CITED

Association of Research Libraries. Office of Management Studies. *Collection Analysis Project Manual*. Washington, DC, 1977.

Bradford, S. C. *Documentation*. London: Crosby Lockwood, 1948.

Harris, Sherry S., ed. *1983–84 Accredited Institutions of Postsecondary Education*. New York: American Council on Education/Macmillan, 1984.

Kantor, Paul B. "Availability and Accessibility Measures." In Association of Research Libraries. Office of Management Studies. *Collection Analysis Project Manual*. Washington, DC, 1977.

Line, Maurice B. *Library Surveys: An Introduction to Their Use, Planning, Procedure and Presentation*. London: Clive Bingley, 1967.

Line, Maurice B., and Sandison, A. " 'Obsolescence' and Changes in the Use of Literature with Time." *Journal of Documentation* 30 (Sept. 1974): 283–321.

Mosher, Paul H. "Managing Library Collections: The Process of Review and Pruning." In *Foundations in Library Science*, 10, Part A. Greenwich, CT: JAI Press, 1980.

National Council for Accreditation of Teacher Education. *Standards for the Accreditation of Teacher Education*. Washington, DC, 1982.

New England Association of Schools and Colleges. Commission on Vocational, Technical, Career Institutions. *Self-Study Outline for Specialized Institutions of Higher Education Awarding an Associate Degree at the Technical Level*. Winchester, MA, January 1982.

Northwest Association of Schools and Colleges. Commission on Colleges. *Accreditation Handbook*. Seattle, WA, 1984.

Orr, Richard H., et al. "Development of Methodologic Tools for Planning and Managing Library Services: II. Measuring a Library's Capability for Providing Documents." *Medical Library Association Bulletin* 56 (1968): 242–67.

Reed-Scott, Jutta. *Draft Manual for the National Inventory of Research Collections.* Washington, DC: Office of Management Studies, Association of Research Libraries, 1984. (Typewritten draft.)

SCI Journal Citation Reports. Vol. 14 of *Science Citation Index,* 1982 Annual. Eugene Garfield, ed. Philadelphia: Institute for Scientific Information, 1982.

Schwarz, Philip, and Olson, Linda. "Management Decisions Based upon a Core Collection Derived from Last Circulation Date." Research Report No. 1, November 1981. ED 214 496.

Shaw, W. M., Jr. "A Practical Journal Usage Technique." *College and Research Libraries* 39 (Nov. 1978): 478–79.

Subramanyam, Kris. "Citation Studies in Science and Technology." In *Foundations in Library Science,* 10, Part B. Greenwich, CT: JAI Press, 1980.

Titles Classified by the Library of Congress Classification: National Shelflist Count. Berkeley, CA: General Library, University of California, 1977.

Trueswell, Richard W. *Analysis of Library User Circulation Requirements.* U.S. Clearinghouse for Federal Scientific and Technical Information. NTIS Document PB 186 482, January 1968.

Virgo, Julie Carroll, and Yuro, David Alan, eds. *Libraries and Accreditation in Institutions of Higher Education.* Proceedings of a conference held in New York City, June 26–27, 1980. Chicago: Association of College and Research Libraries, 1981.

SURVEYS AND REVIEWS OF THE LITERATURE

Bonn, George S. "Evaluation of the Collection." *Library Trends* 22 (Jan. 1974): 265–304.

Lancaster, F. W. "Evaluation of the Collection." (Chapter 5). *The Measurement and Evaluation of Library Services.* Washington, DC: Information Resources Press, 1977.

Mosher, Paul H. "Quality and Library Collections: New Directions in Research and Practice in Collection Evaluation." In *Advances in Librarianship,* 13. Orlando, FL: Academic Press, 1984.

Perkins, David L., ed. *Guidelines for Collection Development.* Chicago: American Library Association, 1979.

Wiemers, Eugene, Jr., et al. "Collection Evaluation: A Practical Guide to the Literature." *Library Acquisitions: Practice and Theory* 8 (1984): 65–76.

SUPPLEMENTARY SOURCES

Ash, Lee. *Yale's Selective Book Retirement Program.* Hamden, CT: Archon Books, 1963.

Backstrom, Charles H., and Hursh, Gerald D. *Survey Research.* Chicago: Northwestern University Press, 1963.

Broadus, Robert N. "The Applications of Citation Analyses to Library Collection Building." In *Advances in Librarianship,* 7. New York: Academic Press, 1977.

Johnson, Marcia K., and Liebert, Robert M. *Statistics: Tool of the Behavioral Sciences.* Englewood Cliffs, NJ: Prentice-Hall, 1977.

Kantor, Paul B. "Availability Analysis." *Journal of the American Society for Information Science* (Sept.–Oct. 1976): 311–19.

Metz, Paul. *The Landscape of Literatures: Use of Subject Collections in a University Library.* ACRL Publications in Librarianship, no. 43. Chicago: American Library Association, 1983.

Slote, Stanley, J. *Weeding Library Collections—II.* 2d rev. ed. Littleton, CO: Libraries Unlimited, 1982.

True, Jane Audrey. *Finding Out: Conducting and Evaluating Social Research.* Belmont, CA: Wadsworth, 1983.

White, Jan V. *Using Charts and Graphs: 1000 Ideas for Visual Persuasion.* New York: R. R. Bowker, 1984.

Appendix B
Statistical Aids

SAMPLING

Upon occasion, it becomes necessary to test or study a population or set of data. Sometimes the magnitude of data is so great that checking every element becomes impractical. When this occurs, the data can be studied, with some qualifications, using techniques of statistical sampling and inference.

A population is the totality of elements having common characteristics. A sample is some representative portion of elements drawn from the population. If, for example, a library had 24,000 titles classified in the Dewey 650's and wanted to know how many of these titles had blue bindings, instead of counting the blue bindings from the entire population of 24,000 titles, the blue bindings from a sample of the population can be more easily counted. The result of the sample can then be "inferred" or generalized to the entire population. If in a valid sample of 24,000 titles were found to be 600 titles and if 200 (or one-third) of the 600 titles were bound in blue, then generalizing the one-third to the entire population suggests that 8,000 of the 24,000 titles are bound in blue.

Sample Size Determination

Although formulas exist for determining sample size, it is usually easier to use a sample size table. Table B.1 is based on a confidence level of 95% with a degree of accuracy of ± 5% and an expected rate of occurrence of 50%. A greater confidence level will require a larger sample and may not justify the additional work involved. Sample size tables are also available for use when you have a reliable estimate that the variables you are measuring have a better than 50/50 chance of occurring in the population you want to sample. But the 50% table included in this manual should be adequate for most collection assessment samples.

As you can see from the table, the smaller the population, the larger the percentage of the population required for the sample. It also shows that even for very large populations, your sample need not be larger than 383. To use the table, simply find the size of your population in the left-hand column. The number to the right is the necessary sample size for that population.

> EXAMPLE: Assume a need to determine the number of French language books in a collection of 44,000 books. The table shows no entry for 44,000, but since this falls between 40,000 and 50,000, select the higher number. The sample size is 381.

Sampling Techniques

In libraries, it is usually necessary to sample in one of 2 ways. One method of sampling is by entering the population via a random number and counting to the sample. The other method entails measuring to a sample as in a shelflist.

Counting to a Sample

This technique is also referred to as "system sampling." It is conducted as follows: Suppose it is necessary to select a sample of 300 books from a population of 15,000 books. Dividing 15,000 by 300, we find we should select about every fiftieth item for inclusion.

In selecting a sample by this technique, we must first choose a number at random from a random number table. (The technique for choosing this number will be explained below.) Assuming the number turned out to be 27, the first book in the sample would be the twenty-seventh one, then 77, 127, 177, 227, . . . 14,977. This would complete the sample.

Measuring to a Sample

Many times, the number of elements between samples in a population is so great that it is difficult to count to the sample. These can be selected by measuring (Altman, pp. 2.12–2.16). When this is necessary, the population elements must be uniform in size. This is the situation that usually exists in files such as a library shelflist.

In obtaining samples from shelflist (or similar files), proceed through the following steps, using the Shelflist Distribution Form, p. 121.

1. To determine the number of cards in the shelflist population, take 7 one-inch samples. This is done by counting the cards in each of 7 one-inch samples. Each sample should be taken in a different position and, where possible, in a different drawer. The total number of cards counted in each sample is tabulated and totaled. The sum of the 7 cards counted in each sample is tabulated and totaled. The sum of the 7 samples is then divided by 7. The quotient is the number of cards per inch. Note: If there are more than 4 cards' difference in any one or more of the 7 samples, the sampling must be repeated as the samples were apparently not measured under uniform pressure.

2. (a) Measure the entire section of shelflist within which the population under examination exists. This is done by pressing the cards in each drawer fairly tightly and measuring them with a retractable metal ruler. The measurement of each drawer is tabulated and totaled to get the overall length.
   (b) Then, multiply the overall length by the number of cards per inch to obtain the number of cards in the shelflist.

3. Determine the number of samples necessary for the study by following the procedures under ''Sample Size Determination'' on p. 115.
   (a) Divide the total number of cards in the entire population by the total number of samples necessary. This result is the number of cards between samples.
   (b) Divide this result (number of cards between samples) by the average number of cards per inch which was determined in step 2. This final result will be the number of inches between samples in hundredths.

4. Convert inches from hundredths to sixteenths by using the interval conversion table on the Shelflist Distribution Form (see p. 121).

5. Determine the entry point into the population by using a random number table. Select a number that falls within the number of cards between samples determined in step 2 (a). Begin the sampling process by counting to this number and then measuring to each additional sample within the population, using the sampling interval obtained in step 4. For example:
   1. Measure the entire shelflist of the Dewey 650's. (Assume this total is 300 inches.)
   2. Take 7 one-inch samples from 7 different drawers or from 7 different places, if fewer than 7 different drawers within the shelflist, and average them.

3. If this average were 100 cards per inch, multiply 100 cards per inch by 300 inches of Dewey 650's and get 30,000 cards for a total population.
4. Determine the number of samples necessary by applying the procedure in "Sample Size Determination." (Assume this yields 500 samples.)
5. Divide the total number of cards in the population by the number of samples: 30,000 divided by 500=60. This is the number of cards between samples.
6. Divide the number of cards between samples by the number of cards per inch: 60 divided by 100=.6 inches. (See conversion table on Shelflist Distribution Form, p. 121).
7. Select a random number within the number of cards between samples, in this case between 1 and 60, using a random number table (see Table B.2). Begin at the first of the population and count to the card that corresponds to the random number. This is the first sample.
8. From the first sample, measure .6 inches (10/16" or 5/8") and take another sample. Repeat this sampling throughout the entire population until you have your 500 sample items.

SELECTING A RANDOM NUMBER FROM A RANDOM NUMBER TABLE

A major problem in using a random number table (see Table B.2) is obtaining an unbiased selection of the first random number. Most methods for accomplishing this are arbitrary. The most important consideration is that the method of selection be determined before turning to the table (Lynch and Huntsberger, p. 247).

If it were necessary to take 100 samples from a population of 800 books, it would be necessary to sample every eighth book (800 divided by 100=8). To arrive at the entry point using a random number table, it is necessary to choose from the table a number between 1 and 8. A predetermined arbitrary method to derive this number involves several steps:

1. Put your pencil down on any number in a random number table.
2. Count 3 numbers to the right.
3. Count 4 numbers down and, proceeding downward, select the first number between 1 and 8.

Assuming the number 3 is the first number encountered between 1 and 8, then the *third* book would be the first sample taken. Proceeding, then, with every eighth sample thereafter, the numbers 11, 19, 27, 35, etc., would also be selected.

The use of the random number table to begin the sampling is necessary if every element within the population is to have an equally likely chance of being selected. To grant integrity to the study, every book selected at random *must* be used in the study. Any temptation to skip a properly selected sample must be overcome.

SUMMARY

Use of the above procedures will allow a collection of statistical samples for most library purposes. If needs arise in the process of collection assessment which are not met by the above, most basic statistics texts or handbooks can provide answers.

BIBLIOGRAPHY

Altman, Ellen and others. *A Data Gathering and Instructional Manual for Performance Measures in Public Libraries*. Chicago: Celadon Press, 1976.

Lynch, Mervin D. and Huntsberger, David V. *Elements of Statistical Inference for Education and Psychology*. Boston: Allyn and Bacon, 1976.

TABLE B.1. Sample Size Table

Confidence Level: 95%   Reliability ± 5%
% in Population Assumed to be 50%

Population Size	Sample Size	Population Size	Sample Size	Population Size	Sample Size
10	9	230	144	1400	301
15	14	240	147	1500	305
20	19	250	151	1600	309
25	23	260	155	1700	313
30	27	270	158	1800	316
35	32	280	162	1900	319
40	36	290	165	2000	322
45	40	300	168	2200	327
50	44	320	174	2400	331
55	48	340	180	2600	334
60	52	360	186	2800	337
65	55	380	191	3000	340
70	59	400	196	3500	346
75	62	420	200	4000	350
80	66	440	205	4500	354
85	69	460	209	5000	356
90	73	480	213	6000	361
95	76	500	217	7000	364
100	79	550	226	8000	366
110	85	600	234	9000	368
120	91	650	241	10000	369
130	97	700	248	15000	374
140	102	750	254	20000	376
150	108	800	259	30000	379
160	113	850	264	40000	380
170	118	900	269	50000	381
180	122	950	273	60000	381
190	127	1000	277	70000	382
200	131	1100	284	120000	382
210	136	1200	291	160000	383
220	140	1300	296	1000000	383

FIGURE B.1. Shelflist Distribution Form

SHELFLIST DISTRIBUTION FORM

Shelflist Sections Measured:

Step 1: Take seven different samples from shelflist and record the number of cards per inch in each sample.

Sample 1	_____	Sample 5	_____
Sample 2	_____	Sample 6	_____
Sample 3	_____	Sample 7	_____
Sample 4	_____	Sum:	_____

Divide sum above by seven = _____ (Average number of cards/inch)

Step 2: (a) Measure length of
shelflist in inches = _____ (Inches in shelflist)

(b) Multiply total inches of shelflist by average number cards per inch (Step 1 × Step 2) = _____ (Total cards in shelflist)

Step 3: (a) Divide total cards in shelflist by number of sample items necessary= _____ (Number of cards between samples)
(b) Divide number of cards per sample interval by average number of cards per inch (Step 3÷Step 1)= _____ (Inches per sample interval in hundredths)

Step 4: Convert inches per interval from "hundredths" to "sixteenths" by means of Index table below = _____ (Inches per sample interval in sixteenths)

Interval Index

Quotient/Sixteenths	Quotient/Sixteenths
0.0625 = 1/16	0.5625 = 9/16
.1250 = 2/16	.6250 = 10/16
.1875 = 3/16	.6875 = 11/16
.2500 = 4/16	.7500 = 12/16
.3125 = 5/16	.8125 = 13/16
.3750 = 6/16	.8750 = 14/16
.4375 = 7/16	.9375 = 15/16
.5000 = 8/16	1.0000 = 16/16

Ellen Altman et al. *A Data Gathering and Instructional Manual for Performance Measures in Public Libraries*, 1976.

TABLE B.2.   Random Number Table

```
                        TABLE OF RANDOM DIGITS

00200   19612 78430   11661 94770   77603 65669   86868 12665   30012 75989
00201   39141 77400   28000 64238   73258 71794   31340 26256   66453 37016
00202   64756 80457   08747 12836   03469 50678   03274 43423   66677 82556
00203   92901 51878   56441 22998   29718 38447   06453 25311   07565 53771
00204   03551 90070   09483 94050   45938 18135   36908 43321   11073 51803

00205   98884 66209   06830 53656   14663 56346   71430 04909   19818 05707
00206   27369 86882   53473 07541   53633 70863   03748 12822   19360 49088
00207   59066 75974   63335 20483   43514 37481   58278 26967   49325 43951
00208   91647 93783   64169 49022   98588 09495   49829 59068   38831 04838
00209   83605 92419   39542 07772   71568 75673   35185 89759   44901 74291

00210   24895 88530   70774 35439   46758 70472   70207 92675   91623 61275
00211   35720 26556   95596 20094   73750 85788   34264 01703   46833 65248
00212   14141 53410   38649 06343   57256 61342   72709 75318   90379 37562
00213   27416 75670   92176 72535   93119 56077   06886 18244   92344 31374
00214   82071 07429   81007 47749   40744 56974   23336 88821   53841 10536

00215   21445 82793   24831 93241   14199 76268   70883 68002   03829 17443
00216   72513 76400   52225 92348   62308 98481   29744 33165   33141 61020
00217   71479 45027   76160 57411   13780 13632   52308 77762   88874 33697
00218   83210 51466   09088 50395   26743 05306   21706 70001   99439 80767
00219   68749 95148   94897 78636   96750 09024   94538 91143   96693 61886

00220   05184 75763   47075 88158   05313 53439   14908 08830   60096 21551
00221   13651 62546   96892 25240   47511 58483   87342 78818   07855 39269
00222   00566 21220   00292 24069   25072 29519   52548 54091   21282 21296
00223   50958 17695   58072 68990   60329 95955   71586 63417   35947 67807
00224   57621 64547   46850 37981   38527 09037   64756 03324   04986 83666

00225   09282 25844   79139 78435   35428 43561   69799 63314   12991 93516
00226   23394 94206   93432 37836   94919 26846   02555 74410   94915 48199
00227   05280 37470   93622 04345   15092 19510   18094 16613   78234 50001
00228   95491 97976   38306 32192   82639 54624   72434 92606   23191 74693
00229   78521 00104   18248 75583   90326 50785   54034 66251   35774 14692

00230   96345 44579   85932 44053   75704 20840   86583 83944   52456 73766
00231   77963 31151   32364 91691   47357 40338   23435 24065   08458 95366
00232   07520 11294   23238 01748   41690 67328   54814 37777   10057 42332
00233   38423 02309   70703 85736   46148 14258   29236 12152   05088 65825
00234   02463 65533   21199 60555   33928 01817   07396 89215   30722 22102

00235   15880 92261   17292 88190   61781 48898   92525 21283   88581 60098
00236   71926 00819   59144 00224   30570 90194   18329 06999   26857 19238
00237   64425 28108   16554 16016   00042 83229   10333 36168   65617 94834
00238   79782 23924   49440 30432   81077 31543   95216 64865   13658 51081
00239   35337 74538   44553 64672   90960 41849   93865 44608   93176 34851

00240   05249 29329   19715 94082   14738 86667   43708 66354   93692 25527
00241   56463 99380   38793 85774   19056 13939   46062 27647   66146 63210
00242   96296 33121   54196 34108   75814 85986   71171 15102   28992 63165
00243   98380 36269   60014 07201   62448 46385   42175 88350   46182 49126
00244   52567 64350   16315 53969   80395 81114   54358 64578   47269 15747

00245   78498 90830   25955 99236   43286 91064   99969 95144   64424 77377
00246   49553 24241   08150 89535   08703 91041   77323 81079   45127 93686
00247   32151 07075   83155 10252   73100 88618   23891 87418   45417 20268
00248   11314 50363   26860 27799   49416 83534   19187 08059   76677 02110
00249   12364 71210   87052 50241   90785 97889   81399 58130   64439 05614
```

Reprinted from page 5 of *A Million Random Digits with 100,000 Normal Deviates* by The Rand Corporation (New York: The Free Press, 1955). Copyright 1955 and 1983 by The Rand Corporation. Used by permission.

Appendix C
Accrediting Groups Recognized by Council on Postsecondary Accreditation (COPA)

NATIONAL INSTITUTIONAL ACCREDITING BODIES

American Association of Bible Colleges
  Randall E. Bell, Executive Director
  PO Box 1523 130-F North College St.
  Fayetteville, AR 72701
  (501) 521-8164

Association of Independent Colleges and Schools
  James M. Phillip, Executive Director
  Accrediting Commission
  One Dupont Circle, Suite 350
  Washington, DC 20036
  (202) 659-2460

National Association of Trade and Technical Schools
  Lee Kirschner, Secretary
  Accrediting Commission
  2021 K St., N.W., Room 305
  Washington, DC 20006
  (202) 296-8892

National Home Study Council
  William A. Fowler, Executive Secretary
  Accrediting Commission
  1601 Eighteenth St., N.W.
  Washington, DC 20009
  (202) 234-5100

Reprinted by permission of the American Council on Education, Washington, DC, 1984.

REGIONAL INSTITUTIONAL ACCREDITING BODIES

Middle States Association of Colleges and Schools
Delaware, District of Columbia, Maryland, New Jersey, New York, Pennsylvania, Puerto Rico, Virgin Islands
Robert Kirkwood, Executive Director
Commission on Higher Education
3624 Market St.
Philadelphia, PA 19104
(215) 662-5606

New England Association of Schools and Colleges
Connecticut, Maine, Massachusetts, New Hampshire, Rhode Island, Vermont
The Sanborn House
15 High St.
Winchester, MA 01890
(617) 729-6762
Charles M. Cook, Director of Evaluation, Commission on Institutions of Higher Education
Daniel S. Maloney, Director of Evaluation Commission on Vocational, Technical, Career Institutions

North Central Association of Colleges and Schools
Arizona, Arkansas, Colorado, Illinois, Indiana, Iowa, Kansas, Michigan, Minnesota, Missouri, Nebraska, New Mexico, North Dakota, Ohio, Oklahoma, South Dakota, West Virginia, Wisconsin, Wyoming
Thurston E. Manning, Director
Commission on Institutions of Higher Education
159 North Dearborn St.
Chicago, IL 60601
(312) 263-0456

Northwest Association of Schools and Colleges
Alaska, Idaho, Montana, Nevada, Oregon, Utah, Washington
James F. Bemis, Executive Director
Commission on Colleges
3700-B University Way, N.E.
Seattle, WA 98105
(206) 543-0195

Southern Association of Colleges and Schools
Alabama, Florida, Georgia, Kentucky, Louisiana, Mississippi, North
Carolina, South Carolina, Tennessee, Texas, Virginia
795 Peachtree St., N.E.
Atlanta, GA 30365
(404) 897-6126
Gordon W. Sweet, Executive Director
Commission on Colleges
Kenneth W. Tidwell, Executive Director
Commission on Occupational Education Institutions
(404) 897-6163

Western Association of Schools and Colleges
American Samoa, California, Guam, Hawaii, Trust Territory of the Pacific
Kay J. Andersen, Executive Director
Accrediting Commission for Senior Colleges and Universities
c/o Mills College
Box 9990
Oakland, CA 94613
(415) 632-5000
Robert E. Swenson, Executive Director
Accrediting Commission for Community and Junior Colleges
PO Box 70, 9053 Soquel Dr.
Aptos, CA 95003
(408) 688-7575

SPECIALIZED ACCREDITING BODIES

Allied Health
(Representing 40 collaborating health organizations)
American Medical Association Committee on Allied Health Education
and Accreditations
John J. Fauser, Director
Department of Allied Health
Education and Accreditation, AMA
535 North Dearborn St.
Chicago, IL 60610
(312) 751-6272

Architecture
(First professional degree programs)
    National Architectural Accrediting Board
    John Wilson-Jeronimo, Executive Director
    1735 New York Ave., N.W.
    Washington, DC 20006
    (202) 783-2007

Art and Design
(Institutions offering professional preparation)
    National Association of Schools of Art and Design
    Samuel Hope, Executive Director
    Commission on Accreditation
    11250 Roger Bacon Dr., Suite 5
    Reston, VA 22090
    (703) 437-0700

Business Administration and Management
(Bachelor's and master's degree programs)
    American Assembly of Collegiate Schools of Business
    William K. Laidlaw, Jr., Executive Vice President
    605 Old Ballas Rd., Suite 220
    St. Louis, MO 63141
    (314) 872-8481

Chiropractic Education
(Institutions offering professional degrees)
    The Council on Chiropractic Education
    Ralph G. Miller, Executive Secretary
    3209 Ingersoll Ave.
    Des Moines, IA 50312
    (515) 255-2184

Construction Education
(Baccalaureate programs)
    American Council for Construction Education
    I. Eugene Thorson, Executive Vice President
    PO Box 1266, 2805 Claflin Rd., Suite 200
    Manhattan, KS 66502
    (913) 776-1544 or (913) 537-7032

Dentistry and Dental Auxiliary Programs
(First professional programs in dental education; degree and certificate
programs in dental auxiliary education)
American Dental Association
Mario V. Santangelo, Secretary
Commission on Dental Accreditation
211 East Chicago Ave.
Chicago, IL 60611
(312) 440-2708

Dietetics
(Coordinated baccalaureate programs)
The American Dietetic Association
Phillip Lesser, Administrator
Department of Education
430 North Michigan Ave.
Chicago, IL 60611
(312) 280-5023

Engineering
(Professional engineering programs at the baccalaureate and master's level;
baccalaureate programs in engineering technology; and 2-year associate
degree programs in engineering technology)
Accreditation Board for Engineering and Technology
David R. Reyes-Guerra, Executive Director
345 East 47th St.
New York, NY 10017
(212) 705-7685

Forestry
(Professional schools)
Society of American Foresters
Ronald R. Christensen, Director of Professional Programs
5400 Grosvenor Lane
Bethesda, MD 20814
(301) 897-8720

Health Services Administration
(Graduate programs)
Accrediting Commission on Education for Health Services
Administration

Steven M. Sundre, Executive Secretary
1911 North Fort Myer Dr., Suite 503
Arlington, VA 22209
(703) 524-0511

Home Economics
(Undergraduate programs)
American Home Economics Association
Judith A. Jax, Director
Office of Professional Education
2010 Massachusetts Ave., N.W.
Washington, DC 20036
(202) 862-8355

Interior Design
(Programs at the 2-year, 3-year, baccalaureate, and master's levels)
Foundation for Interior Design Education
Edna Kane, Director of Administration
242 West 27th St., Suite 6B
New York, NY 10001
(212) 929-8366

Journalism
(Units and programs leading to undergraduate and master's degrees in journalism)
Accrediting Council on Education in Journalism and Mass Communication
Roger Gafke, Executive Secretary
Accrediting Committee, School of Journalism, University of Missouri
PO Box 838
Columbia, MO 65205
(314) 882-6362

Landscape Architecture
(Professional programs)
American Society of Landscape Architects
Karen Rosenfeld, Director of Education and Research
Landscape Architectural Accreditation Board
1733 Connecticut Ave., N.W.
Washington, DC 20009
(202) 466-7730

Law
(Professional schools)
  American Bar Association
  James P. White, Consultant on Legal Education
  Indianapolis Law School, Indiana University—Purdue University at Indianapolis
  735 West New York St., Room 237
  Indianapolis, IN 46202
  (317) 264-8071

  Association of American Law Schools
  Millard H. Ruud, Executive Director
  One Dupont Circle, N.W., Suite 370
  Washington, DC 20036
  (202) 296-8851

Librarianship
(First professional degree programs)
  American Library Association
  Elinor Yungmeyer, Accreditation Officer
  Committee on Accreditation
  50 East Huron St.
  Chicago, IL 60611
  (312) 944-6780

Medical Assistant and Medical Laboratory Technician
(Diploma, certificate, and associate degree programs)
  Accrediting Bureau of Health Education Schools
  Hugh A. Woosley, Administrator
  Oak Manor Offices, 29089 U.S. 20 West
  Elkhart, IN 46514
  (219) 293-0124

Medicine
(Programs leading to first professional degree and programs in the basic medical sciences)
  Liaison Committee on Medical Education (in odd-numbered years beginning each July 1, contact)
  Edward S. Petersen, Secretary
  Council on Medical Education, AMA
  535 North Dearborn St.

Chicago, IL 60610
(312) 751-6310
or (in even-numbered years beginning each July 1, contact)
J. R. Schofield, Secretary
Association of American Medical Colleges
One Dupont Circle, N.W., Suite 200
Washington, DC 20036
(202) 828-0670

Music
(Baccalaureate and graduate degree programs, also nondegree granting institutions)
National Association of Schools of Music
Samuel Hope, Executive Director
11250 Roger Bacon Dr., Suite 5
Reston, VA 22090
(703) 437-0700

Nursing
(Associate, baccalaureate, and higher degree programs; also diploma and practical nurse programs)
National League for Nursing
Virginia O. Allen, Director of Accreditation Services
10 Columbus Circle
New York, NY 10019
(212) 582-1022

(Practical nursing programs only)
National Association for Practical Nurse Education and Service
Terence Roderick, Director of Accreditation Services
254 West 21st St.
New York, NY 10001
(212) 736-4540

Optometry
(Professional programs in optometry and optometric technology)
American Optometric Association
Sally A. Bowers, Executive Secretary
Council on Optometric Education
243 North Lindbergh Blvd.
St. Louis, MO 63141
(314) 991-4100

Osteopathic Medicine
(First professional degree programs)
American Osteopathic Association
Douglas Ward, Director, Bureau of Professional Education
212 East Ohio St.
Chicago, IL 60611
(312) 280-5800

Pharmacy
(First professional degree programs)
American Council on Pharmaceutical Education
Daniel A. Nona, Executive Director
311 West Superior St.
Chicago, IL 60610
(312) 664-3575

Physical Therapy
(First professional degree programs)
American Physical Therapy Association
Patricia Yarbrough, Director
Department of Educational Affairs
Transpotomac Plaza, 1111 North Fairfax St.
Alexandria, VA 22314
(703) 684-2782

Podiatry
(Professional schools)
American Podiatry Association
Warren G. Ball, Director
Council on Podiatry Education
20 Chevy Chase Circle, N.W.
Washington, DC 20015
(202) 537-4970

Psychology
(Doctoral programs leading to professional practice of psychology)
American Psychological Association
Paul D. Nelson, Administrative Officer for Accreditation
1200 Seventeenth St., N.W.
Washington, DC 20036
(202) 833-7692

Public Health
(Graduate schools of public health and master's degree programs in community health education)
   Council on Education for Public Health
   Patricia P. Evans, Executive Director
   1015 Fifteenth St., N.W., Suite 403
   Washington, DC 20005
   (202) 789-1050

Rabbinical and Talmudic Education
(Postsecondary programs in advanced Rabbinical and Talmudic education)
   Association of Advanced Rabbinical and Talmudic Schools
   Bernard Fryshman, Executive Director
   175 Fifth Ave., Room 711
   New York, NY 10010
   (212) 477-0950 or (212) 645-1814

Rehabilitation Counseling
(Master's degree programs)
   Council on Rehabilitation Education
   Charlene McGrath, Executive Director
   162 North State St., Room 317
   Chicago, IL 60601
   (312) 346-6027

Social Work
(Baccalaureate and master's degree programs)
   Council on Social Work Education
   Sidney Berengarten, Director
   Division of Education
   Standards and Accreditation
   111 Eighth Ave., Suite 501
   New York, NY 10011
   (212) 242-3800

Speech Pathology and Audiology
(Master's degree programs)
   American Speech—Language—Hearing Association
   Billie Ackerman, Director
   Standards and Ethics Dept.

10801 Rockville Pike
Rockville, MD 20852

Teacher Education
(Baccalaureate and graduate degree programs)
National Council for Accreditation of Teacher Education
George Denemark, Interim Director
1919 Pennsylvania Ave., N.W., Suite 202
Washington, DC 20006
(301) 897-5700

Theology
(Graduate professional schools and programs)
Association of Theological Schools in the United States and Canada
Leon Pacala, Executive Director
42 East National Rd., P.O. Box 130
Vandalia, OH 45377
(513) 898-4654

Veterinary Medicine
(First professional degree programs)
American Veterinary Medical Association
R. Leland West, Director of Scientific Activities
930 North Meacham Rd.
Schaumburg, IL 60196
(312) 885-8070

(This listing current as of September 1, 1983)

Appendix D
Sample Survey Instruments

BYU FACULTY SURVEY OF ENGLISH COLLECTION

1. How many times per week do you usually use the English Collection in the library? (check one only)
   a. _____ Never (if you checked this response, please skip to Question 14 of this survey)
   b. _____ Less than once per week
   c. _____ 1–2 times per week
   d. _____ 3–4 times per week
   e. _____ 5–6 times per week
   f. _____ 7 or more times per week

2. How many hours per week do you spend using the English Collection? (check one only)
   a. _____ Less than 2 hours
   b. _____ 2–5 hours
   c. _____ 6–10 hours
   d. _____ 11–15 hours
   e. _____ More than 15 hours

3. If you have ever used an English Collection at any college or university library other than BYU's, please respond to this question:

   How well does the English Collection in the Harold B. Lee Library compare with those of other libraries?

   1=BYU much poorer
   2=BYU poorer
   3=BYU about the same
   4=BYU better
   5=BYU much better

Please answer for both "Books" and "Journals" below by placing a number for each college collection you have used.

Name of College or University	Books	Journals
1. Arizona State University		
2. Cal Tech		
3. Colorado State University		
4. Harvard University		
5. Indiana University		
6. Iowa State University		
7. MIT		
8. New Mexico Highlands University		
9. Oregon State University		
10. Stanford		
11. University of Calgary, Canada		
12. University of California, Berkeley		
13. University of California, Davis		
14. University of California, Irvine		
15. University of California, Los Angeles		
16. University of Cincinnati		
17. University of Illinois		
18. University of Lethbridge, Canada		
19. University of Liege, Belgium		
20. University of Utah		
21. University of Virginia		
22. Utah State University		
23. University of Washington, Seattle		
24. Vanderbilt University		
25. Washington University, St. Louis		

4. How often do you use the English Collection for each of the following activities? (please respond to all items a–h by circling the appropriate number)

	Rarely or Never	Sometimes	Often
a. To keep up in my field	1	2	3
b. To prepare for class	1	2	3
c. To do research	1	2	3

d.	To use journals	1	2	3
e.	To have students do research for me	1	2	3
f.	To use manuscripts	1	2	3
g.	To use primary sources (novels, poetry, etc.)	1	2	3
h.	To use secondary sources (criticism, etc.)	1	2	3

5. How adequate is the English Collection in each of the following areas? (please circle appropriate number)

		Inadequate	Poor	Fair	Good	Excellent
a.	Current	1	2	3	4	5
b.	Books more than 10 years old	1	2	3	4	5
c.	Current journals	1	2	3	4	5
d.	Journals more than 10 years old	1	2	3	4	5
e.	Manuscripts	1	2	3	4	5
f.	Indexes, bibliographies, reference books	1	2	3	4	5

6. How good should the English Collection be in each of these to meet your needs adequately? (please circle appropriate number)

		Very Poor	Poor	Fair	Good	Excellent
a.	Current books	1	2	3	4	5
b.	Books more than 10 years old	1	2	3	4	5
c.	Current journals	1	2	3	4	5
d.	Journals more than 10 years old	1	2	3	4	5
e.	Manuscripts	1	2	3	4	5
f.	Indexes, bibliographies, reference books	1	2	3	4	5

7. How often do you find yourself having to go to another library or using interlibrary loan because the Harold B. Lee Library's English Collection does not have what you need? (please circle appropriate number)

Rarely or Never	Sometimes	Often
1	2	3

8. a. Are you satisfied with the acquisitions and processing of materials for the English Collection? (check one only)

_____Usually satisfied _____Occasionally _____Usually not
                                        not satisfied   satisfied

b. How easy is it to get materials ordered? (please circle number)

Hard to Order   Easy to Order
   1   2   3

c. Do you personally participate in the library material selection process in your department? _____Yes _____No

d. How often are you refused the purchase of what you feel to be needed library materials for the English Collection? (please circle number)

Rarely or Never   Sometimes   Often
   1   2   3

e. How soon are you notified when the materials you have special ordered are received? (please circle number)

Not notified   Slowly   Fair   Quickly
   1   2   3   4

f. Is the present "book list" method of listing new acquisitions an adequate way of informing you about new books?

_____Yes   _____No If no, can you recommend a better method?

9. If you had control of the budget for the English Collection, how would you allocate it? (give a percentage in the space provided)

a. _____ Current books
b. _____ Current journals
c. _____ Retrospective books
d. _____ Retrospective journals
e. _____ Indexes, bibliographies, and reference books
f. _____ Nonprint media
g. _____ Other _____

10. How adequate is the English Collection for each of the following? (circle appropriate number)

	Inadequate	Poor	Fair	Good	Excellent
a. Undergraduates	1	2	3	4	5
b. Master's candidates	1	2	3	4	5
c. Ph.D candidates	1	2	3	4	5
d. Faculty	1	2	3	4	5

11. How would you rate the English Collection for (please circle number)

	Very Poor	Poor	Fair	Good	Excellent
a. Instructional purposes	1	2	3	4	5
b. Research purposes	1	2	3	4	5

12. Which of the following present problems to you with the English Collection? (check all that apply)

a. _____ Not enough journals
b. _____ Not enough books
c. _____ Time lag between ordering and receiving
d. _____ Misfiled books and/or journals
e. _____ Lost books and/or journals
f. _____ Spread out on different levels of the library
g. _____ Journals gone too long for binding
h. _____ Ease of locating and obtaining books, journals, etc.
i. _____ Service at the Humanities Reference Desk
j. _____ Insufficient copies of individual titles
k. _____ Other (please explain):

13. Please list any suggestions you may have for improving the English Collection.

14. How many years have you taught at BYU? (check one only)
a. _____ Less than 2 years
b. _____ 2–5 years
c. _____ 5–10 years
d. _____ More than 10 years

CAP FACULTY RESEARCH SURVEY

Name _____

Department _____

AREAS OF RESEARCH

1. What are your areas of specialization?

_____
_____

2. What are your current areas of research interests or activities?

_____
_____

3. What future research projects are you anticipating that would involve library materials?

_____
_____

COLLECTION ASSESSMENT

1. How adequate do you find the library collection in your areas of specialization?

_____
_____
_____

2. What deficiencies are you aware of in the library collections or services that support your research?

_____
_____
_____
_____
_____

Association of Research Libraries. Office of Management Studies. *Collection Analysis Project Manual*. Washington, DC, 1977.

CAP GRADUATE STUDENT LIBRARY RESEARCH SURVEY

NAME _____

MAJOR _____

LEVEL OF GRADUATE STUDY_____

AREAS OF RESEARCH

1. What are your areas of specialization?

   _____

   _____

   _____

2. What are your current areas of research interests or activities?
   a. Course work

   _____

   _____

   _____

   b. Thesis or dissertation

   _____

   _____

COLLECTION ASSESSMENT

1. How adequate do you find the library collection in your areas of specialization?

   _____

   _____

   _____

2. What deficiencies are you aware of in the library collections or services that support your research?

   _____

   _____

   _____

Association of Research Libraries. Office of Management Studies. *Collection Analysis Project Manual*. Washington, DC, 1977.

CAP NEEDS SURVEY OF MAJOR ACADEMIC UNITS

College: _____

I.   Please indicate anticipated changes in your college's instructional program during the next five years (e.g., significant enrollment shifts; new courses or degree programs; discontinued courses or degree programs; etc.).

II. Please indicate any major anticipated changes in your college's research programs during the next five years (e.g., shifts in emphasis in current research activities; new research programs; discontinued or completed programs; etc.).

III. We would like a general idea of your view of the adequacy of the library's collections in supporting your college's major programs. (please circle appropriate number in each scale)

   A. Adequacy of collection in support of college's *Instructional* Program.

1	2	3	4	5	6	7	8	9	10

   10=Entirely adequate;   1=Entirely inadequate

   B. Adequacy of collection in support of college's *Research* Programs.

1	2	3	4	5	6	7	8	9	10

   10=Entirely adequate;   1=Entirely inadequate

   C. Please provide additional comment regarding the above rating if you so desire.

IV. In future phases of this study, we will be conducting detailed interviews with selected faculty on the adequacy of the library's collections. Who in your college would you recommend for this type of interview in terms of knowledge of and interest in the library's collections program?

   _____

   _____

Association of Research Libraries. Office of Management Studies. *Collection Analysis Project Manual*. Washington, DC, 1977.

CAP IMPORTANCE/SUCCESS SURVEY

The library is seeking to answer two questions. First, we would like to know what type of library collections needs are most important to your work. We realize that different groups and individuals have different needs and we want to focus on what library users consider most important. You can help us by distinguishing those needs which are most important from those which are less important. Second, we would like to determine how well the library is presently meeting your needs.

You are asked to provide two answers to each of the questions appearing below. Answer in the following manner: (1) indicate how important the need is to you by placing the letter "I" on the scale where it best indicates that importance; (2) indicate how successful the library has been in providing for that need by placing the letter "S" on the scale where it best indicates that success.

"I" = Importance   "S" = Success

Example:

Need for foreign dissertations   (min) _____I___S___ (max)

Need for reports on microfiche   (min) _____I,S___ (max)

Need for local newspapers   (min) _S___I_____ (max)

1. The need to consult or borrow the following types of material:

   a. Handbooks and encyclopedias   (min) _____ (max)

   b. Indexes to journals and periodicals   (min) _____ (max)

   c. Books   (min) _____ (max)

   d. Technical reports   (min) _____ (max)

   e. U.S. government documents   (min) _____ (max)

   f. Scholarly journals   (min) _____ (max)

Association of Research Libraries. Office of Management Studies. *Collection Analysis Project Manual*. Washington, DC, 1977.

g. Trade Journals

h. General interest materials (e.g.,   (min) _____ (max)
novels, local newspapers, news
magazines, etc.)   (min) _____ (max)

i. Microfilms and microfiche   (min) _____ (max)

j. Other (specify)   (min) _____ (max)

2. The need to consult or borrow material in the following languages:

a. English   (min) _____ (max)

b. Romance languages (e.g., French,   (min) _____ (max)
Italian, Spanish, Portuguese)

c. Germanic (e.g., German, Dutch,   (min) _____ (max)
Swedish, Danish)

d. Slavic (e.g., Czech, Russian, Polish)   (min) _____ (max)

e. Oriental (e.g., Chinese, Japanese)   (min) _____ (max)

f. Arabic   (min) _____ (max)

g. Other (specify)   (min) _____ (max)

3. The need to consult or borrow material published within the following
time frame:

a. Published in the last 5 years   (min) _____ (max)

b. Published prior to 5 years ago   (min) _____ (max)

4. The need to consult or borrow material for the following purposes:

a. For course purposes (assigned   (min) _____ (max)
reading, recommended course
reading)

b. For academic research (publication,   (min) _____ (max)
dissertation, course research)

c. For sponsored research (grant or
contract supported research)   (min)＿＿＿＿＿＿ (max)

d. For general interest or recreation   (min)＿＿＿＿＿＿ (max)

e. Other (specify)   (min)＿＿＿＿＿＿ (max)

5. Because the libraries cannot have all published material available in their collections, cooperative programs are maintained with other libraries so that materials can be borrowed from them or, in some instances, our users can use these materials at these other libraries.

   a. How important are these cooperative services to you?

                       (min) ＿＿＿＿＿＿ (max)

   b. How successful is the library in making you aware of these services?

                       (min) ＿＿＿＿＿＿ (max)

6. a. How important is your need to actively influence the library's selection of library materials? (e.g., books, journals, etc.)

                       (min)＿＿＿＿＿＿ (max)

   b. How successful is the library in providing the opportunity to influence the library's selection of materials?

                       (min) ＿＿＿＿＿＿ (max)

The following information will help the library determine the relative success of the various parts of its collection program.

Your Status:

Faculty ＿＿＿＿＿＿＿＿＿＿   Master's degree candidate ＿＿＿＿＿
Research staff ＿＿＿＿＿＿＿   Doctoral degree candidate ＿＿＿＿＿
Undergraduate ＿＿＿＿＿＿   Other ＿＿＿＿＿＿＿＿＿＿＿＿

Your general area(s) of interest:

Humanities _____   Social Sciences _____
Engineering _____   Sciences _____
Art & Architecture _____   Other (specify) _____

Using the scale below, please indicate the frequency with which you use the MIT Libraries.

1=more than once a week
2=once or twice a month
3=a few times each semester
4=once or twice a year
5=never

_____ Humanities Library
_____ Science Library
_____ Fine Arts Library
_____ Social Sciences
_____ Engineering Library

Name (optional) _____

THE M.I.T. LIBRARIES SEEK YOUR HELP

In connection with a research project sponsored by the Association of Research Libraries, we want to find out to what extent the library collections are meeting the information needs of M.I.T. students, faculty, and research staff. You can assist us by responding to the questions listed below.

Thank you for your participation.

Jay K. Lucker
Director of Libraries

Part I Question	Card Column	Response
D What is your status at M.I.T.?	8–9	_____

FX (Faculty)
RX (Research Staff)
MO (Masters Degree Candidate)
MT (Masters/Teaching Asst.)
MR (Masters/Research Asst.)
DO (Doctoral Degree Candidate)
DT (Doctoral/Teaching Asst.)
DR (Doctoral/Research Asst.)
U1 (Undergrad–1st yr)
U2 (Undergrad–2nd yr)
U3 (Undergrad–3rd yr)
U4 (Undergrad–4th yr)
XX (non-Degree Program)

E What is your M.I.T. DEPT/LAB/CENTER affiliation?

_____

F What is your Subject Specialty(ies) or Major Field(s)?

_____   _____

G In which of these broad categories does   10   _____
   your main interest lie?

E (Engineering)
D (Social Science)

R (Architecture)
U (Urban Planning)
H (Humanities)
M (Management)
S (Science)
X (Other–specify) _____

H How often do you visit the M.I.T. Libraries?   11   _____

W (Weekly)
M (Once or twice a month)
S (A few times a semester)
X (Seldom)

Part II

Please express your opinions on the following questions of importance/satisfaction by using a scale of:

1–minimum or lowest
2
3
4
5–maximum or highest

If you do not know or have no opinion, please use 6.

I How important to you is material for the following purposes?
a. Reserve use (assigned readings)   12   _____
b. Other course purposes (recommended
readings, independent study, preparation for
course teaching)   13   _____
c. Research (publication, dissertation, grant
or contract supported research)   14   _____
d. General interest or recreation   15   _____
e. Other (specify)   15   _____

J How well do the M.I.T. Libraries serve your needs for materials for the purposes?
a. Reserve use (assigned readings)   17   _____
b. Other course purposes (recommended
readings, independent study, preparation for

course teaching)   18   _____
c. Research (publication, dissertation, grant or
contract supported research)   19   _____
d. General interest or recreation   20   _____
e. Other (specify) _____

K How effective do you find the Libraries' collections in your subject
specialty or major field?
a. Scope   22   _____
b. Depth   23   _____

L What are the deficiencies, if any, in the collections in your subject
specialty or major field?

_____

_____

M How well do the M.I.T. Libraries meet your needs for foreign language
materials:
a. Romance languages   24   _____
b. Germanic languages   25   _____
c. Slavic languages   26   _____
d. Oriental languages   27   _____
e. Other (specify)   28   _____

N Is English your native language?   29   _____
Y (Yes)
N (No)

O How important to you is material
published more than 5 years ago?   30   _____

P How well does the library meet this need
for material older than 5 years?   31   _____

Q Because the libraries cannot have all published material available in
their collections, cooperative programs are maintained with other libraries so that materials can be borrowed from them or, in some instances,
our users can use these materials at these other libraries.
a. How successful has the library been in
making you aware of these services?   32   _____
b. How important are these cooperative
services to you?   33   _____

c. If you have used these services,
how satisfied are you with the
effectiveness of the service?   34   _____

R How interested are you in influencing the
selection of library materials? (e.g., books,
journals, etc.)   35   _____

S How successful has the library been in
giving you the opportunity to
influence selection of library materials?   36   _____

T How satisfied have you been with the libraries'
response to your suggestions or requests?   37   _____

BYU FACULTY PERIODICALS SURVEY

NAME: _____

DEPARTMENT: _____

1. Please list the periodical titles you read regularly:

2. What other titles do you consider to be significant in your field?

3. To which journals do you frequently refer your students?

4. Check the boxes indicating the years of periodical coverage you consider important in your field:

   ____Pre–1950   ____1950–1960   ____1960–1970   ____1970–

5. List any titles to which the library *does not* subscribe that you think are
   important to your program:

CAP FACULTY INTERVIEW

NAME: _____

DEPARTMENT: _____

AREA OF SPECIAL INTEREST: _____

A. PERSONAL USE OF THE LIBRARY
   1. How often do you use the University Library?

      ____daily ____weekly ____monthly ____other

   2. Do you usually ____ come in person ____ call by telephone
      ____ send secretary or research assistant

   3. Do you usually find the materials or information you are looking for?
      ____-yes ____ no

      When you are unsuccessful, is it because:
      ____ library lacks title

      ____ materials checked out

      ____ materials not on shelf

      ____ nothing yet published

      ____ other

   4. Are you currently engaged in research which is hampered by library resources, services, or facilities?   Elaborate.

B. INSTRUCTIONAL AND STUDENT USE OF THE LIBRARY
   1. Have your students complained to you of inadequacies in seating, lighting, or other physical facilities? (Specific areas of complaint)

   2. Have your students complained to you regarding library service? (Specific areas)

3. Are you satisfied with the present system of handling Reserves? Specific suggestions?

4. Do you frequently lend students materials from your office? If so, what kinds of materials?

    How frequently?

    Is it a matter of convenience, or is it because of a library lack?

5. Do you ever have to restrict any assignments because of inadequacy in library materials?

    If so, what kinds of materials?

6. How do you go about evaluating adequate access to needed library materials before approving student research topics? (Dissertations, theses, practica, reading and conference, etc.)

7. Do you believe that the students would benefit educationally if there were a separate collection for undergraduates?

C. FUTURE PLANS (INSTRUCTION AND RESEARCH)

1. What new *programs* of instruction are you planning which will involve library resources (materials)? Services (reserve, reference, etc.)? Facilities?

2. Do you anticipate any changes or developments in your teaching *methods* (independent study, etc.) which would affect students' use of the library?   How?

3. Do you feel restricted in planning research because of a lack of library resources, services, or facilities?   Elaborate.

4. Do you include provision for library support in proposals for research grants?   Is this feasible?

D. RESOURCES

1. To what extent have the resources and facilities of the Library affected your decision to join the faculty? To remain here? (greatly, moderately, none, etc.)

2. Is there a need for retrospective buying in your field? How much? To what extent can ILL, CRL, etc., substitute for purchase?

3. To what extent do you rely on your personal collection rather than on the collections of the Library? (greatly, moderately, none)

4. Should the University Library acquire materials in fields not now directly covered by courses and research?

5. Roles of Library Representative and Subject Specialist

   a. How do you perceive the function of the Library Representative in your department? (Collection development responsibilities or processor of orders?)

   b. To whom do you make recommendations for library acquisitions?

   _____ Library Representative

   _____ Subject Specialist in Library

   _____ Other

   c. How do you perceive the role of the subject specialist from the Library within the area of collection development?

   d. Is this arrangement (Library Representative/Subject Specialist) satisfactory?   Any specific recommendations for improving?

6. The Library utilizes several approval plans and blanket orders. Does this function satisfactorily for your areas of interest?

7. Has the Library usually been able to secure the materials you have requested?   When unsuccessful, what type of material is involved (foreign language, o.p., current titles, etc.)

8. Should the faculty have a role in assisting the staff of the Library in weeding obsolete materials from the collections?

9. Microforms

   a. For what types of materials in your field do you find micro-
      forms acceptable?

      _____ deteriorating materials

      _____ dissertations

      _____ expensive materials which can be acquired in microform
      at greatly reduced cost

      _____ little used materials

      _____ other (please specify)

   b. Do you have any suggestions for encouraging the use of micro-
      forms?

10. Resource Sharing

    a. How satisfactory would you find the cooperative buying of
       certain expensive sets with other nearby libraries with access
       through courier service?

    b. Do you use the services of the Interlibrary Loan?

       Successfully?   Suggestions for improvement?

       How often are you charged?   How do you feel about
       charges?

    c. Do you use the materials available on loan from the Center for
       Research Libraries? Should they continue to buy very expen-
       sive, rarely used materials for their members to access on
       demand?

Do you have any additional suggestions for the development of the Library
in the areas of Resources?   Physical facilities?   Services?   Personnel?

CAP STUDENT USER SURVEY

You can assist the University Library in making the best possible service available to students by answering the questions which follow. You do not need to sign your name, but please answer as many of the questions as possible:

Class Standing:

Major Subject _____ _____ Freshman _____ Sophomore

College _____ _____ Junior _____ Senior

Candidate for _____ degree _____ Graduate Student

---

1. How often do you use the University Library?

_____ Daily

_____ Once a week

_____ Once a month

_____ First visit

2. Why do you usually come to the library? (Mark all that apply to you)

_____ Assigned readings

_____ Research; term papers

_____ Place to study

_____ "Fun" reading (fiction, etc.)

_____ Typing rooms, copy machines

_____ Other (Freshman Library Projects, etc., or specify)

3. When you look for books in the library, do you find that:
   Book not owned by library:
   _____ Often _____ Seldom

Book checked out:
_____Often _____Seldom

Book not on shelf:
_____Often _____Seldom

4. Did you find the books and magazines you needed today?

_____ Yes _____No _____Some

   If not, what subject were you interested in?

5. What would help you to find library materials?

_____ More library tours

_____More copies of the book I needed

_____ More reference help in service areas

_____ More instruction in library use

6. How can we improve our services?

_____Longer hours

_____ More staff assistance

_____Change due date to:

_____longer period

_____ shorter period

_____ other (please specify)

Appendix E
ACRL Academic Library Standards

Standards for University Libraries

FOREWORD

The following statement of university library standards has been prepared by a joint committee established by the Association of Research Libraries and the Association of College and Research Libraries. A draft of the statement appeared in the April 1978 issue of *College & Research Libraries News*.

In August 1978, the Joint ARL-ACRL Committee on University Library Standards revised this draft. On October 26, 1978, the ARL membership unanimously endorsed the statement as revised. At the ALA Midwinter Meeting in January 1979, the ACRL Board also voted to ratify the revised statement. "Standards for University Libraries" is being published in its final form in this issue of *C&RL News* for the information of ACRL members.

STANDARDS
FOR UNIVERSITY LIBRARIES

Prepared by a joint committee of the Association of Research Libraries and the Association of College and Research Libraries, a division of the American Library Association.

Introduction

These standards have been prepared to assist faculty, university administrators, librarians, accrediting agencies, and others in the evaluation and improvement of university library services and resources. These statements are intended to apply only to those institutions of higher education which have been characterized by the Carnegie Commission on Higher Education as "doctoral granting institutions."[1] All of these institutions emphasize graduate study, professional education, and research. Despite these basic similarities, university libraries are also characterized by a high degree of individuality, particularly with respect to policies, programs, responsibilities, and traditions. Hence, these standards are not intended to establish normative prescriptions for uniform application. Rather, they are meant to provide a general framework within which informed judgment can be applied to individual circumstances.

The fundamental assumption of these standards is that the library has a central and critical importance in a university. This importance has been recognized repeatedly by analysts of higher education. In his 1966 report to the American Council on Education, Allan M. Cartter, for example, stated:

"The library is the heart of the university; no other single non-human factor is as closely related

to the quality of graduate education. A few universities with poor library resources have achieved considerable strength in several departments, in some cases because laboratory facilities may be more important in a particular field than the library, and in other cases because the universities are located close to other great library collections such as the Library of Congress and the New York Public Library. But institutions that are strong in all areas invariably have major national research libraries."[2]

As with all institutions, universities and their libraries have experienced considerable change over time. Further changes are taking place now, and others clearly lie ahead. Particularly noteworthy is the increasing sense of interdependence and commitment to coordination among universities generally. With regard to university libraries, the following developments are particularly important: the growth of interlibrary cooperation, especially resource sharing; the strengthening and expansion of service programs, such as bibliographic instruction; the increasing importance of recorded information in nonprint formats; the application of automated systems to library operations and the growth of machine-readable data bases; the closer interaction between librarians and faculty and the improved status of librarians within the university; increased stress on the effectiveness and efficiency of operations. A recognition of such trends and their importance is fundamental to these standards.

Recognizing the increasing interdependence of universities in developing and maintaining scholarly resources, these standards are intended to provide guidance in identifying that level of library self-sufficiency which is essential to the health and vigor of a university and its academic programs. The general assumption is that the primary obligation of a university library is to meet the instructional and research needs of the students and faculty at that university. However, no university library can acquire all of the recorded information that its clientele may find useful. An attempt is made, therefore, to recognize the mechanisms being developed to promote cooperative access to scholarly information, to identify the current limitations of interdependence, and to enumerate the factors which are essential in maintaining an environment in which instruction and research can flourish.

Care has been taken to limit the standards to succinct statements focusing on the elements judged to be most critical in determining the adequacy of a university library. Amplification of the principles identified in the standards is provided in the form of commentary.

SECTION A: SERVICES

Standard A.1

In order to support the instructional, research, and public service programs of the university, the services offered by a university library shall promote and facilitate effective use of recorded information in all formats by all of the library's clientele.

Commentary on Standard A.1

In developing and implementing its program of service, a university library should give priority to the needs of the students, faculty, and other academic staff of the university, who may be said to constitute the library's "primary clientele." While it may also have obligations or commitments to other clienteles or constituencies, the library should recognize that these are secondary.

A university library should provide the following services: reference and information services which are available at adequately identified and designated points during established service hours; specialized and in-depth assistance to individuals in the use of the library's resources; bibliographic instruction programs; services which will facilitate access to nonprint media and machine-readable data bases; and services which will facilitate access to recorded information in other library collections.

These services should be designed to meet effectively the whole range of different informational and bibliographical needs that arise in the various academic areas and in all other parts of the university.

While universities should place great emphasis on meeting the intensive library needs of graduate students and faculty, they should be careful to provide adequately for the needs of undergraduate students.

Finally, university libraries should recognize that, to one degree or another, they share a responsibility with all research libraries to support higher education in general and each other in particular through cooperative efforts.

Standard A.2

In order to ensure maximum access to its collections and their contents, a university library shall maintain records of its collections that are complete, consistent, and in conformity with national bibliographical standards and requirements.

Commentary on Standard A.2

The extent of bibliographical coverage that must be provided in a particular library will depend on many factors, such as whether or not the library has open or closed access stacks, the extent and nature of the library's specialized collections, the history and traditions of the library and of the university, and the nature of specific

cooperative arrangements that the library may have entered into with other libraries and library consortia.

To ensure effective access to its collections as well as to increase its operational efficiency, a university library's bibliographic records should conform to recognized standards of cataloging and classification, and its bibliographic apparatus should be internally consistent. Its bibliographic records should be adjusted in conjunction with periodic inventories of the collections. Every multi-unit university library should have a union catalog of its cataloged holdings.

Standard A.3

Within the limits of the university's particular responsibilities and priorities, a university library shall provide maximum access to its collections for all of its clientele.

Commentary on Standard A.3

Various factors are involved in providing access to a library's collections, such as circulation policies and procedures, service hours, security arrangements, and actual operating efficiency. While practices vary significantly from library to library, certain principles should be followed in each library. Most items in the library collections should be readily available both for consultation in the library and for circulation to authorized clientele. Access to and circulation of rare, fragile, and high-demand materials should be appropriately controlled and restricted. To ensure maximum availability of the collections to those authorized to use them, terms of loan should be carefully set and should generally be similar for all user categories.

Adequate precautions should be taken to control loss of or damage to the library's collections. The prompt return in good condition of all circulated materials should be effectively enforced for all borrowers.

Circulation procedures and stack maintenance operations in a university library should be effective and efficient. There should be a regular and continuing program of shelf reading. Library service hours should be responsive to high- and low-use periods, to the number of branch, departmental, and other special libraries in the system as well as to the availability of alternative study space.

SECTION B: COLLECTIONS

Standard B.1

A university library's collections shall be of sufficient size and scope to support the university's total instructional needs and to facilitate the university's research programs.

Commentary on Standard B.1

A university library should provide all of the resources that are necessary for direct support of the university's full instructional programs at both the undergraduate and the graduate levels. If these resources are not readily available in the library, the instructional programs cannot be carried out successfully. These resources include required and assigned readings, reference and bibliographical materials, basic journals and serials, as well as any other library materials that undergraduate or graduate students are expected to be able to consult readily in their courses of study, or in the preparation of theses and dissertations.

Weak collections can hamper research. The accumulation and preservation of substantial collections and the implementation of comprehensive acquisition programs must be recognized as providing a resource whose presence within a university is essential to the conditions under which knowledge is effectively increased and transmitted. It is clear that no university library can be expected to possess in its collections all of the recorded information which faculty or doctoral students may need to consult as they pursue their research. Nevertheless, it is essential that collections be of such size, scope, and quality that they promote rather than restrict research. While every library should take care to develop collections whose areas of concentration reflect and support the academic priorities and strengths within the university, interlibrary arrangements, which have long been established for the mutual support of exceptional research needs, must continue to be relied upon to supplement even the most comprehensive research collections.

The continued rapid growth of scholarly literature and the costs of providing access to this literature for those in the university community have necessitated formal and informal arrangements among libraries to ensure maximum access to this literature. Common methods of sharing resources and improving access have been loans between libraries, provision of visiting privileges for scholars, agreements on the acquisitions of materials, and sharing of bibliographic information.

While interlibrary cooperation, as presently practiced, may not promise large cost savings in the immediate future, significant improved methods of supplementing local resources are in the active planning stages. University libraries must participate in the development of these new access mechanisms to ensure that local, regional, national, and international interests are effectively served.

Attempts have been made to identify precise quantitative measures of adequate collection size and growth rates for a university library. No such formula has yet been developed which can be generally applied. At present, such formulas as exist can only yield approximations which indicate a general level of need. If they are applied arbitrarily and mechanically, they can distort the realities of a given situation. Nevertheless, quantitative measures are increasingly important in guiding the qualitative judgment that must ultimately be applied to university libraries and their collections. One technique is the use of regression analysis to facilitate the comparison of similar libraries to one another;[3] another of some general applicability is the "index of quality" developed by the American Council on Education for relating library collection size to graduate program quality.[4]

Standard B.2

A university library's collections shall be developed systematically and consistently within the terms of explicit and detailed policies.

Commentary on Standard B.2

Given the great breadth of university library collections and the wide variations in depth of collections among subjects held, it is essential that there be a collections development policy to guide the selection and acquisition of materials.

By establishing such a policy, librarians seek to ensure that the library's collections are planned and developed in relation to the university's academic, research, and service goals and priorities and within the limits of resources available.

Working in close consultation with faculty and administration, librarians, particularly subject specialists, should assume the responsibility for drafting and implementing this policy.

Recognizing the inherent difficulties in collection development, it is imperative that the library have full and continuous access to information about all developments, actual and planned, in the academic, research, and service programs of the university and its components which affect the library.

Once codified, the library's collection development policy should be made known to and endorsed by the university faculty and administration. To ensure that this policy reflects changes within the university, the policy should be regularly and carefully reviewed.

Standard B.3

A university library's collections shall contain all of the varied forms of recorded information.

Commentary on Standard B.3

The university library has traditionally been recognized as the repository within the university for the printed information needed to support the university's instructional and research programs. As recorded information becomes increasingly available in a variety of nonprint formats, such as films, sound recordings, and video tapes, it is appropriate that this material, except where needed exclusively for classroom use, also be acquired, organized, and made available through the university library.[5]

SECTION C: PERSONNEL

Standard C.1

A university library shall have a sufficient number and variety of personnel to develop, organize, and maintain such collections and to provide such reference and information services as will meet the university's needs.

Commentary on Standard C.1

The size of a university library's staff is determined by many factors, including the number of physically separate library units, the number of service points requiring staff, the number of service hours provided, the number and special characteristics of items processed annually, the nature and quality of the processing to which they are subjected, the size of the collections, and the rate of circulation of the collections. Interinstitutional cooperative arrangements may also affect staff size. As such factors vary widely from one institution to another, no single model or formula can be provided for developing an optimum staff size.

A university library should have on its staff a variety of personnel: professional, clerical, and student-assistant staff. The librarians should perform the core academic and professional functions of the library: collection development, reference and information services, and substantive activities related to the bibliographic control of materials. All categories of personnel should have appropriate education and experience, including, when necessary, graduate or professional degrees in their particular specialties. The recognized terminal degree for librarians is the master's degree from an American Library Association accredited library school program, although additional graduate degrees may sometimes be desirable.

The deployment of personnel within a specific university library is related to the range of operations and services provided by that library and to its total workload requirements.

Standard C.2

Personnel practices within a university library shall be based on sound, contemporary administrative practice and shall be consistent with personnel practices within the university as well as the goals and purposes of the library.

Commentary on Standard C.2

The terms and conditions of employment of the several categories of staff in a university library should be consonant with the established terms and conditions of employment of staff in related categories elsewhere within the university. Terms and conditions of employment for librarians, for example, should parallel those of the rest of the university's academic staff, just as terms and conditions of employment for the library's clerical and student staff should parallel those of similar employees within the university as a whole.

A comprehensive university library personnel management program should address recruitment, appointment, promotion, tenure, dismissal, appeal, definition of position responsibilities, classification and pay plans, orientation and training programs, review of employee performance, staff development, and counseling.

More specific guidance on these matters is provided in the following documents: "Statement on Faculty Status of College and University Librarians"[6] and "Library Education and Personnel Utilization."[7]

SECTION D: FACILITIES

Standard D.1

A university library shall have facilities which meet the present and anticipated future requirements of the university and its programs.

Commentary on Standard D.1

A university library's buildings should be of sufficient size and quality to house the collections and to provide sufficient space for their use by students, faculty, and other clientele. There should also be adequate space for the library operations necessary for the provision of its services. Adequacy of facilities cannot be determined simply on the basis of present requirements. The size and composition of the university's enrollment, the nature of its instructional and research programs, the form and publication rate of library materials strongly influence library requirements, and it is necessary that these requirements be subject to continuous evaluation and planning.

A university library should be attractive, inviting, and carefully designed to promote operational efficiency and effectiveness of use. Specific factors relevant here include general environmental features that affect clientele, staff, and collections (light, ventilation, temperature and humidity control, vertical and horizontal transportation, safety features, etc.), layout of the stacks, number and variety of reader stations, relationship between stacks and reader stations, relationship among service points, effective flow of materials, and adequacy of space for staff and operations.

The fundamental consideration in designing a library building should be its function. Since the nature of collections, services, operations, and the needs of a library's clientele can change significantly over time, present and future flexibility is an important element in library design. Although the architectural style and traditions of a university may dictate certain design features for a library building, such factors should not be allowed to compromise basic functional considerations.[8]

Standard D.2

Libraries shall be so located that the university community will have convenient access to them.

Commentary on Standard D.2

The requirements of interdisciplinary studies and research, recognition of the needs of undergraduate students, the urgency of achieving operating economies—these and other factors have revived interest in centralizing physically dispersed library units in order to improve access to resources and avoid costly duplication in the development and maintenance of collections. There are circumstances, however, such as campus geography, intensity of use, and size of collections which may continue to justify the maintenance of multiple library units. Remote storage facilities may also be established in attempting to deal with space inadequacies although this usually inhibits convenience of access. Where the pattern of decentralization persists in any form, it is important that libraries be located so as to minimize inconvenience to all library users.[9]

SECTION E: ADMINISTRATION AND GOVERNANCE

Standard E.1

The place of the university library within the administrative and governance structure of the university shall be clearly identified, and the responsibilities and authority of the library administration and its chief administrative officer shall be defined.

Commentary on Standard E.1

If there is ambiguity within the university community as to the particular place occupied by the library within the administrative and governance structure of the university, and if the authority and responsibilities of the library's chief administrative officer are not clearly identified, misunderstanding, conflict, and confusion can sometimes result to the detriment of both the university and its library., Because it is closely related to instruction and research, the university library should be formally recognized as one of the major academic units within the university, and its chief administrative officer should participate regularly and directly in university-wide academic planning and decision making. For similar reasons, this person should report directly to the chief academic officer of the university.

The long-recognized need in institutions of higher education to involve faculty in library matters has led to the institutionalization of the advisory library committee. Because of the fundamental importance of the library to instruction and research and the consequent need for close, continuing interaction between the faculty and the library, the existence of the library committee is

valuable. The committee should be advisory, and its responsibilities should be clearly delineated.

Standard E.2

The university library's own administrative and governance structure shall be clearly specified and shall be consonant with the governance structure of the university as well as with the particular needs and requirements of the library.

Commentary on Standard E.2

In order to facilitate effective organizational activity and decision making, it is essential that the administrative and governance structure of the university library itself be clearly specified. This will involve identifying the roles and responsibilities of all categories of library personnel in the governance of the library. It is essential that library governance reflect the principles and practice followed elsewhere within the university, although they should be modified as necessary to embody those conditions and issues peculiar to an academic library.

Standard E.3

There shall be a close administrative relationship among all libraries within the university to the end that library users may make full and effective use of library resources and services.

Commentary on Standard E.3

No single pattern of library administration will serve all universities equally well, but whatever pattern an institution chooses should have as its principal purpose the equitable distribution of library resources and services. The needs of scholars differ from discipline to discipline and often the needs of students differ from those of faculty. These competing interests cannot always be reconciled, but one important task of library administration is to achieve as much balance as possible in the provision of services to all groups.

However administrative relationships among library units within a university are determined, it is essential that adequate coordinating mechanisms be established and enforced to ensure that service policies are in reasonable harmony, that costs related to duplication are controlled, and that access to all library collections is maximized.

Standard E.4

A university library's major policies and procedures shall be clearly defined and regularly reviewed.

Commentary on Standard E.4

In order to ensure that it is effective internally and understood externally, a university library should clearly define its major policies and procedures and record them in written form. The written statements of policy should be readily available to all members of the library staff, and policies which have external relevance (such as the library's collection development policy or circulation policy) should be accessible to the library's clientele and to others who may need or desire to consult them. These policies, as well as the practices that implement them, should be regularly reviewed to ensure that they continue to be appropriate.

SECTION F: FINANCE

Standard F.1

Budgetary support for the university library shall be sufficient to enable it to fulfill its obligations and responsibilities as identified in the preceding standards.

Commentary on Standard F.1

The total budgetary needs of a university library can be determined only in relation to its responsibilities. Many attempts have been made to develop formulas or other "objective" measures for determining the budgetary requirements of a university library. These measures range from matching funding with student enrollment to defining a minimum percentage of the total university G and E budget which should be devoted to the library. Such "objective" approaches to budget determination do not always take cognizance of the range and complexity of demands which any university library must meet, as well as the significantly different library needs of different universities.

These conditions also make it impossible to identify a viable model that can be applied to all university libraries for allocating their budgets by major category (salaries and wages, acquisitions, binding, miscellaneous supplies, and other expense). Allocation ultimately depends on local requirements and priorities. For example, if a university library is expected to operate a substantial number of discrete units with parallel and duplicative activities, its expenditures for salaries and wages will be higher than if this were not the case.

Under any circumstances, it is essential that a university library be provided with sufficient funding to enable it to develop appropriate collections, provide appropriate services, carry out necessary operations, and satisfy identified expectations and requirements. If funding is less than is necessary to fulfill these obligations, the library will be unable to meet university needs.

A university library should be expected to operate on a sound financial basis. To do this, the library and its administration must be able to identify and support its fiscal request effectively and to report adequately on expenditure of funds.

Standard F.2

The university library budget shall be a distinct part of the university's budget, and it shall

be developed and managed by the chief administrative officer of the university library.

Commentary on Standard F.2

The authority to prepare, submit, defend, and administer the university library budget should be delegated clearly and explicitly to the chief administrative officer of the university library. He or she should have full responsibility for managing this budget as well as the authority necessary to maximize the use of the library's total resources. He or she should have the same degree of latitude and responsibility that is exercised by other major administrative officers within the university. The library should be responsible for preparing adequate and regular reports on expenditures throughout the year. These reports should conform to the university's requirements and, where necessary, to its standardized procedures and practices.

· Because of the importance of the library within the university and the need that it respond effectively to changing demands, priorities, and academic programs, it is essential that the library budget be developed in relationship to and with full cognizance of the total university budget-planning process, and that the library's chief administrative officer be directly and significantly involved in this process.

REFERENCES

1. Carnegie Commission on Higher Education, *A Classification of Institutions of Higher Education* (Berkeley, Calif.: The Commission, 1973), p.1–2, 9–22. This publication identifies 173 "doctoral granting institutions."
2. Allan M. Cartter, *An Assessment of Quality in Graduate Education* (Washington, D.C.: American Council on Education, 1966), p.114.
3. William J. Baumol and Matityahu Marcus, *Economics of Academic Libraries* (Washington, D.C.: American Council on Education, 1973).
4. Cartter, *An Assessment of Quality in Graduate Education*, p.114.
5. The best recent discussion of the importance of nonprint media for higher education is Carnegie Commission on Higher Education, *The Fourth Revolution: Instructional Technology in Higher Education* (New York: McGraw-Hill, 1972).
6. In *Faculty Status for Academic Librarians: A History and Policy Statement* (Chicago: American Library Assn., 1975), p.35–38.
7. "Library Education and Personnel Utilization" (Chicago: American Library Assn., 1976).
8. Considerable valuable information is available in several publications, the best of which remains Keyes D. Metcalf, *Planning Academic and Research Library Buildings* (New York: McGraw-Hill, 1965).
9. This issue has been the subject of considerable

analysis. See, particularly, Ralph E. Ellsworth, *The Economics of Book Storage in Academic Libraries* (Metuchen, N.J.: The Association of Research Libraries and the Scarecrow Press, 1969). Also useful is Jeffrey A. Raffel and Robert Shishko, *Systematic Analysis of University Libraries* (Cambridge, Mass.: MIT Press, 1969).

APPENDIX

QUANTITATIVE ANALYTICAL TECHNIQUES FOR UNIVERSITY LIBRARIES

The university libraries[1] to which quantitative measures might be applied are so complex, so diverse in the programs they support, and so different from each other that it is extremely difficult, if not impossible, to devise a common statistical measure which could be applied to all of them. This problem is further complicated by the character and inadequacy of the currently available data. Herman Fussler, for example, observes that "libraries, like universities, tend to have very inadequate analytical data on their own operations and performance. Such data, especially as they relate to costs and system responses to user needs, are critically important in any effort to improve a library's efficiency and responsiveness."[2] Fritz Machlup, in the course of his recent efforts to measure the holdings and acquisitions of libraries on a broad scale, has complained about the lack of adequate data.[3] Other observers have challenged the utility of present library data collection.[4] They focus on perceived failures to measure performance or effectiveness. Nevertheless, academic institutions do compete for faculty and students, and one of the elements in this competition is the adequacy of library services and collections. Comparative judgments about academic libraries are made, and these comparisons can be aided by quantitative measures.

Unfortunately, much of the data which are needed to actually make interinstitutional comparisons is not easily available, although some useful data can be obtained from ARL statistics. The LIBGIS and HEGIS surveys also supply data, but these are usually too old for current needs or in a form which is difficult to use. Consequently, the analyst is compelled to rely on what is available: ARL statistics, authorities who have written on the subject, and such limited surveys as he or she can make. All of these methods have varying degrees of utility, but with the possible exception of the ARL data, none provide the raw data on which empirically derived measures can be based. Certain "common" practices can be discerned, and the advice of authorities can be weighed, but these, however valuable, do not constitute quantitative measures in an empirically derivable, logically justifiable sense. To have reliable quantitative measures, the categories to be measured must be defined, and a mechanism for gathering the necessary data must be developed.

In the absence of either of these necessary conditions, it is difficult to do more than perform what analyses can be performed on ARL data. Briefly, these fall into three categories: (a) insights obtained by simple inspection of the data; (b) the construction of ratios which reduce the quantity of data to be comprehended and facilitate comparison; and (c) regression analysis which performs roughly the same function from the analyst's point of view as the construction of ratios but also requires an effort on the part of the analyst to group like institutions together and gives the analyst some indication of how well this has been accomplished (coefficient of determination).

Simple inspection of ARL data, aided by rankings, ranges, averages, and medians, does provide useful insights for the experienced library manager who can mentally discount obvious discrepancies and differences between institutions and can restrict comparisons to a homogeneous group. However, to read, for example, that in 1976–77 the number of volumes in ARL libraries ranged between Harvard's 9,547,576 and McMaster's 906,741, that the average library held 2,127,047, and the median was 1,653,000 may give the reader a sense of perspective, which is valuable, but it is of limited use in drawing comparisons between rather different institutions.

A reduction of data can be achieved by the use of ratios or percentages, as is shown in the example of ratio analysis below. Some of those which can be generated from existing data include:

1. The ratio of professional to nonprofessional staff
2. Expenditure for library materials as a percent of total library operating expenditure
3. Ratio of salary expenditures to library material expenditures

This kind of data reduction aids analysis by making the data more comprehensible. For example, among ARL libraries in 1976–77, the ratio of professional to nonprofessional staff ranged from 1.08 to 0.24; the average was 0.51 and the median 0.49. The overwhelming majority of libraries tended toward a pattern of one professional to two nonprofessionals. Among ARL libraries in 1976–77, expenditures for library materials as a percent of total library expenditures ranged from 19.14 percent for Toronto to 50.61 percent for Houston. The average was 31.46 percent and the median 30.09 percent. The vast majority of ARL libraries tended to spend 30 percent of their budgets on acquisitions. The obverse of materials expenditure for libraries is salary expenditure. Expressed as a ratio of salary to materials it ranged from 3.6 in the case of Toronto, to 0.8 in the case of Houston, with the median 1.9 and the average 1.93.

From ratios such as these, a deeper insight into

library operations can be obtained, but it would be rash to conclude that all libraries should spend 30 percent of their budgets for books and 60 percent for salaries or that the ratio of professional to nonprofessional should always be 1:2. Local conditions dictate differing policies. A library with many branches may require a higher ratio of professionals to nonprofessionals. Conversely, differing operating conditions, different types of staffing may dictate different ratios. An example of a more extended kind of ratio analysis is that of Allan Cartter's Library Resources Index, which is described in a following section. Yet, even this kind of ratio analysis should be viewed cautiously. At best, ratio analysis can serve only as a background against which local conditions may be evaluated.

Regression analysis also provides a form of data reduction, but it compels the analyst to attempt to group like institutions together. Baumol and Marcus provide a guide to its use in library data analysis.[5] The concluding section of this appendix gives an example of its application. But the same caveats about drawing inferences that apply to ratio analysis apply to regression analysis.

In addition to these, there is a growing literature on performance evaluation of libraries which is expressed in various ways. F. W. Lancaster summarizes some of the possible approaches:

"1. The ability of the library to deliver a particular item when it is needed.

"2. The ability of the catalog and the shelf arrangement to disclose the holdings of particular items or of materials on particular subjects.

"3. The ability of reference staff to answer questions completely and accurately.

"4. The speed with which a particular item can be located when needed.

"5. The speed with which a reference inquiry can be answered or a literature search conducted and the results presented to the library user.

"6. The amount of effort that the user must himself expend in exploiting the services of the library (including factors of physical accessibility of the library and its collections, the size and quality of the library staff, and the way in which the collections are cataloged, indexed, shelved and signposted."[6]

Performance measures are, however, still in the early stages of their development. They may eventually prove to be extremely important to libraries, but they are likely to be most useful in making intrainstitutional rather than interinstitutional decisions. In sum, there are no simple solutions, no ready panaceas, no easily available substitutes for intelligent analysis of available data.

Example of Ratio Analysis

Table 1 below demonstrates the application of ratio analysis to library materials expenditures as a percentage of total library operating expenditures. It is based on the latest (1976–77) ARL data. For the sake of brevity and because this is simply used as an example, only twenty of the total applicable ninety-three institutions have been included.

The Library Resources Index

The Library Resources Index is a specialized index devised by Allan M. Cartter and published

TABLE 1
LIBRARY MATERIALS EXPENDITURES AS A PERCENTAGE
OF TOTAL LIBRARY OPERATING EXPENDITURES (VALUE)
FOR TWENTY UNIVERSITY LIBRARIES, 1976–77

Rank Order Number	Institution Number	Institution Name	Value
1	31	Houston	50.61
2	3	Arizona	44.63
3	82	Texas A & M	44.05
4	87	VPI & SU	42.84
5	81	Texas	42.69
6	28	Georgia	42.21
7	35	Iowa	42.15
8	71	South Carolina	42.08
9	68	Rice	41.67
10	42	Louisiana State	40.19
11	20	Connecticut	40.04
12	60	Oklahoma State	39.51
13	53	Nebraska	39.30
14	80	Tennessee	39.22
15	52	Missouri	38.93
16	4	Arizona State	38.62
17	22	Dartmouth	38.30
18	24	Emory	38.23
19	1	Alabama	38.08
20	57	Notre Dame	37.87

TABLE 2
THE LIBRARY RESOURCES INDEX APPLIED
TO TWENTY ARL LIBRARIES, 1976–77

Rank Order Overall Index	Institution Name	Total Volume Index	Volumes Added Index	Serials Index	Overall Library Resources Index
1	Harvard	4.49	2.25	3.89	3.54
2	Illinois	2.74	1.95	3.43	2.71
3	Yale	3.24	2.40	2.44	2.69
4	Calif., Berkeley	2.31	1.75	3.90	2.65
5	Texas	1.91	2.87	2.41	2.39
6	Indiana	2.07	2.39	1.71	2.05
7	Columbia	2.22	1.57	2.31	2.03
8	Michigan	2.31	1.81	1.92	2.02
9	Stanford	2.05	1.67	2.13	1.95
10	Toronto	1.87	2.15	1.66	1.90
11	Calif., Los Angeles	1.84	1.44	2.26	1.84
12	Washington	1.52	2.16	1.64	1.77
13	'Cornell	1.87	1.33	2.08	1.76
14	Chicago	1.83	1.60	1.76	1.73
15	Wisconsin	1.52	1.30	1.92	1.58
16	Ohio State	1.53	1.50	1.15	1.39
17	Minnesota	1.58	0.93	1.48	1.33
18	Duke	1.35	1.28	1.33	1.32
19	Princeton	1.37	1.18	1.25	1.27
20	Pennsylvania	1.31	1.08	1.10	1.16

in his *An Assessment of Quality in Graduate Education.*[7] It is an average of three indexes and is computed in the following way. First, the pool of institutions to be compared is determined. (In the example, shown as table 2, this pool is all ARL libraries and the data are for 1976–77). Second, three variables are isolated: (a) total volumes; (b) volumes added; and (c) periodicals received. A separate index is formed for each variable by finding the average for each variable and dividing the average value into the value for each institution.

For example, assume that the average number of periodicals held in ARL libraries is 15,000, and three institutions have totals respectively of 60,000, 15,000, and 7,500. Dividing the average, 15,000, into each of these figures yields index values of 4, 1, and .5. Similarly, values are found for each institution for the other two variables: volumes added and total volumes. Then the three index values for each institution are summed, divided by three, and sorted into descending order. For example, refer to institution number 8 in table 2. It is Michigan. It has index values of 2.31, 1.81, and 1.92. The sum of these is 6.04. Dividing this by 3 yields 2.01, the overall library resources index.

Mr. Cartter's index was based on 1963–64 data. His general conclusion at that time was: "Those libraries which fall below .5 are probably too weak to support quality graduate programs in a wide range of fields, although they may be adequate for an institution that specializes in technology or in advanced work in a very limited number of areas."[8]

Table 2 demonstrates an application of the Li-
brary Resources Index to twenty ARL libraries, using 1976–77 ARL data.

Regression Analysis Tables Using ARL Data, 1975–76

In analyzing data from ARL libraries, the strongest statistical relationships are found to exist when these libraries are categorized in some way. Therefore, by way of example, ARL libraries may be grouped in four different ways:

1. All ARL academic libraries.
2. All private ARL academic libraries in the U.S.
3. All public ARL academic libraries in the U.S.
4. All Canadian ARL academic libraries.

Further, for each group additional tables may be developed that predict the values of certain different (dependent) variables based upon the value of other (independent) variables. Six variables, for example, which can be examined are:

1. Professional staff
2. Total staff
3. Gross volumes added
4. Expenditures for library materials
5. Total library expenditures
6. Current periodicals held

For each library in each of the four groups noted above, the following predictions then can be made:

1. Number of professional staff based on number of volumes held
2. Number of total staff based on number of volumes held
3. Number of gross volumes added based on volumes held

TABLE 3
EXAMPLE OF REGRESSION ANALYSIS APPLIED
TO SIZE OF PROFESSIONAL STAFF (Y)

Institution	Y Value	Y Estimate	Residual	Display		
Library A	37	39	−2	X		
Library B	52	48	+4		X	
Library C	63	55	+8			X
Library D	60	72	−12	X		
				least squares		
				line normalized		

4. Expenditures for library materials based on gross volumes added and volumes held
5. Total expenditures based on volumes held, gross volumes added, and total staff
6. Number of current serials based on number of volumes held

Thus, for each table there can be plotted a display of variables, together with observations for each institution, and which include for each dependent variable its actual value, its estimated value, and the residual, which is the difference between the actual and the estimated value. For example, assume we have the display shown above as table 3, which predicts the number of professional staff a library is expected to have based upon the number of volumes held.

The first column identifies each institution; the second shows the actual value for each variable; the third shows the expected value based on the regression equation computation which has been done; the fourth is the difference between columns two and three; and the fifth is a plot of the data.

Looking at Library A, we see that it has thirty-seven professional staff, but based on the other libraries in its comparison class, it would be expected to have thirty-nine. The actual value is two fewer than expected, so its position on the graph is plotted to the left of the least squares line. (See any standard textbook on statistics for detailed explanation of this technique.) Libraries B and C have more professionals than would be expected, so they are plotted to the right of the line. Consequently, by inspection, the library

manager can note any obvious anomalies between his or her institution and others.

REFERENCES FOR APPENDIX

1. Doctoral granting institutions in Carnegie Commission on Higher Education. *A Classification of Institutions of Higher Education* (Berkeley, Calif.: The Commission, 1973). p.1–2, 9–22.
2. Herman H. Fussler, *Research Libraries and Technology, A Report to the Sloan Foundation* (Chicago: Univ. of Chicago Press, 1973), p.61.
3. Fritz Machlup, "Our Libraries: Can We Measure Their Holdings and Acquisitions," *AAUP Bulletin* 62:303–7 (Oct. 1976).
4. See, for example, Morris Hamburg and others, *Library Planning and Decision Making Systems* (Cambridge, Mass.: MIT Press, 1974).
5. William J. Baumol and Matityahu Marcus, *Economics of Academic Libraries* (Washington, D.C.: American Council on Education, 1973).
6. F. W. Lancaster, *The Measurement and Evaluation of Library Services* (Washington, D.C.: Information Resources, 1977), p.323.
7. Allan M. Cartter, *An Assessment of Quality in Graduate Education* (Washington, D.C.: American Council on Education, 1966).
8. *Ibid.*, p.114.

Editor's Note: Members may order single copies by sending a self-addressed label to the ACRL office. Nonmembers should include $1.00 with their order. ■■

Reprinted from the April 1979 issue of *College & Research Libraries News*
Copyright, 1979, American Library Association

Standards for College Libraries

Approved as policy by the Board of Directors of the Association of College and Research Libraries, on July 3, 1975. These Standards supersede and replace the 1959 "Standards for College Libraries" (College & Research Libraries, July 1959, p.274-80).

Introduction

Since the beginning of colleges libraries have been considered an essential part of advanced learning. Their role has ever been to provide access to the human records needed by members of the higher education community for the successful pursuit of academic programs. Total fulfillment of this role, however, is an ideal which has never been and probably never will be attained. Libraries can therefore be judged only by the degree to which they approach this ideal. Expectations moreover of the degree of total success that they should attain are widely various, differing from institution to institution, from individual to individual, from constituency to constituency. It is this diversity of expectations that prompts the need for standards.

The Standards hereinafter presented do not prescribe this unattainable ideal. They rather describe a realistic set of conditions which, if fulfilled, will provide an adequate library program in a college. They attempt to synthesize and articulate the aggregate experience and judgment of the academic library profession as to adequacy in library resources, services, and facilities for a college community. They are intended to apply to libraries serving academic programs at the bachelors and masters degree levels. They may be applied also to libraries serving universities which grant fewer than ten doctoral degrees per year.* They are not designed for use in two-year colleges, larger universities, independent professional schools, specialized programs or other atypical institutions.

These Standards are organized on the basis of the major functions and components of library organization and services and are arranged as follows:

1. Objectives
2. Collections
3. Organization of Materials
4. Staff
5. Delivery of Service

* Specifically these Standards address themselves to institutions defined by the Carnegie Commission on Higher Education as Liberal Arts Colleges I and II and Comprehensive Universities and Colleges I and II, in *A Classification of Institutions of Higher Education* (Berkeley, Cal., 1973).

6. Facilities
7. Administration
8. Budget

A brief explanatory exegesis is appended to each Standard, citing the reasons for its inclusion and providing suggestions and comments upon its implementation. Complete background considerations for these commentaries may be found in the literature of librarianship.

There are a number of additional areas wherein standards are felt to be desirable when it is possible to prepare them, but for which no consensus among librarians is apparent at this time. These include measures of library effectiveness and productivity, the requisite extent and configuration of non-print resources and services, and methods for program evaluation. Research and experimentation should make it possible, however, to prepare standards for them at some future time.

STANDARD 1:
OBJECTIVES OF THE LIBRARY

1 *The college library shall develop an explicit statement of its objectives in accord with the goals and purposes of the college.*

1.1 *The development of library objectives shall be the responsibility of the library staff, in consultation with students, members of the teaching faculty, and administrative officers.*

1.2 *The statement of library objectives shall be reviewed periodically and revised as needed.*

Commentary on Standard 1

The administration and faculty of every college have a responsibility to examine from time to time their education programs and to define the purposes and goals of the institution. Members of the library faculty share in this exercise, and they have thereafter the responsibility to promote library service consistent with institutional aims and methods. Successful fulfillment of this latter responsibility can best be attained when a clear and explicit statement of derivative library objectives is prepared and promulgated so that all members of the college community can understand and evaluate the appropriateness and effectiveness of library activities.

Preparation of library objectives is an obligation of the library faculty with the assistance of the rest of the library staff. In this effort, however, the library should seek in a formal or structured way the advice and guidance of students, of members of the teaching faculty, and of administrative officers. Library objectives should be kept current through periodic review and revision as needed.

In preparing its statement of objectives, the library staff should consider the evolution in recent decades of new roles for the American college library. Although the college library continues as in the past to serve as the repository for the printed information needed by its patrons, its resources have now been extended to embrace new forms of recorded information, and its proper purpose has been enlarged through changes in the scope of the curriculum and by new concepts of instruction. Thus it now serves also as a complementary academic capability which affords to students the opportunity to augment their classroom experience with an independent avenue for learning beyond the course offerings of the institution. Even this instructional objective of the library, however, must be conceived and formulated within the overall academic purpose of the college.

STANDARD 2:
THE COLLECTIONS

2 *The library's collections shall comprise all corpuses of recorded information owned by the college for educational, inspirational, and recreational purposes, including multi-dimensional, aural, pictorial, and print materials.*

2.1 *The library shall provide quickly a high percentage of such materials needed by its patrons.*

2.1.1 *The amount of print materials to be thus provided shall be determined by a formula (See Formula A) which takes into account the nature and extent of the academic program of the institution, its enrollment, and the size of its teaching faculty.*

Commentary on Standard 2

The records of intellectual endeavor appear in a wide range of formats. Books represent extended reports of scholarly investigation, compilations of findings, creative works, and summaries prepared for educational purposes. The journal has become the common medium for scientific communication and usually represents more recent information. Scientific reports in near-print form are becoming an even faster means of research communication. Documents represent compilations of information prepared by governmental agencies, and newspapers contain the systematic recording of daily activities throughout the world.

Many kinds of communication can be better and sometimes faster accomplished through such non-print media as films, slides, tapes, radio and television recordings, and realia. Mi-

---

FORMULA A—

The formula for calculating the number of relevant print volumes (or microform volume-equivalents) to which the library should provide prompt access is as follows (to be calculated cumulatively):

1. Basic Collection . . . . 85,000 vols.
2. Allowance per FTE Faculty Member . . . . . 100 vols.
3. Allowance per FTE Student . . . . . . 15 vols.
4. Allowance per Undergraduate Major or Minor Field* . . . 350 vols.
5. Allowance per Masters Field, When No Higher Degree is Offered in the Field* . . . . 6,000 vols.
6. Allowance per Masters Field, When a Higher Degree is Offered in the Field* . . . . 3,000 vols.
7. Allowance per 6th-year Specialist Degree Field* . . . . . 6,000 vols.
8. Allowance per Doctoral Field* . . . . . . 25,000 vols.

A "volume" is defined as a physical unit of any printed, typewritten, handwritten, mimeographed, or processed work contained in one binding or portfolio, hardbound or paperbound, which has been cataloged, classified, and/or otherwise prepared for use. For purposes of this calculation microform holdings should be included by converting them to volume-equivalents. The number of volume-equivalents held in microform should be determined either by actual count or by an averaging formula which considers each reel of microform as one, and five pieces of any other microformat as one volume-equivalent.

Libraries which can provide promptly 100 percent as many volumes or volume-equivalents as are called for in this formula shall, in the matter of quantity, be graded A. From 80-99 percent shall be graded B; from 65-79 percent shall be graded C; and from 50-64 percent shall be graded D.

* See Appendix I, "List of Fields."

crophotography is an accepted means of compacting many kinds of records for preservation and storage. Recorded information may also come in the form of manuscripts, archives, and machine-readable data bases. Each medium of communication provides unique dimensions for the transmission of information, and each tends to complement the others.

This inherent unity of recorded information, and the fundamental commonality of its social utility, require that regardless of format, all kinds of recorded information needed for academic purposes by an institution be selected, acquired, organized, stored, and delivered for use within the library. In this way the institution's information resources can best be articulated and balanced for the greatest benefit of the entire community.

It is less important that a college hold legal title to the quantity of library materials called for in Formula A than it be able to supply the amount quickly—say within fifteen minutes—as by contract with an adjacent institution or by some other means. An institution which arranges to meet all or part of its library responsibilities in this way, however, must take care that in doing so it not create supernumerary or unreimbursed costs for another institution and that the materials so made available are relevant to its own students' needs.

Since a library book collection once developed, and then allowed to languish, loses its utility very rapidly, continuity of collection development is essential. Experience has shown that even after collections have attained sizes required by this Standard, they can seldom retain their requisite utility without sustaining annual gross growth rates, before withdrawals, of at least five percent.

Higher education has thus far had too little experience with non-print library materials to permit tenable generalizations to be made about their quantitative requirements. Since consensus has not yet been attained among educators as to the range, extent, and configuration of non-print services which it is appropriate for college libraries to offer, no generally applicable formulas are possible here. It is assumed, however, that every college library should have non-print resources appropriate to institutional needs.

The goal of college library collection development should be quality rather than quantity. A collection may be said to have quality for its purpose only to the degree that it possesses a portion of the bibliography of each discipline taught, apropriate in quantity both to the level at which each is taught and to the number of students and faculty members who use it. Quality and quantity are separable only in theory: it is possible to have quantity without quality; it is not possible to have quality without quan-

tity defined in relation to the purposes of the institution. No easily applicable criteria have been developed, however, for measuring quality in library collections.

The best way to assure quality in a college library collection is to gain it at point of input. Thus rigorous discrimination in the selection of materials to be added to the library's holdings, whether as purchases or gifts, is of considerable importance. Care should be exerted to select a substantial portion of the titles listed in the standard, scholarly bibliographies reflecting the curriculum areas of the college and supporting general fields of knowledge. A number of such subjects lists for college libraries have been prepared by learned associations. Among general bibliographies *Books for College Libraries* is useful especially for purposes of identifying important retrospective titles. For current additions, provision should be made to acquire a majority of the significant new publications reviewed in *Choice*. Generous attention should be given also to standard works of reference and to bibliographical tools which provide access to the broad range of scholarly sources as listed in Winchell's *Guide to Reference Books*. Institutional needs vary so widely for periodical holdings that quantitative standards cannot be written for them at this time, but in general it is good practice for a library to own any title that is needed more than six times per year. Several good handlists have been prepared of periodical titles appropriate for college collections.

College library collections should be evaluated continuously against standard bibliographies and against records of their use, for purposes both of adding to the collections and identifying titles for prompt withdrawal once they have outlived their usefulness to the college program. No book should be retained in a college library for which a clear purpose is not evident in terms of the institution's current or anticipated academic program; when such clear purpose is lacking, a book should be retired from the collections.

Although in the last analysis the library staff must be responsible for the scope and content of the collections, it can best fulfill this responsibility with substantial help and consultation from the teaching faculty and from students. Of greatest benefit to the library is continuing faculty assistance in defining the literature requirements of the courses in the curriculum, definitions which should take the form of written selection policies. In addition, members of the teaching faculty may participate in the selection of individual titles to be obtained. If this latter activity, however, is carried out largely by the library, then the teaching faculty should review the books acquired both for their appropriateness and the quality of their contents.

STANDARD 3:
ORGANIZATION OF MATERIALS

3 *Library collections shall be organized by nationally approved conventions and arranged for efficient retrieval at time of need.*

3.1 *There shall be a union catalog of the library's holdings that permits identification of items, regardless of format, by author, title, and subject.*

3.1.1 *The catalog may be developed either by a single library or jointly among several libraries.*

3.1.2 *The catalog shall be in a format that can be consulted by a number of people concurrently and at time of need.*

3.1.3 *In addition to the catalog there shall also be requisite subordinate files, such as serial records, shelf lists, authority files, and indexes to nonmonographic materials.*

3.2 *Except for certain categories of material which are for convenience best segregated by form, library materials shall be arranged on the shelves by subject.*

3.2.1 *Patrons shall have direct access to library materials on the shelves.*

Commentary on Standard 3

The acquisition alone of library materials comprises only part of the task of providing access to them. Collections must be indexed and systematically arranged on the shelves before their efficient identification and retrieval at time of need, which is an important test of a good library, can be assured. For most library materials this indexing can best be accomplished through the development of a union catalog with items entered in accord with established national or international bibliographical conventions, such as rules for entry, descriptive cataloging, filing, classification, and subject headings.

Opportunities of several kinds exist for the cooperative development of the library's catalog, through which economy can be gained in its preparation. These include the use of centralized cataloging by the Library of Congress and the joint compilation of catalogs by a number of libraries. Joint catalogs can take the form of card files, book catalogs, or computer files. Catalogs jointly developed, regardless of format, can satisfy this Standard provided that they can be consulted—under author, title, or subject—by a number of library patrons concurrently at their time of need. Catalogs should be subject to continual editing to keep them abreast of modern terminology, current technology, and contemporary practice.

Proper organization of the collections will also require the maintenance of a number of subordinate files, such as authority files and shelf lists, and of complementary catalogs, such as serial records. Information contained in these files should also be available to library users. In addition, some library materials such as journals, documents, and microforms are often indexed centrally by commercial or quasi-commercial agencies, and in such cases access should be provided to those indexes as needed, whether they be in published or computer-based format.

Materials should be arranged on the shelves by subject matter so that related information can be consulted together. Some kinds of materials, however, such as maps, microforms, and non-print holdings, may be awkward to integrate physically because of form and may be segregated from the main collection. Other materials, such as rarities and manuscripts or archives, may be segregated for purposes of security. Materials in exceptionally active use, such as bibliographies, works of reference, and assigned readings, may be kept separate to facilitate access to them. Except in such cases, however, the bulk of the collections should be classified and shelved by subject in open stack areas so as to permit and encourage browsing.

STANDARD 4:
STAFF

4 *The library staff shall be of adequate size and quality to meet agreed-upon objectives.*

4.1 *The staff shall comprise qualified librarians, skilled supportive personnel, and part-time assistants serving on an hourly basis.*

4.2 *The marks of a librarian shall include a graduate library degree from an ALA-accredited program, responsibility for duties of a professional nature, and participation in professional library affairs beyond the local campus.*

4.2.1 *The librarians of a college shall be organized as an academic department—or, in the case of a university, as a school—and shall administer themselves in accord with ACRL "Standards for Faculty Status for College and University Librarians" (See Appendix II).*

4.3 *The number of librarians required shall be determined by a formula (Formula B, below) which takes into account the enrollment of the college and the size and growth rate of the collections.*

4.3.1 *There shall be an appropriate balance of effort among librarians, supportive personnel, and part-time assistants, so that every staff member is employed as nearly as possible commensurate with his library training, experience, and capability.*

4.4 *Library policies and procedures concerning staff shall be in accord with sound personnel management practice.*

Commentary on Standard 4

The college library will need a staff comprising librarians, supportive personnel, and part-time assistants to carry out its stated objectives. The librarian has acquired through training in a graduate library school an understanding of the principles and theories of selection, acquisition, organization, interpretation, and administration of library resources. Supportive staff members have normally received specialized or on-the-job training for particular assignments within the library; such assignments can range in complexity from relatively routine or business functions to highly technical activities often requiring university degrees in fields other than librarianship. Well managed college libraries also utilize some part-time assistants, many of whom are students. Although they must often perform repetitive and more perfunctory work, given good training and adequate experience such assistants can often perform at relatively skilled levels and constitute an important segment of the library team.

Work assignments, both to these several levels and to individuals, should be carefully conceived and allocated so that all members of the library staff are employed as nearly as possible commensurate with their library training, experience, and capability. This will mean that the librarians will seldom comprise more than 25–35 percent of the total FTE library staff.

The librarians of a college comprise the faculty of the library and should organize and administer themselves as any other departmental faculty in the college (or in the case of the university, the library faculty is equivalent to a school faculty, and should govern itself accordingly). In either case, however, the status, responsibilities, perquisites, and governance of the library faculty shall be fully recognized and supported by the parent institution, and it shall

function in accord with the ACRL "Standards for Faculty Status for College and University Librarians."

The staff represents one of the library's most important assets in support of the instructional program of the college. Careful attention is therefore required to proper personnel management policies and procedures. Whether administered centrally for the college as a whole or separately within the library, these policies and practices must be based upon sound, contemporary management understanding consistent with the goals and purposes of the institution. This will mean that:

1. Recruitment methods should be based upon a careful definition of positions to be filled, utilization of a wide range of sources, qualifications based upon job requirements, and objective evaluation of credentials.
2. Written procedures should be followed in matters of appointment, promotion, tenure, dismissal, and appeal.
3. Every staff member should be informed in writing as to the scope of his responsibilities and the individual to whom he is responsible.
4. Classification and pay plans should give recognition to the nature of the duties performed, training and experience required, and rates of pay and benefits of other positions requiring equivalent background.
5. There should be provided a structured program for the orientation and training of new staff members and opportunities for the continuing education of existing staff.
6. Supervisory staff should be selected on the basis of job knowledge and human relations skills and provide training in these responsibilities as needed.
7. Systems should be maintained for periodic review of employee performance and for recognition of achievement.
8. Career opportunities and counseling should be made available to library staff members at all levels and in all departments.

FORMULA B—

The number of librarians required by the college shall be computed as follows (to be calculated cumulatively):

For each 500, or fraction thereof, FTE students up to 10,000	1 librarian
For each 1,000 or fraction thereof, FTE students above 10,000 . . .	1 librarian
For each 100,000 volumes, or fraction thereof, in the collection	1 librarian
For each 5,000 volumes, or fraction thereof, added per year	1 librarian

Libraries which provide 100 percent of these formula requirements can, when they are supported by sufficient other staff members, consider themselves at the A level in terms of staff size; those that provide 75-99 percent of these requirements may rate themselves as B; those with 55-74 percent of requirements qualify for a C; and those with 40-54 percent of requirements warrant a D.

STANDARD 5:
DELIVERY OF SERVICE

5   *The college library shall establish and maintain a range and quality of services that will promote the academic program of the institution and encourage optimal library use.*

5.1 *Proper service shall include: the provision of continuing instruction to patrons in the effective exploitation of libraries; the guidance of patrons to the library materials they need; and the provision of information to patrons as appropriate.*

5.2 *Library materials shall be circulated to qualified patrons under equitable policies and for as long periods as possible without jeopardizing their availability to others.*

5.2.1 *The availability of reading materials shall be extended wherever possible by the provision of inexpensive means of photocopying.*

5.2.2 *The quality of the collections available locally to patrons shall be enhanced through the use of "National Interlibrary Loan Code 1968" (See Appendix II) and other cooperative agreements which provide reciprocal access to multi-library resources.*

5.3 *The hours of public access to the materials on the shelves, to the study facilities of the library, and to the library staff, shall be consistent with reasonable demand, both during the normal study week and during weekends and vacation periods.*

5.4 *Where academic programs are offered away from a campus, library services shall be provided in accord with ACRL's "Guidelines for Library Services to Extension Students"* (See Appendix II).

Commentary on Standard 5

The primary purpose of college library service is to promote the academic program of the parent institution. The successful fulfillment of this purpose will require that librarians work closely with teaching faculty to gain an intimate knowledge of their educational objectives and methods and to impart to them an understanding of the services which the library can render. Both skill in library use and ease of access to materials can encourage library use, but the major stimulus for students to use the library has always been, and likely always will be, the instructional methods used in the classroom. Thus close cooperation between librarians and classroom instructors is essential.

Such cooperation does not come about fortuitously; it must be a planned and structured activity, and it must be assiduously sought. It

will require not only that librarians participate in the academic planning councils of the institution but also that they assist teaching faculty in appraising the actual and potential library resources available, work closely with them in developing library services for new courses and new pedagogical techniques, and keep them informed of new library capabilities.

A key service of a college library is the introduction and interpretation of library materials to patrons. This activity takes several forms. The first form is instruction in bibliography and in the use of information tools. It will also familiarize patrons with the physical facilities of the library, its services and collections, and the policies and conditions which govern their use. Bibliographic instruction and orientation may be given at many levels of sophistication and may use a variety of instructional methods and materials, including course-related instruction, separate courses with or without credit, group or individualized instruction, utilizing print or non-print materials.

The second basic form which interpretation will take is conventional reference work wherein individual patrons are guided by librarians in their appraisal of the range and extent of the library resources available to them for learning and research, in the most effective marshalling of that material, and in the optimal utilization of libraries. Most library interpretative work is of this kind.

The third major genre of library interpretation is the delivery of information itself. Although obviously inappropriate in the case of student searches which are purposeful segments of classroom assignments, the actual delivery of information—as distinct from guidance to it—is a reasonable library service in almost all other conceivable situations.

As regards the circulation of library materials, the general trend in recent years has been toward longer loan periods, but these periods must be determined by local conditions which will include size of the collections, the number of copies of a book held, and the extent of the user community. Circulation should be for as long periods as are reasonable without jeopardizing access to materials by other qualified patrons. This overall goal may prompt some institutions to establish variant or unique loan periods for different titles or classes of titles. Whatever loan policy is used, however, it should be equitably and uniformly administered to all qualified categories of patrons.

Locally-held library resources should be extended and enhanced in every way possible for the benefit of library patrons. Both the quantity and the accessibility of reading materials can be extended through the provision of inexpensive means of photocopying within the laws regarding copyright. Local resources should aso be extended through the provision and. encouragement of reciprocal arrangements with other libraries as through the "National Interlibrary Loan Code 1968" and joint-access consortia. Beyond its own local constituency every library also has a responsibility to make its holdings available to other students and scholars in at least three ways—in-house consultation, photocopy, and through interlibrary loan.

The number of hours per week that library services should be available will vary, depending upon such factors as whether the college is in an urban or rural setting, teaching methods used, conditions in the dormitories, and whether the student body is primarily resident or commuting. In any case, library scheduling should be responsive to reasonable local need, not only during term-time week-days but also on weekends, and, especially where graduate work is offered, during vacation periods. In many institutions readers may need access to study facilities and to the collections during more hours of the week than they require the personal services of librarians. The public's need for access to librarians may range upward to one hundred hours per week, whereas around-the-clock access to the library's collections and/or facilities may in some cases be warranted.

Special library problems exist for colleges that provide off-campus instructional programs. Students in such programs must be provided with library services in accord with ACRL's "Guidelines for Library Services to Extension Students." These Guidelines require that such services be financed on a regular basis, that a librarian be specifically charged with the delivery of such services, that the library implications of such programs be considered before program approval, and that courses so taught encourage library use. Such services, which are especially important at the graduate level, must be furnished despite their obvious logistical problems.

STANDARD 6:
FACILITIES

6   The college shall provide a library building containing secure facilities for housing its resources, adequate space for administration of those resources by staff, and comfortable quarters and furnishings for their utilization by patrons.

6.1   The size of the library building shall be determined by a formula (See Formula C) which takes into account the enrollment of the college, the extent and nature of its collections, and the size of its staff.

6.2   The shape of the library building and the internal distribution of its facilities and services shall be determined by function.

6.3   Except in unusual circumstances, the college library's collections and services shall be administered within a single structure.

Commentary on Standard 6

Successful library service presupposes an adequate library building. Although the type of building provided will depend upon the character and the aims of the institution, it should in all cases present secure facilities for housing the library's resources, sufficient space for their administration by staff, and comfortable quarters and furnishings for their utilization by the public, all integrated into a functional and esthetic whole. The college library building should represent a conscious planning effort, involving the librarian, the college administration, and the architect, with the librarian responsible for the preparation of the building program. The needs of handicapped patrons should receive special attention in the designing of the library building.

Many factors will enter into a determination of the quality of a library building. They will include such esthetic considerations as its location on the campus, the grace with which it relates to its site and to neighboring structures, and the degree to which it contributes esthetically to the desired ambience of the campus. They will also include such internal characteristics as the diversity and appropriateness of its accommodations and furnishings, the functional distribution and interrelationships of its spaces, and the simplicity and economy with which it can be utilized by patrons and operated by staff. They will include moreover such physical characteristics as the adequacy of its acoustical treatment and lighting, the effectiveness of its heating and cooling plant, and the selection of its movable equipment.

Decentralized library facilities in a college have some virtues, and they present some difficulties. Primary among their virtues is their adjacency to the laboratories and offices of some teaching faculty members within their service purview. Primary among their weaknesses are their fragmentation of unity of knowledge, their relative isolation from library users (other than aforementioned faculty), the fact that they can seldom command the attention of qualified staff over either long hours during a week or over a sustained period of time, and the excessive costs of creating duplicate catalogs, periodical lists, circulation services, and attendant study facilities. Where decentralized library facilities are being considered, these costs and benefits must be carefully compared. In general, experience has shown that except where long distances are involved, decentralized library facilities are at the present time unlikely to be in the best pedagogical or economic interests of a college.

STANDARD 7:
ADMINISTRATION

7 *The college library shall be administered in a manner which permits and encourages the fullest and most effective use of available library resources.*

7.1 *The statutory or legal foundation for the library's activities shall be recognized in writing.*

7.2 *The college librarian shall be a member of the library faculty and shall report to the president or the chief academic officer of the institution.*

7.2.1 *The responsibilities and authority of the college librarian and procedures for his appointment shall be defined in writing.*

7.3 *There shall be a standing advisory committee comprising students and members of the teaching faculty which shall serve*

as the main channel of formal communication between the library and its user community.

7.4 *The library shall maintain written policies and procedure manuals covering internal library governance and operational activities.*

7.4.1 *The library shall maintain a systematic and continuous program for evaluating its performance and for identifying needed improvements.*

7.4.2 *The library shall develop statistics not only for purposes of planning and control but also to aid in the preparation of reports designed to inform its publics of its accomplishments and problems.*

7.5 *The library shall develop, seek out, and utilize cooperative programs for purposes of either reducing its operating costs or enhancing its services, so long as such programs create no unreimbursed or unreciprocated costs for other libraries or organizations.*

FORMULA C—

The size of the college library building shall be calculated on the basis of a formula which takes into consideration the size of the student body, requisite administrative space, and the number of physical volumes held in the collections. In the absence of consensus among librarians and other educators as to the range of non-book services which it is appropriate for libraries to offer, no generally applicable formulas have been developed for calculating space for them. Thus, space required for a college library's non-book services and materials must be added to the following calculations:

a. *Space for readers.* The seating requirement for the library of a college wherein less than fifty percent of the FTE enrollment resides on campus shall be one for each five FTE students; the seating requirement for the typical residential college library shall be one for each four FTE students; and the seating requirements for the library in the strong, liberal arts, honors-oriented college shall be one for each three FTE students. In any case, each library seat shall be assumed to require twenty-five square feet of floor space.

b. *Space for books.* Space required for books depends in part upon the overall size of the book collection, and is calculated cumulatively as follows:

	Square Feet/Volume
For the first 150,000 volumes	0.10
For the next 150,000 volumes	0.09
For the next 300,000 volumes	0.08
For holdings above 600,000 volumes	0.07

c. *Space for administration.* Space required for such library administrative activities as acquisition, cataloging, staff offices, catalogs, and files shall be one-fourth of the sum of the spaces needed for readers and books as calculated under (a) and (b) above.

This tripartite formula indicates the net assignable area necessary for all library services except for non-book services. (For definition of "net assignable area" see "The Measurement and Comparison of Physical Facilities for Libraries," produced by ALA's Library Administration Division. See Appendix II.) Libraries which provide 100 percent as much net assignable area as is called for by the formula shall qualify for an A rating as regards quantity; 75–99 percent shall warrant a B; 60–74 percent shall be due a C; and 50–59 percent shall warrant a D.

7.6 The library shall be administered in accord with the spirit of the ALA "Library Bill of Rights." (See Appendix II.)

Commentary on Standard 7

Much of the commentary on general administration of the college library is gathered under the several other Standards. Matters of personnel administration, for example, are discussed under Standard 4, and fiscal administration is glossed under Standard 8. Some important aspects of library management, however, must be considered apart from the other Standards.

Primary among administrative considerations which are not part of other Standards is the matter of the responsibilities and authority both of the library as an organization and of the college librarian as a college officer. No clear set of library objectives, no tenable program of collection development, no defensible library personnel policy can be developed unless there is first an articulated and widespread understanding within the college as to the statutory, legal or other basis under which the library is to function. This may be a college bylaw, or a trustee minute, or a public law which shows the responsibility and flow of authority under which the library is empowered to act. There must also be a derivative document defining the responsibility and authority vested in the office of the college librarian. This document may also be statutorily based and should spell out, in addition to the scope and nature of his duties and powers, the procedures for his appointment and the focus of his reporting responsibility. Experience has shown that, for the closest coordination of library activities with the instructional program, the college librarian should report either to the president or to the chief officer in charge of the academic affairs of the institution.

Although the successful college library must strive for excellence in all of its communications, especially those of an informal nature, it must also have the benefit of an advisory committee representing its user community. This committee—of which the college librarian should be an *ex officio* member—should serve as the main channel of formal communication between the library and its publics and should be used to convey both an awareness to the library of its patrons' concerns, perceptions, and needs, and an understanding to patrons of the library's capabilities and problems. The charge to the committee should be specific, and it should be in writing.

Many of the precepts of college library administration are the same as those for the administration of any other similar enterprise. The writing down of policies and the preparation of procedures manuals, for example, are required for best management of any organization so as to assure uniformity and consistency of action, to aid in training of staff, and to contribute to public understanding. Likewise sound public relations are essential to almost any successful service organization. Although often observed in their omission, structured programs of performance evaluation and quality control are equally necessary. All of these administrative practices are important in a well managed library.

Some interlibrary cooperative efforts have tended in local libraries to enhance the quality of service or reduce operating costs. Labor-sharing, for example, through cooperative processing programs has been beneficial to many libraries, and participation in the pooled ownership of seldom-used materials has relieved pressure on some campuses for such materials to be collected locally. The potential values of meaningful cooperation among libraries are sufficient to require that libraries actively search out and avail themselves of cooperative programs that will work in their interests. Care should be taken, however, to assure that a recipient library reimburse, either in money or in kind, the full costs of any other institution that supplies its service, unless of course the supplying institution is specifically charged and funded so to make its services available.

College libraries should be impervious to the pressures or efforts of any special interest groups or individuals to shape their collections and services in accord with special pleadings. This principle, first postulated by the American Library Association in 1939 as the "Library Bill of Rights," should govern the administration of every college library and be given the full protection of all parent institutions.

STANDARD 8:
BUDGET

8 The college librarian shall have the responsibility for preparing, defending, and administering the library budget in accord with agreed-upon objectives.

8.1 The amount of the library appropriation shall express a relationship to the total institutional budget for educational and general purposes.

8.2 The librarian shall have sole authority to apportion funds and initiate expenditures within the library approved budget, in accord with institutional policy.

8.3 The library shall maintain such internal accounts as are necessary for approving its invoices for payment, monitoring its encumbrances, and evaluating the flow of its expenditures.

Commentary on Standard 8

The library budget is a function of program planning and tends to define the library's objectives in fiscal terms and for a stated interval of time. Once agreed to by the college administration, the objectives formulated under Standard 1 should constitute the base upon which the library's budget is developed. The degree to which the college is able to fund the library in accord with its objectives is reflected in the relationship of the library appropriation to the total educational and general budget of the college. Experience has shown that library budgets, exclusive of capital costs and the costs of physical maintenance, which fall below six percent of the college's total educational and general expenditures are seldom able to sustain the range of library programs required by the institution. This percentage moreover will run considerably higher during periods when the library is attempting to overcome past deficiencies, to raise its "grade" on collections and staff as defined elsewhere in these Standards, or to meet the information needs of new academic programs.

The adoption of formulas for preparation of budget estimates and for prediction of library expenditures over periods of time are relatively common, especially among public institutions. Since such formulas can often provide a gross approximation of needs, they are useful for purposes of long-range planning, but they frequently fail to take into account local cost variables, and they are seldom able to respond promptly to unanticipated market inflation or changes in enrollment. Thus they should not be used, except as indicators, in definitive budget development.

Among the variables which should be considered in estimating a library's budget requirements are the following:

1. The scope, nature, and level of the college curriculum;

2. Instructional methods used, especially as they relate to independent study;

3. The adequacy of existing collections and the publishing rate in fields pertinent to the curriculum;

4. The size, or anticipated size, of the student body and teaching faculty;

5. The adequacy and availability of other library resources in the locality to which the library has contracted access;

6. The range of services offered by the library, the number of service points maintained, the number of hours per week that service is provided, etc.;

7. The extent to which the library already meets the Standards defined in these pages.

Procedures for the preparation and defense of budget estimates, policies on budget approval, and regulations concerning accounting and expenditures may vary from one institution or jurisdiction to another, and the college librarian must know and conform to local practice. In any circumstance, however, sound prac-

tices of planning and control require that the librarian have sole responsibility and authority for the allocation—and within college policy, the reallocation—of the library budget and the initiation of expenditures against it. Depending upon local factors, between 35 and 45 percent of the library's budget is normally allocated to the purchase of materials, and between 50 and 60 percent is expended for personnel.

The preparation of budget estimates may be made on the basis of past expenditures and anticipated needs, comparison with similar libraries, or statistical norms and standards. More sophisticated techniques for detailed analysis of costs by library productivity, function, or program—as distinct from items of expenditure—have been attempted in some libraries. Such procedures require that the library develop quantitative methods by which to prepare estimates, analyze performance, and determine the relative priority of services rendered. Although this kind of budgeting, once refined, may lead to more effective fiscal control and greater accountability, libraries generally have thus far had too limited experience with program budgeting or input-output analysis to permit their widespread adoption at this time.

APPENDIX I
List of Fields
(Count each line as one program)

Advertising
Afro-American/Black Studies
Agriculture & Natural Resources
   Agricultural Biology
   Agricultural Business
   Agricultural Chemistry
   Agricultural Economics
   Agricultural Education
   Agricultural Engineering:
     See Engineering
   Agriculture
   Agronomy
   Animal Science
   Crop Science: See Agronomy
   Dairy Science
   Fisheries
   Food Industries
   Forestry
   Fruit Science and Industry
   International Agriculture
   Mechanized Agriculture
   National Resources Management
   Ornamental Horticulture
   Poultry Industry
   Range Management
   Soil Science
   Veterinary, Pre-
   Watershed Management
   Wildlife Management
American Studies
Anthropology
Architecture (See also City Plg.; Engr.; Landscape Arch)

Art
Art History
Asian Studies (See also East Asian)
Astronomy
Behavioral Sciences
Bilingual Studies
Biochemistry
Biology, Biological Sciences (See also Botany,
    Microbiology, etc.)
Biology and Mathematics
Black Studies: See Afro-American
Botany
Business Administration
  Accounting
  Business Administration
  Business Economics
  Business Education
  Business, Special interest
  Business Statistics
  Data Processing
  Finance
  Hotel and Restaurant Management
  Industrial Relations
  Information Systems: Listed alphabetically
    under "I"
  Insurance
  International (World) Business
  Management (Business)
  Marketing (Management)
  Office Administration
  Operations Research
    (Management Science)
  Personnel Management
  Production/Operations Management
  Public Relations
  Quantitative Methods
  Real Estate
  Secretarial Studies
  Transportation Management
Cell Biology
Chemical Physics
Chemistry
Chinese
City/Regional/Urban Planning
Classics
Communications
Communicative Disorders
    See Speech Pathology
Comparative Literature
Computer Science
Corrections: See Criminal Justice
Creative Writing
Crime, Law and Society
Criminalistics (Forensic Science)
Criminal Justice Administration
Criminal Justice—Corrections
Criminal Justice—Security
Criminology
Cybernetic Systems
Dance
Dietetics and Food Administration
Drama (Theater Arts)
Earth Sciences
East Asian Studies
Ecology/Environmental Biology
    (See also Environmental Studies)
Economics

Education
  Adult Secondary
  Child Development
  Counseling/Guidance
  Curriculum and Instruction
  Culturally Disadvantaged
  Deaf
  Education
  Educational Administration
  Educational Foundations and Theory
  Educational Psychology
  Educational Research
  Educational Supervision
  Elementary Education
  Gifted
  Health and Safety
  Instructional Media
    (Audio-Visual)
  Learning Disabilities
    (Handicapped)
  Mentally Retarded
  Orthopedically Handicapped
  Reading Instruction
  School Psychology: See Psychology
  Secondary Education
  Special Education
  Special Education Supervision
  Special Interest
  Visually Handicapped
  Visually Handicapped:
    Orientation and Mobility
Engineering
  Aeronautical Engineering, Aerospace and
    Maintenance
  Aeronautics (Operations)
  Agricultural
  Air Conditioning, Air Pollution:
    See Environmental Engineering
  Architectural
  Biomedical Engineering
  Chemical
  Civil
  Computer
  Construction
  Electrical
  Electrical/Electronic
  Electronic
  Engineering
  Engineering Materials
  Engineering Mechanics
  Engineering Science
  Engineering Technology
  Environmental
  Environmental Resources
  Industrial Administration
  Industrial Engineering
  Measurement Science
  Mechanical
  Metallurgical
  Nuclear
  Ocean
  Structural
  Surveying and Photogrammetry
  Systems
  Transportation
  Water Pollution: See Environmental
  Water Resources

English
English as a Second Language
Entomology
Environmental Studies
Ethnic Studies (See also Afro-American and Mexican-American)
European Studies
Expressive Arts: See Fine and Creative Arts
Film
Fine and Creative Arts
Foods and Nutrition: See Dietetics
French
Genetics
Geography
Geology
German
Government: See Political Science
Government—Journalism
Graphic Communications (Printing)
Graphic Design
Health and Safety: See Education
Health, Public (Environmental)
Health Science
History
Home Economics
Hotel Management: See Business
Humanities
Human Development
Human Services
Hutchins School
India Studies
Industrial Arts
Industrial Design
Industrial Technology
Information Systems
Interior Design
International Relations
Italian
Japanese
Journalism (see also Communications)
Landscape Architecture
Language Arts
Latin American Studies
Law Enforcement: See Criminal Justice
Liberal Studies
Library Science
Linguistics
Literature (See also English)
Marine Biology
Marriage and Family Counseling
Mass Communications: See Communications
Mathematics
Mathematics, Applied
Medical Biology: See Medical Laboratory Technology
Medical Laboratory Technology (Clinical Science)
Meteorology
Mexican-American/La Raza Studies
Microbiology
Music Education
Music (Liberal Arts)
Music (Performing)
Natural Resources: See Agriculture
Natural Science
Nursing (See also Health Sciences)
Occupational Therapy

Oceanography
Park Administration
Philosophy
Philosophy and Religion
Physical Education
(Men)
(Women)
Physical Science
Physical Therapy
Physics
Physiology
Police Science: See Criminal Justice
Political Science
Psychology
Clinical
College Teaching
Developmental
Educational: See Education
Industrial
Physiological
Psychology
Research
School
Social
Public Administration
Public Relations: See Business category or Communications degrees
Radiological and Health Physics
Radio—Television (Telecommunications)
Recreation Administration
Rehabilitation Counseling
Religious Studies
Russian
Russian Area Studies
Social Sciences (See also Anthropology, Sociology, etc.)
Social Welfare and Services
Sociology
Spanish
Special Major
Speech and Drama
Speech Communication
Speech Pathology and Audiology
Communicative Disorders
Statistics
Theater Arts: See Drama
Urban Planning: See City Planning
Urban Studies
Vocational Education
Zoology

APPENDIX II
Other Works Cited

"[ACRL] Standards for Faculty Status for College and University Librarians." *College and Research Libraries News* (September 1972), 33:210–12.

"[ACRL] Guidelines for Library Services to Extension Students." *ALA Bulletin* (January 1967), 61:50–55.

"The Measurement and Comparison of Physical Facilities for Libraries"; typescript. Chicago: American Library Association, Library Administration Division, 1969. 17pp.

"Library Bill of Rights." *ALA Handbook of Organization 1974–1975*, p.93.

"National Interlibrary Loan Code, 1968." Chicago: American Library Association, Reference and Adult Services Division. 4pp.

The "Standards for College Libraries" were first prepared by a committee of ACRL and promulgated in 1959. The present 1975 revision was prepared by the ACRL Ad Hoc Committee to Revise the 1959 Standards. Members were Johnnie Givens, Austin Peay State University (Chairman); David Kaser, Graduate Library School, Indiana University (Project Director and Editor); Arthur Monke, Bowdoin College; David L. Perkins, California State University, Northridge; James W. Pirie, Lewis & Clark College; Jasper G. Schad, Wichita State University; and Herman L. Totten, School of Librarianship, University of Oregon.

The effort was supported by a J. Morris Jones—World Book Encyclopedia—ALA Goals Award.

Copies of these Standards are available, upon request, from the ACRL Office, 50 E. Huron St., Chicago, IL 60611. ■■

An Evaluative Checklist for Reviewing a College Library Program

Editor's Note: At the ALA Annual Conference in June 1979 the ACRL Board of Directors approved the recommendation of the Standards and Accreditation Committee that "An Evaluative Checklist for Reviewing a College Library Program" be adopted as a supplement to "Standards for College Libraries." The Standards and Accreditation Committee developed the checklist and then evaluated it by asking a representative sample of fifty college libraries to test it in the field. The checklist appears in this issue of C&RL News for the information of ACRL members.

INTRODUCTION

The Evaluative Checklist is based on the 1975 "Standards for College Libraries" developed by the Association of College and Research Libraries, a division of the American Library Association. The standards "describe a realistic set of conditions which, if fulfilled, will provide an adequate library program in a college. They attempt to synthesize and articulate the aggregate experience and judgment of the academic library profession as to adequacy in library resources, services, and facilities for a college community."[1] The standards cover libraries serving academic programs at the bachelor's and master's degree levels as defined by the Carnegie Commission on Higher Education as Liberal Arts Colleges I and II and Comprehensive Universities and Colleges I and II.[2,3] The checklist has been validated and field-tested. When properly applied it will discriminate among the several levels of quality in library programs.

The status of a library program is not likely to be known without periodic evaluation. Before

completing the checklist, the evaluator should review the Application Procedures and Directions for Use that precede the checklist. He or she may also wish to study the text of the "Standards for College Libraries" covered by the checklist.

The checklist follows the organization of the standards stated at the head of the following sections:

1. Objectives
2. Collections
3. Organization of Materials
4. Staff
5. Delivery of Service
6. Facilities
7. Administration
8. Budget

It is acknowledged that it would be desirable to include more precise measures of library effectiveness and productivity, nonprint resources and services, and program evaluation in the checklist. However, there is no consensus among academic librarians for their preparation at this time.

APPLICATION PROCEDURES

Evaluation in general is a process, a complex of tools, used to produce a picture of what's happening, with some further goals in mind. The primary concern of the checklist is with evaluating how well a college library is performing some of its key functions to enable it to chart a course for improvement. The collection of checklist scores without providing the evaluators with operational information, analyzing accurately the results, and formulating appropriate recommendations will result in a simplistic comparison rather than producing a framework for improving library services. To accomplish its purpose, the checklist should be the instrument of an evaluating process which includes the following components—

1. Widespread participation and input of the total college community in the evaluation of library programs, and the review of the results.
2. The evaluators' review and understanding of the broad goals and specific objectives of the college and its library.
3. The use of the Evaluative Checklist in recording judgments concerning levels of library services.
4. The collection of information not furnished by the checklist which describes program effectiveness in terms of the objectives set forth.

1. "Standards for College Libraries," *College & Research Libraries News* 36:277 (Oct. 1975).
2. Carnegie Foundation for the Advancement of Teaching, *A Classification of Institutions of Higher Education* (Berkeley, Calif.: The Foundation, 1973).
3. Libraries serving junior and community colleges should consult: "AAJC-ACRL Guidelines for Two-Year College Library Learning Resource Centers," *College & Research Libraries News* 33:305–15 (Dec. 1972).
   Recently developed University Library Standards cover libraries serving comprehensive universities: ARL/ACRL Joint Committee on University Library Standards, "University Library Standards," *College & Research Libraries News* 40:101–10 (April 1979).

5. The interpretation of the results and drawing of conclusions which furnish information about the growth, progress, and effectiveness of the library's programs.
6. The formulation of recommendations that will support revised objectives and improve library services.

The college community and its library evaluators should be aware of the limitations of any evaluating process. These include the coverage of the evaluating instrument (the checklist does not pretend to cover everything), and the objectivity of the evaluation process. Judgmental decisions are involved throughout all phases of the evaluation as the participants adjust their activities in terms of the feedback received. An alert evaluator is aware of the influence of his or her own experience, the impact of personalities, and potential errors in methodology, data collection, and interpretation. The community itself, and the library in particular, are in the best position to evaluate what the study means, and to utilize it in improving library programs.

DIRECTIONS FOR USE

Circle *one* of the numbers at the left of the statement that most accurately represents conditions in the library you are evaluating. If a statement accurately describes the library, circle the middle number (2, 5, 8, or 11) at the left of that statement. If you think conditions are below what is described, circle the higher number (3, 6, 9, or 12). If the conditions at the library are above, circle one of the lower numbers (1, 4, 7, or 10). Circle *only one* of the numbers in the 1 to 12 grouping.

EXAMPLE

Standard 5: Delivery of Service

A. *Library Instruction*

1 2 3   Librarians routinely work closely with the teaching faculty in identifying instructional needs and teach the use of library resources and services to meet these needs.

4 5 6   Librarians are regularly called on for consultative assistance and instruction in the use of library resources and services.

7 8 9   Librarians provide consultative assistance in the use of library resources and services when requested and free from other duties.

10 11 12   Librarians are rarely available to provide library instruction services.

Directions for use and interpretation of the Profile graph accompany the Profile on pages 313–15.

EVALUATIVE CHECKLIST

Standard 1: Objectives of the Library

1   The college library shall develop an explicit statement of its objectives in accord with the goals and purposes of the college.

1.1   The development of library objectives shall be the responsibility of the library staff, in consultation with students, members of the teaching faculty, and administrative officers.

1.2   The statement of library objectives shall be reviewed periodically and revised as needed.

(Circle only one of the twelve numbers)

1 2 3   The college library's statement of objectives is conceived and formulated within the overall academic purpose of the college, is recognized by the college community as supporting its educational goals and instructional needs, and is kept current through periodic reviews and revisions by the library faculty, teaching faculty, and administrative staff.

4 5 6   The library's statement of objectives generally conforms with the overall academic purpose of the college, but requires minor revisions or better dissemination so that all members of the college community can understand and evaluate the appropriateness and effectiveness of library services.

7 8 9   The college library's statement of objectives requires substantial revision and updating to coordinate it with the educational goals and instructional needs of the college.

10 11 12   The college library does not have a statement of objectives conceived and formulated within the overall academic purpose of the college and consistent with the institution's educational goals and instructional needs.

Standard 2: The Collections

2   The library's collections shall comprise all corpora of recorded information owned by the college for educational, inspirational, and recreational purposes, including multi-dimensional, aural, pictorial, and print materials.

2.1   The library shall provide quickly a high percentage of such material needed by its patrons.

2.1.1   The amount of print materials to be thus provided shall be determined by Formula A (see Appendix) which takes into account the nature and extent of the academic program of the institution, its enrollment, and the size of its teaching faculty.

A. *Availability of Library Materials**

1 2 3   The library acquires, organizes, stores, and delivers for use within, or circulation from, the library all college-owned forms of recorded information required to support the college's educational programs and interests.

4 5 6   The library acquires and organizes most college-owned recorded information, but the delivery of this information is somewhat restricted by storage and access conditions at the library or other campus locations.

7 8 9   College-owned materials required to support several curriculum areas of the college are not acquired and organized by the library, and delivered through its services.

10 11 12   A substantial corpus of college-owned recorded information is not acquired, organized, stored, and delivered for use within, or circulated from, the library.

B. *Accessibility of Library Materials**

1 2 3   The library is able to deliver, from its own collection or via interlibrary systems, a substantial quantity of materials satisfying the user's needs and assignment schedules.

4 5 6   The library is frequently able to deliver, from its own collection or via interlibrary systems, a sufficient quantity of materials satisfying the user's needs and assignment schedules.

7 8 9   The quantity/quality of available library materials is uneven, thereby limiting the library's ability to supply materials requested, or to deliver them without significant delays.

10 11 12   The quantity/quality of library materials is so limited that the library is unable to supply many materials requested, or deliver them without intolerable delays.

C. *Selection of Materials**

1 2 3   The library selects an adequate portion of the bibliography of the disciplines represented by the curriculum, appropriate in quantity to both the level of instruction and to the number of students and faculty who use it. The collection's annual

growth rate, before withdrawals, exceeds 5 percent.

4 5 6   The library collection generally supports the college's curriculum and interests except for the need to improve coverage in a few subject areas. The annual growth rate approaches 5 percent.

7 8 9   The library collection is uneven in its support of the college's curriculum and interests. Basic collections should be developed for several disciplines.

10 11 12   The library collection is generally inadequate in its support of the college's academic program. A substantial portion of titles listed in standard, scholarly bibliographies, or considered by the faculty as supporting their instructional needs, are not represented in the library collection.

D. *Withdrawal of Materials**

1 2 3   Continuous evaluation of the collection provides for the withdrawal of materials which do not contribute to the college's current or anticipated academic programs.

4 5 6   The collection is periodically evaluated to identify outdated or nonsupportive materials. More frequent reviews are required in a few subject areas.

7 8 9   Several subject collections contain much material which should be withdrawn because it is outdated or nonsupportive of current or anticipated academic programs.

10 11 12   The collection generally contains material which has outlived its usefulness to the college's programs.

E. *Quantity of Materials**

Using Formula A (see Appendix) for calculating the number of relevant print volumes (or microform volume-equivalents) to which the library should provide prompt access—

1 2 3   The library can provide promptly 90–100 percent called for.

4 5 6   The library can provide promptly 80–90 percent called for.

7 8 9   The library can provide promptly 65–70 percent called for.

10 11 12   The library can provide promptly 50–64 percent called for.

Standard 3: Organization of Materials

3   Library collections shall be organized by nationally approved conventions and arranged for efficient retrieval at time of need.

*Circle only one of the twelve numbers.

3.1 There shall be a union catalog of the library's holdings that permits identification of items, regardless of format, by author, title, and subject.

3.1.1 The catalog may be developed either by a single library or jointly among several libraries.

3.1.2 The catalog shall be in a format that can be consulted by a number of people concurrently and at time of need.

3.1.3 In addition to the catalog there shall also be requisite subordinate files, such as serial records, shelf lists, authority files, and indexes to nonmonographic materials.

3.2 Except for certain categories of material which are for convenience best segregated by form, library materials shall be arranged on the shelves by subject.

3.2.1 Patrons shall have direct access to library materials on the shelves.

A. Indexing of Library Materials*

1 2 3   The library has a bibliographic control system for the classification, bibliographic identification, location, and retrieval of all library materials which conforms to national conventions and includes author, title, and subject entries.

4 5 6   The library has a bibliographic control system that is adequate most of the time, but excludes some materials according to form or location.

7 8 9   The college community reports some difficulties in identifying, locating, and retrieving specific library materials because of deficiencies in the organization and coverage of the bibliographic control system.

10 11 12   Library materials are consistently difficult to identify, locate, and retrieve because the bibliographic control system requires major reorganization.

B. Arrangement of Library Materials*

1 2 3   Most library materials are arranged on the shelves by subject and the college community locates, browses, and selects these materials with ease.

4 5 6   Library materials are generally arranged on open shelves by subject, although the complexities of classification or storage arrangements of some materials reduce easy access to them.

7 8 9   The complexities or disorganization of the arrangement of library materials discourage the college community from using the materials.

10 11 12   Library materials are very difficult

*Circle only one of the twelve numbers.

to locate and retrieve, and their inaccessibility seriously deters their optimum use.

Standard 4: Staff

4   The library staff shall be of adequate size and quality to meet agreed-upon objectives.

4.1 The staff shall comprise qualified librarians, skilled supportive personnel, and part-time assistants serving on an hourly basis.

4.2 The marks of a librarian shall include a graduate library degree from an ALA-accredited program, responsibility for duties of a professional nature, and participation in professional library affairs beyond the local campus.

4.2.1 The librarians of a college shall be organized as an academic department—or, in the case of a university, as a school—and shall administer themselves in accord with ACRL "Standards for Faculty Status for College and University Librarians" (see Appendix II [of "Standards for College Libraries"]).

4.3 The number of librarians required shall be determined by a formula (Formula B, [Appendix]) which takes into account the enrollment of the college and the size and growth rate of the collections.

4.3.1 There shall be an appropriate balance of effort among librarians, supportive personnel, and part-time assistants, so that every staff member is employed as nearly as possible commensurate with his library training, experience, and capability.

4.4 Library policies and procedures concerning staff shall be in accord with sound personnel management practice.

A. Staff Size*

1 2 3   The library has sufficient professional, technical, and clerical staff to provide satisfactory services meeting the library's objectives. Using Formula B (see Appendix) for calculating the number of librarians, the library provides 90–100 percent of the requirements.

4 5 6   Using Formula B for calculating the number of librarians, the library provides 75–90 percent of the requirements.

7 8 9   Using Formula B for calculating the number of librarians, the library provides 55–74 percent of the requirements.

10 11 12   Using Formula B for calculating the number of librarians, the library provides 40–54 percent of the requirements.

B. Professional Responsibilities*

1 2 3   Leadership and instructional and consultative services are provided by qualified librarians who have faculty status and administer themselves in accord with the ACRL "Standards for Faculty Status for College and University Librarians."

4 5 6   The administration and delivery of library services are provided by qualified librarians recognized and supported by the college, but without full coverage of the ACRL "Standards for Faculty Status."

7 8 9   The responsibility for library services is delegated to librarians without professional status and departmental organization.

10 11 12   The responsibility for administering library services is assigned to institutional staff members not qualified as librarians.

C. Support Staff*

1 2 3   The qualified clerical and technical staff is sufficient in number, with assignment of responsibilities commensurate with job requirements, training, and experience.

4 5 6   Clerical and technical assistance is usually sufficient. Mismatching of job assignments among clerical and professional staff infrequently occurs.

7 8 9   Clerical and technical assistance is available, but there are frequent shortages or mismatching of job assignments among support and professional staff.

10 11 12   Clerical and technical assistance is generally not available.

D. Personnel Management*

1 2 3   Written policies and procedures consistent with the goals and responsibilities of the college direct the recruiting, appointment, training, evaluation, promotion and tenure, or dismissal of the library staff.

4 5 6   Library personnel policies are consistent with the goals and responsibilities of the college, although several procedures require revision and updating.

7 8 9   Library personnel policies are frequently inconsistent with the goals and responsibilities of the college. Policy and procedural improvements are necessary.

10 11 12   Major revisions are required in library personnel policies and procedures to establish sound management practices.

Standard 5: Delivery of Service

5   The college library shall establish and maintain a range and quality of services that will promote the academic program of the institution and encourage optimal library use.

5.1   Proper service shall include: the provision of continuing instruction to patrons in the effective exploitation of libraries, the guidance of patrons to the library materials they need, and the provision of information to patrons as appropriate.

5.2   Library materials shall be circulated to qualified patrons under equitable policies and for as long periods as possible without jeopardizing their availability to others.

5.2.1   The availability of reading materials shall be extended wherever possible by the provision of inexpensive means of photocopying.

5.2.2   The quality of the collections available locally to patrons shall be enhanced through the use of "National Interlibrary Loan Code, 1968" (see Appendix II [of "Standards for College Libraries"]) and other cooperative agreements which provide reciprocal access to multi-library resources.

5.3   The hours of public access to the materials on the shelves, to the study facilities of the library, and to the library staff shall be consistent with reasonable demand, both during the normal study week and during weekends and vacation periods.

5.4   Where academic programs are offered away from a campus, library services shall be provided in accord with ACRL's "Guidelines for Library Services to Extension Students" (see Appendix II [of "Standards for College Libraries"]).

A. Library Instruction*

1 2 3   Librarians routinely work closely with the teaching faculty in identifying instructional needs and teach the use of library resources and services to meet these needs.

4 5 6   Librarians are regularly called on for consultative assistance and instruction in the use of library resources and services.

7 8 9   Librarians provide consultative assistance in the use of library resources and services when requested and free from other duties.

10 11 12   Librarians are rarely available to provide library instruction services.

*Circle only one of the twelve numbers

B. Information Services*

1 2 3   The library staff provides a variety of information, instruction, and interpretative services, and meets most of its community's demands for these services.

4 5 6   The library staff provides a variety of information, instruction, and interpretative services, but is unable to meet some demands for these services.

7 8 9   Limited information services are available to the college community, and may be restricted to certain clientele.

10 11 12   Information services are not available to the college community.

C. Circulation*

1 2 3   Uniformly administered circulation policies regulate use of library materials for periods that are reasonable without jeopardizing the college community's access to materials.

4 5 6   Circulation policies regulate the use of library materials for periods that are usually acceptable. A review of the policies is desirable to correct minor problems.

7 8 9   Circulation policies are frequently restrictive without cause. Regulations are confusing and inconsistently administered.

10 11 12   Circulation policies do not facilitate access to library materials, and are poorly administered.

D. Access to Multi-Library Resources*

1 2 3   The library efficiently delivers materials and services provided by local, state, and national libraries via interlibrary loan codes and joint access consortia to students, faculty, and staff.

4 5 6   The library delivers materials and services provided by other libraries to students, faculty, and staff, but delays and/or access difficulties sometimes restrict service effectiveness.

7 8 9   The library delivers materials and services provided by other libraries only to selected individuals or groups in the academic community.

10 11 12   The library seldom provides its college community with access to the materials and services of other libraries.

E. Hours*

1 2 3   The number of hours per week that

*Circle only one of the twelve numbers.

library services and facilities are available meets the study and research needs of the college community.

4 5 6   Library hours are usually responsive to the community's needs for library services and facilities. There are requests for minor changes in these hours.

7 8 9   There are periods during the week (e.g., evenings, weekends) and the academic year (e.g., vacations, exams) when library hours are not responsive to the community's needs.

10 11 12   An insufficient number of library hours seriously deters the college community from achieving its educational goals.

Standard 6: Facilities

6   The college shall provide a library building containing secure facilities for housing its resources, adequate space for administration of those resources by staff, and comfortable quarters and furnishings for their utilization by patrons.

6.1 The size of the library building shall be determined by a formula (see Formula C [Appendix]) which takes into account the enrollment of the college, the extent and nature of its collections, and the size of its staff.

6.2 The shape of the library building and the internal distribution of its facilities and services shall be determined by function.

6.3 Except in unusual circumstances, the college library's collections and services shall be administered within a single structure.

A. The Building*

1 2 3   The building housing the library collection and services is fully equipped to support a quality program, functional in arrangement, accommodating to users and staff, and flexible in accommodating growth needs.

4 5 6   The design and arrangement of the library building generally supports service, storage, and growth requirements, but would be improved by renovations, expansions, or rearrangement.

7 8 9   The library building has a number of deficiencies which limit its contribution to and support of library services.

10 11 12   The library building is deficient in several critical areas, e.g., storage space, security, service, facilities, efficient design. These deficiencies

seriously handicap the library in its delivery of service to the community.

B. Building Size*

Using Formula C (see Appendix) for calculating the net assignable area necessary for all library services except non-book services—

1 2 3   The library's facilities provide 90–100 percent of the space called for.

4 5 6   The library's facilities provide 75–90 percent of the space called for.

7 8 9   The library's facilities provide 60–74 percent of the space called for.

10 11 12 The library's facilities provide 50–59 percent of the space called for.

Standard 7: Administration

7   The college library shall be administered in a manner which permits and encourages the fullest and most effective use of available library resources.

7.1   The statutory or legal foundation for the library's activities shall be recognized in writing.

7.2   The college librarian shall be a member of the library faculty and shall report to the president or the chief academic officer of the institution.

7.2.1 The responsibilities and authority of the college librarian and procedures for his appointment shall be defined in writing.

7.3   There shall be a standing advisory committee comprising students and members of the teaching faculty which shall serve as the main channel of formal communication between the library and its user community.

7.4   The library shall maintain written policies and procedure manuals covering internal library governance and operational activities.

7.4.1 The library shall maintain a systematic and continuous program for evaluating its performance and for identifying needed improvements.

7.4.2 The library shall develop statistics not only for purposes of planning and control but also to aid in the preparation of reports designed to inform its publics of its accomplishments and problems.

7.5   The library shall develop, seek out, and utilize cooperative programs for purposes of either reducing its operating costs or enhancing its services, so long as such programs create no unreimbursed or unreciprocated costs for other libraries or organizations.

7.6   The library shall be administered in accord

*Circle only one of the twelve numbers.

with the spirit of the ALA "Library Bill of Rights" (see Appendix II [of "Standards for College Libraries"]).

A. Administration of the Library*

1 2 3   The library program is directed by a well-qualified librarian with faculty appointment who administers library services which support the full range of the college's educational program.

4 5 6   The library program is directed by a well-qualified librarian; a better orientation of library services to the college's educational program is desirable.

7 8 9   The library director does not attend to the full range of the library's responsibilities, and a review of the causes should be initiated.

10 11 12 The college community generally believes the library is not serving its educational program, and a major reorganization appears desirable.

B. Organization Authority*

1 2 3   The library's responsibilities and flow of authority under which it is empowered to act are described in official college documents such as bylaws, trustee documents, or public laws.

4 5 6   The library's responsibilities and flow of authority under which it is empowered to act are described in official college documents such as organizational charts, reporting structure diagrams, and job descriptions.

7 8 9   The library's responsibilities and flow of authority are inadequately covered by official college and administrative documents.

10 11 12 The library's responsibilities and flow of authority are not covered in official college and administrative documents.

C. Librarian's Authority*

1 2 3   The scope and nature of the college librarian's duties and powers, the procedures for his appointment, and the focus of his reporting responsibilities are defined in writing.

4 5 6   Some of the college librarian's duties and powers, appointment procedures, and reporting responsibilities are defined in writing.

7 8 9   The written description of the responsibilities and authority of the college librarian is generally inadequate and incomplete.

10 11 12 There is a minimal or no written description of the responsibilities and authority of the college librarian.

D. Reporting Structure*

1 2 3   The college librarian reports to either the president or the chief officer in charge of academic affairs of the college.

4 5 6   The college librarian reports to the office of academic affairs, but does not always review reports and recommendations with the chief academic officer.

7 8 9   The college librarian reports to a learning resources director or dean who reports to the chief academic officer.'

10 11 12   No person has been given the administrative responsibility for receiving reports from the college librarian.

E. Library Committee*

1 2 3   A committee composed of representatives of the college community meets regularly to advise the librarian on matters of policy, user needs, and concerns, and effectively assists the community in understanding the library's capabilities and problems.

4 5 6   A committee composed of representatives of the college community advises the librarian on policy matters, user needs, and concerns, and conveys library information to the community. Its effectiveness could be improved.

7 8 9   A committee meets to advise the librarian on policy matters, user needs, and concerns, but is frequently ineffective as a channel of communication between the library and its community.

10 11 12   There is no committee or representative group to advise the librarian and channel communications between the library and its community.

F. Policy and Procedure Records*

1 2 3   Written policies and procedure manuals assuring uniformity and consistency of action and aiding staff training cover most of the library's technical and reader service operations.

4 5 6   Written policies and procedure manuals cover many of the library's operations, but several require revision and updating to incorporate policy and procedural changes.

7 8 9   A number of library operations require written policies and procedure manuals to assist administrative and training activities.

*Circle only one of the twelve numbers.

10 11 12   Generally the library does not have written policies and procedure manuals.

G. Evaluation of Services*

1 2 3   The library staff is continually involved in monitoring and evaluating the productivity, use of, and needs for library services, and uses this information to revise and develop library programs.

4 5 6   The library periodically monitors and evaluates its services and reviews user needs, and uses this information in program revisions and development.

7 8 9   The library conducts evaluations of its services and reviews user needs only in response to critical problems, or to provide data for reports.

10 11 12   Evaluations of library services and user needs are rarely conducted by the library, or used in program planning.

H. Public Relations*

1 2 3   Information concerning library service accomplishments and problems is regularly disseminated to the faculty, students, and administration. The forms of this information include news releases, reports, handbooks, brochures, reading lists, and displays.

4 5 6   Information concerning library services is occasionally disseminated to faculty, students, and staff or by request.

7 8 9   Information concerning library services is seldom disseminated to the community, but is sometimes supplied upon request.

10 11 12   Information concerning library services is rarely disseminated to the community or provided upon request.

I. Interlibrary Cooperation*

1 2 3   The library engages in and seeks interlibrary cooperative activities which enhance the qualities of its services and benefit its interests. The costs of these services are equitably distributed among the cooperating institutions.

4 5 6   The library engages in interlibrary cooperative activities which enhance the quality of its services and benefit its interests. However, the benefits of these services do not always balance their costs.

7 8 9   The library engages in interlibrary cooperative activities, but should im-

10 11 12   prove its use of these services, and/or their cost-effectiveness.

The library does not seek or engage in interlibrary activities although services are available which would enhance the quality of its services and benefit its interests.

J. Bill of Rights*

1 2 3   The library is not restricted by partisan or doctrinal disapprovals in its selection of library materials, upholds the user's right of access to information, and has college support for the "Library Bill of Rights."

4 5 6   Partisan or doctrinal disapprovals seldom affect the selection of library materials or the user's access to information. Usually the "Library Bill of Rights" is supported by the library and the college.

7 8 9   The library supports the provisions of the "Library Bill of Rights," but the college does not always support these rights.

10 11 12   The library excludes materials or restricts access to information contrary to the provisions of the "Library Bill of Rights," and does not seek college support of the policy.

Standard 8: Budget

8   The college librarian shall have the responsibility for preparing, defending, and administering the library budget in accord with agreed-upon objectives.

8.1   The amount of the library appropriation shall express a relationship to the total institutional budget for educational and general purposes.

8.2   The librarian shall have sole authority to apportion funds and initiate expenditures within the library approved budget, in accord with institutional policy.

8.3   The library shall maintain such internal accounts as are necessary for approving its invoices for payment, monitoring its encumbrances, and evaluating the flow of its expenditures.

A. Budget Contents*

1 2 3   The budget of the library program developed by the librarian in consultation with library staff and college administrators reflects the library's priorities and objectives.

4 5 6   The budget of the library program developed by the librarian generally reflects most of the library's objec-

*Circle only one of the twelve numbers.

tives. Several allotments do not conform to program priorities.

7 8 9   The library budget partially reflects the library's objectives and priorities. The budgeting process requires revision.

10 11 12   The library budget is based on an arbitrary or undefined allotment of funds with minimal reference to the library's objectives and priorities. The budgeting process requires major revision.

B. Financial Support Requirements*

1 2 3   The library's annual appropriation, exclusive of capital and physical maintenance costs, is at least 6 percent of the college's total educational and general expenditures.

4 5 6   The library's annual appropriation, exclusive of capital and physical maintenance costs, is 5 to 6 percent of the college's total educational and general expenditures.

7 8 9   The library's annual appropriation, exclusive of capital and physical maintenance costs, is 4 to 5 percent of the college's total educational and general expenditures.

10 11 12   The library's annual appropriation, exclusive of capital and physical maintenance costs, is below 4 percent of the college's total educational and general expenditures.

C. Fiscal Accountability*

1 2 3   Regular reports reflect the status of allocations, encumbrances, and expenditures, and support sound practices of planning and control.

4 5 6   Reports reflecting the status of library accounts are issued periodically, but could be improved in scope, content, or frequency to support the administrative process.

7 8 9   Reports reflecting the status of library accounts are inadequate in scope and content, and/or issued too irregularly to provide accountability and support the administrative process.

10 11 12   There are few or no reports reflecting the status of library accounts, or those that exist fail the test of fiscal accountability.

PROFILE SHEET

This chart [fig. 1] is provided to tabulate and summarize the judgments recorded on the Evaluative Checklist. To develop a profile, transfer the marks from each item of the checklist to this sheet. Connect the marked circles by straight

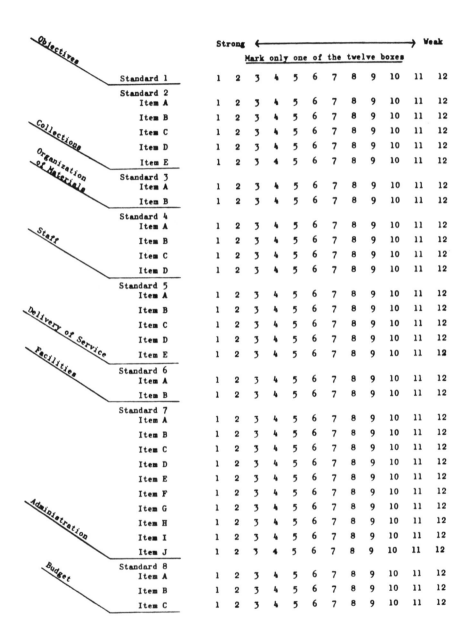

Fig. 1
Profile Sheet

lines. Then turn the sheet to a horizontal position to observe the resulting graph. Interpretive guidelines are provided [below].

USE OF THE PROFILE SHEET

Interpreting evaluations recorded on one profile sheet is a relatively simple task; summarizing and describing a number of profile sheets requires the application of regular frequency distributions. To construct such a distribution—

1. List every score value in the first column (denoted by symbol X) with the lowest number at the top.
2. Note the frequency (denoted by symbol f) of each score (the number of times a given score was obtained) to the right of the score in the second column of the table.

The table reveals at a glance how often each score was obtained; modalities, groupings, and skewings are easily identified. The scores could also be recorded in a grouped frequency distribution, using interval sizes of 4, although loss of information will occur with such groupings since they will not provide the exact value of each score.

	EXAMPLE	
Standard 1	*Score (X)*	*Frequency (f)*
	1	0
	2	0
	3	1
	4	3
	5	3
	6	4
	7	1
	8	0
	9	1
	10	0
	11	0
	12	0

The number of evaluations in this sample was 13.

Computations of central tendencies (means, medians, modes) are not advised because an evaluation cannot be described by a single number. After all scores are tabulated, trends and interrelationships should be observed to identify areas in which services might be improved, or new goals developed.

APPENDIX

Editor's Note: Appendix I, referred to in Formula A, and Appendix II, in Formula C, are published in the 1975 "Standards for College Libraries" (College & Research Libraries News 36:299–301 [Oct. 1975]).

FORMULA A—

The formula for calculating the number of relevant print volumes (or microform volume-equivalents) to which the library should provide prompt access is as follows (to be calculated cumulatively):

1. Basic Collection . . . . 85,000 vols.
2. Allowance per FTE Faculty Member . . . . 100 vols.
3. Allowance per FTE Student . . . . 15 vols.
4. Allowance per Undergraduate Major or Minor Field* . . . . 350 vols.
5. Allowance per Masters Field, When No Higher Degree is Offered in the Field* . . . . 6,000 vols.
6. Allowance per Masters Field, When a Higher Degree is Offered in the Field* . . . . 3,000 vols.
7. Allowance per 6th-year Specialist Degree Field* . . . . 6,000 vols.
8. Allowance per Doctoral Field* . . . . 25,000 vols.

A "volume" is defined as a physical unit of any printed, typewritten, handwritten, mimeographed, or processed work contained in one binding or portfolio, hardbound or paperbound, which has been cataloged, classified, and/or otherwise prepared for use. For purposes of this calculation microform holdings should be included by converting them to volume-equivalents. The number of volume-equivalents held in microform should be determined either by actual count or by an averaging formula which considers each reel of microform as one, and five pieces of any other microformat as one volume-equivalent.

Libraries which can provide promptly 100 percent as many volumes or volume-equivalents as are called for in this formula shall, in the matter of quantity, be graded A. From 80–99 percent shall be graded B; from 65–79 percent shall be graded C; and from 50–64 percent shall be graded D.

* See Appendix I, "List of Fields."

FORMULA B—

The number of librarians required by the college shall be computed as follows (to be calculated cumulatively):

For each 500, or fraction thereof, FTE students up to 10,000	1 librarian
For each 1,000 or fraction thereof, FTE students above 10,000	1 librarian
For each 100,000 volumes, or fraction thereof, in the collection	1 librarian
For each 5,000 volumes, or fraction thereof, added per year	1 librarian

Libraries which provide 100 percent of these formula requirements can, when they are supported by sufficient other staff members, consider themselves at the A level in terms of staff size; those that provide 75–99 percent of these requirements may rate themselves as B; those with 55–74 percent of requirements qualify for a C; and those with 40–54 percent of requirements warrant a D.

FORMULA C—

The size of the college library building shall be calculated on the basis of a formula which takes into consideration the size of the student body, requisite administrative space, and the number of physical volumes held in the collections. In the absence of consensus among librarians and other educators as to the range of non-book services which it is appropriate for libraries to offer, no generally applicable formulas have been developed for calculating space for them. Thus, space required for a college library's non-book services and materials must be added to the following calculations:

    a. *Space for readers.* The seating requirement for the library of a college wherein less than fifty percent of the FTE enrollment resides on campus shall be one for each five FTE students; the seating requirement for the typical residential college library shall be one for each four FTE students; and the seating requirements for the library in the strong, liberal arts, honors-oriented college shall be one for each three FTE students. In any case, each library seat shall be assumed to require twenty-five square feet of floor space.

    b. *Space for books.* Space required for books depends in part upon the overall size of the book collection, and is calculated cumulatively as follows:

	Square Feet/Volume
For the first 150,000 volumes	0.10
For the next 150,000 volumes	0.09
For the next 300,000 volumes	0.08
For holdings above 600,000 volumes	0.07

    c. *Space for administration.* Space required for such library administrative activities as acquisition, cataloging, staff offices, catalogs, and files shall be one-fourth of the sum of the spaces needed for readers and books as calculated under (a) and (b) above.

This tripartite formula indicates the net assignable area necessary for all library services except for non-book services. (For definition of "net assignable area" see "The Measurement and Comparison of Physical Facilities for Libraries," produced by ALA's Library Administration Division. See Appendix II.) Libraries which provide 100 percent as much net assignable area as is called for by the formula shall qualify for an A rating as regards quantity; 75–99 percent shall warrant a B; 60–74 percent shall be due a C; and 50–59 percent shall warrant a D.

Editor's Note: ACRL Members may order single copies of the Evaluative Checklist by sending a self-addressed label and $.30 in postage to the ACRL office. Nonmembers should include $1 with their order.

Guidelines for Two-Year College Learning Resources Programs (Revised)

PART ONE

Approved by the ACRL Board of Directors on June 30, 1981. These guidelines supersede and replace the previous guidelines which appeared in C&RL News, December 1972.

Association of College and
Research Libraries
Association for Educational Communications
and Technology

Two-Year College. Includes publicly-supported community colleges, privately-supported junior colleges, two-year technical colleges, and two-year branch campuses.

Learning Resources. Includes library, audio-visual and telecommunications and encompasses instructional development functions and instructional system components. (See Glossary for expanded definitions.)

Introduction. Two-year colleges constitute one of the most dynamic sectors in American higher education. They are probably the most diverse of all postsecondary institutions in the country, ranging from highly specialized technical or vocational schools to comprehensive multi-unit community colleges. In addition, there are two-year branch campuses of colleges and universities, proprietary institutions with similar missions, and other specialized institutions. A statement describing adequate learning resources and services has been difficult to formulate for such institutions because of factors such as the widely diversified purposes and sizes of the institutions—private and public, the high proportion of commuting students, the comprehensiveness of the curricula, the willingness of administrators and faculty to experiment unhampered by tradition, and the heterogeneity of background among those enrolled. Although the diversity among the institutional patterns makes the establishment of generally applicable guidelines difficult, all two-year institutions need qualitative recommendations based on professional expertise and successful practices in leading institutions which can be used for self-evaluation and projective planning.

The evolution of libraries away from their traditional function as repositories of books has been parallel to the evolution of audiovisual centers away from their traditional function as agencies for showing films. There has been a confluence of accelerated development in both areas which is inextricably interwoven in the technological revolution in education. Contemporary Learning Resources Programs in two-year colleges are supportive of institution-wide efforts. Such programs should provide innovative leadership coupled with a multiplicity of varied resources which are managed by qualified staff who serve to facilitate the attainment of institutional objectives. Paramount to the success of such programs is the involvement of Learning Resources staff with teaching, administrative, and other staff members in the design, implementation, and evaluation of instructional and educational systems of the institution.

These guidelines are diagnostic and descriptive in nature. They have been prepared to give direction to two-year colleges desiring to develop comprehensive Learning Resources Programs. This document is designed to provide criteria for information, self-study, and planning, not to establish minimal (or accreditation) standards. Application of the criteria should be governed by the purposes and objectives of each college. Since they represent recommended practices, any variant procedures should be supported by cogent reasons directly related to institutional objectives.

Nothing in these guidelines should be construed as an effort to superimpose an administrative or organizational structure upon an institution. There is no expectation that every institution should be forced into the same mold. The guidelines are more concerned with functions related to the instructional program rather than with specific organizational patterns. Although it is expected that these functions will be grouped into administrative (or supervisory) units within the Learning Resources Program, the nature of grouping and the resulting number of units must be determined by the unique requirements, resources, facilities, and staff of the college. The degree of autonomy granted each unit will also vary considerably. In some institutions, perhaps because of size, the units may be fairly task specific, with supervisory (rather than administrative) heads, and with little budgetary autonomy.

Examples of such units include: an audio-tutorial laboratory; a bibliographic control center; media production; technical processes; etc. In other institutions, each unit may subsume a number of related activities, or carry out direct instructional assignments of a broad scope, and have an administrative head and a high degree of budgetary autonomy. Examples of such units include: an audiovisual center; a computing center; a library; a telecommunications center; etc. In all institutions, however, the units report to a chief administrator responsible for overall coordination of the Learning Resources Program. The extent of direct supervision of the units will be determined by the nature of the units and the degree of autonomy granted them.

Many aspects of traditional library and audiovisual services in the two-year college and the integration of these services have not been studied adequately for long-range projection of needs. Until such studies have been made these guidelines may serve as the foundations for research and for experimentation in organization, structure, and services.

The changing and expanding role of two-year colleges in America today may well result in institutions quite different from those in operation at the present time. These guidelines, therefore, may require significant upward revision when such institutions reach a new stage in their development. At that point, they may well need greater resources and greatly extended services. All concerned should be alert to this coming challenge.

The Role of the Learning Resources Program

Many diverse elements contribute to the quality of instruction as it contributes to the development of two-year college students. No one of these is dominant or isolated from the others. Faculty, students, finances, teaching methods, facilities, resources, and educational philosophy all play significant roles in the educational environment of the institution.

Education is more than exposure through lectures and rote learning to the knowledge, ideas, and values current in society. Education is a process for communicating means for resolving the range of problems continuously encountered by man in living and in pursuing an occupation. Students must be able to explore fields of knowledge which will enhance their potential and be relevant to them. The means of exploration include active participation in the classroom and the laboratory, self-directed study, and the use of individualized instructional resources. Trained professional assistance is necessary in the design of instructional systems which contribute to the enrichment of the learning environment as well as to the support of students and faculty. The design of the instructional system, utilizing a configuration of resources, is a joint responsibility of administration, teaching faculty, and the Learning Resources staff.

The student's success in achieving instructional objectives is heavily dependent on access to materials. Both student and faculty member function at their best when Learning Resources Programs are adequately conceived, staffed, and financed. More than almost any other element in the institution, Learning Resources Programs express the educational philosophy of the institution they serve.

Because of its direct relationship to the institutional and instructional objectives, the Learning Resources Program has a fourfold role: (1) to provide leadership and assistance in the development of instructional systems which employ effective and efficient means of accomplishing those objectives; (2) to provide an organized and readily accessible collection of materials and supportive equipment needed to meet institutional, instructional, and individual needs of students and faculty; (3) to provide a staff qualified, concerned, and involved in serving the needs of students, faculty, and community; (4) to encourage innovation, learning, and community service by providing facilities and resources which will make them possible.

Glossary

The terms listed below are used throughout these guidelines as defined.

Two-year college. Any postsecondary associate degree-granting public or private educational institution which serves one or more of the following purposes: (1) providing the first two years of college work in anticipation of transfer to another institution at the junior or third-year level; (2) providing vocational and technical education in preparation for job entry; (3) offering a comprehensive program of liberal arts, occupational education, general education, and developmental education; (4) offering readily-accessible lifelong learning opportunities of all types; and (5) providing, through branches or extension centers of four-year colleges or universities, the first two years of postsecondary education. Thus the term "two-year college" includes publicly-supported community colleges, privately-supported junior colleges, two-year technical colleges, and two-year branch campuses.

Learning Resources Program. An administrative configuration within the institution responsible for the supervision and management of Learning Resources Units, regardless of the location of these components within the various physical environments of the institution.

Learning Resources Unit. A subordinate agency within the Learning Resources Program sufficiently large to acquire organizational identification as distinct from individual assignment and with an administrative or supervisory head, and which may have its own facilities, staff, and budget. How many of these units would make up the Learning Resources Program, and the functions assigned to each, will vary from institution to institution.

Instructional development functions. The solution of instructional problems through the design and application of instructional system components.

Instructional system components. All of the resources which can be designed, utilized, and combined in a systematic manner with the intent of achieving learning. These components include: persons, machines, facilities, ideas, materials, procedures, and management.

Instructional product design. The process of creating and/or identifying the most effective materials to meet the specific objectives of the learning experience as defined by instructional development.

Production. The design and preparation of materials for institutional and instructional use. Production activities may include graphics, photography, cinematography, audio and video recording, and preparation of printed materials.

Staff. The personnel who perform Learning Resources Program functions. These persons have a variety of abilities and a range of educational backgrounds. They include professional and supportive staff.

Professional staff. Personnel who carry on responsibilities requiring professional training at the graduate level and experience appropriate to the assigned responsibilities.

Supportive staff. Personnel who assist professional staff members in duties requiring specific skills and special abilities. They make it possible for the professional staff to concentrate their time on professional services and activities. Their training may range from four-year degrees and two-year degrees to a one-year certificate, or extensive training and experience in a given area or skill.

System(s) approach. A process for effectively and efficiently applying the instructional systems component to achieve a required outcome based on agreed-upon institutional goals.

Materials. Divided into three categories: written, recorded, and other materials (see below).

Written materials. All literary, dramatic, and musical materials or works, and all other materials or works, published or unpublished, copyrighted and copyrightable at any time under the Federal Copyright Act as now existing or hereafter amended or supplemented in whatever format.

Recorded materials. All sound, visual, audiovisual, films or tapes, videotapes, kinescopes or other recordings or transcriptions, published or unpublished, copyrighted or copyrightable at any time under the Federal Copyright Act as now existing or hereafter amended or supplemented.

Other material. All types of pictures, photographs, maps, charts, globes, models, kits, art objects, realia, dioramas, and displays.

I. OBJECTIVES AND PURPOSES

A. *The college makes provision for a Learning Resources Program.*

The kinds of educational programs offered at nearly every two-year college require that adequate provisions be made for a Learning Resources Program, which should be an integral part of each institution. Learning Resources Programs should efficiently meet the needs of the students and faculty and be organized and managed for users. The effect of combining all learning resources programs under one administrative office provides for the maximum flexibility, optimum use of personnel, material, equipment, facilities, and systems to permit increased opportunities for the materials best suited for the user's needs.

B. *Learning Resources Programs have a statement of defined purpose and objectives.*

The need for clear definition of the role and purposes of the college and its various programs is highly desirable. Since Learning Resources Programs are a vital part, the objectives within the college they serve need to be defined and disseminated in an appropriate college publication. Within this framework, the following overall purposes of the Learning Resources Program are delineated:

1. *Learning Resources Programs exist to facilitate and improve learning.*

The emphasis is upon the improvement of the individual student, with a wide choice of materials to facilitate learning. Such emphasis requires a staff committed to effective management of instructional development functions and effective utilization of instructional system components.

2. *Learning Resources Programs, like the instructional staff, are an integral part of instruction.*

Students who discover by themselves, or who are encouraged by the staff or faculty to seek out, the materials appropriate to their curriculum sequence of courses should be provided options to regular classroom instruction to achieve credit for a particular course. *Such alternatives should be developed and made available to the students.* The staff provides information on new materials, acquires them, or produces them, working cooperatively with the faculty on instructional development.

3. *Learning Resources Programs provide a variety of services as an integral part of the instructional process.*

a. Instructional development functions, which include task analysis, instructional design, evaluation, and related research.

b. Acquisition of learning materials, including cataloging and other related services.

c. Production.

d. User services which include reference, circulation (print and nonprint material), transmission or dissemination, and assistance to both faculty and students with the use of Learning Resources.

e. Other services, such as the computer operation, bookstore, campus duplicating or printing service, the learning or developmental lab, various auto-tutorial carrels or labs, telecommunications, or other information networks might be included within the functions and purposes of the college's overall organization and objectives.

4. *Learning Resources Programs cooperate in the development of area, regional, and state networks, consortia or systems.*

Every two-year college, whether privately or publicly supported, has a responsibility to help meet the resource material need of the larger community in which it resides. Attention is placed on ways in which each college can serve that community; in turn, the community serves as a reservoir of material and human resources which can be used by the college.

If the internal needs of the college and its students and staff are met, then coordination of its resources and services with those of other institutions to meet wider needs is mandatory. Reciprocal participation in consortia with other institutions for the development of exchanges, networks, or systems provides the colleges with materials and services that otherwise could not practically be provided.

II. ORGANIZATION AND ADMINISTRATION

A. *The responsibilities and functions of Learning Resources Programs within the institutional structure and the status of the chief administrator and heads of Learning Resources Units are clearly defined.*

The effectiveness of services provided depends on the understanding by faculty, college administrators, students, and Learning Resources staff of their responsibilities and functions as they relate to the institution. A written statement, endorsed by the institution's trustees or other policy-setting group, should be readily available.

To function adequately, the chief administrator of a Learning Resources Program (whose title may vary in different institutions) reports to the administrative officer of the college responsible for the instructional program and has the same administrative rank and status as others with similar institution-wide responsibilities. These responsibilities are delineated as part of a written statement so that the chief administrator has adequate authority to manage the internal operations and to provide the services needed.

B. *The relationship of a Learning Resources Program to the total academic program necessitates involvement of the professional staff in all areas and levels of academic planning.*

Provision of learning materials is central to the academic program. As a result, the professional staff has interests which are broad and go beyond the scope of its day-to-day operations. The professional staff members are involved in all areas and levels of academic planning. The chief administrator and heads of Learning Resources Units work closely with other chief administrators of the college, and all professional staff members participate in faculty affairs to the same extent as other faculty.

The professional staff members are involved in major college committees. As far as possible, the professional staff members ought to function as liaison participants in staff meetings of the various departments.

C. *Advisory committees composed of faculty and students are essential for the evaluation and extension of services.*

As a rule, there should be a faculty advisory committee appointed by the appropriate administrative officer of the college, elected by the faculty, or selected by the procedure generally followed in the formation of a faculty committee. It should include representatives of the various academic divisions of the college and consist of both senior and junior members of the faculty, chosen carefully for their demonstrated interest beyond their own departmental concerns. The committee functions in an advisory capacity and acts as a connecting link between the faculty as a whole and the Learning Resources Program. It should not concern itself with details of administration.

A student advisory committee (or a joint advisory committee with the faculty) serves as a liaison between the student body and the Learning Resources Program. The committee should work closely with the chief administrator and should be used as a sounding board for new ideas in developing a more effective program of services.

D. *The chief administrator is responsible for the administration of the Learning Resources Program, which is carried out by means of established lines of authority, definition of responsibilities, and channels of communication through heads of Learning Resources Units as defined in writing.*

E. *Internal administration of a Learning Resources Program is based on staff participation in policy, procedural, and personnel decisions.*

The internal organization is appropriate to the institution, and within this framework is based upon a considerable amount of self-determination, guided by the need for meeting common goals. Regular staff meetings and clearly devised lines of authority and responsibility are necessary. All staff members share in the process by which policies and procedures are developed; all staff members have access to heads of Learning Resources Units and the chief administrator.

Each professional and supportive staff member is provided with a position description which clearly identifies the position duties and responsibilities, and superior and subordinate relationships. Each Learning Resources Unit requires a staff manual which provides policy and procedural statements, duty assignments, and other organizational matters, and items of general information which would compliment instructional policies.

F. *Budget planning and implementation of a Learning Resources Program is the responsibility of the chief administrator.* (See Section III.)

G. *The accumulation of pertinent statistics and maintenance of adequate records is a management responsibility.*

Adequate records are needed for internal analysis and management planning and to provide data for annual and special reports needed by the college, accrediting associations, and government agencies. Effective planning can be made only on the basis of available information. Statistics providing a clear and undistorted picture of activities, acquisitions of materials and equipment, utilization of materials, equipment and personnel, and annual expenditures are essential for federal, state, and college use. These statistics and records are collected in terms of the definitions and methods of reporting set forth in federal and professional publications. Appropriate data must also be collected and analyzed with regard to the instructional programs and the effectiveness of Learning Resources on these programs. Data of this type serve as the basis for important instructional decisions affecting the institution, faculty, students, and Learning Resources Program.

H. *Adequate management includes the preparation and dissemination of information to administration, faculty, and students concerning activities, services, and materials.*

The close interrelationship which exists with instructional departments on the campus demands that information about the Learning Resources Program be readily available. An annual report and other planned informational reports are essential for this purpose. Among other possible publications are bibliographies, acquisitions bulletins, current awareness lists, handbooks for faculty and students, releases to student and community publications through regular college channels, campus broadcasts, and utilization of other communications services which will reach students and faculty.

I. *Responsibilities for all learning resources and services should be assigned to a central administrative unit.*

Centralized administration is desirable in order to provide coordination of resources and services, to develop system approaches to needs, and to effectively utilize staff. Material and equipment, on the other hand, may be located in the areas where learning takes place. Inventory control of all materials and equipment should be the responsibility of the Learning Resources Program and its units. All such collections of materials should be considered the resources of the entire college and not limited in utilization to separate departments.

J. *Multicampus districts take advantage of the opportunity for close cooperation, exchange of resources, and shared technical processes while providing full resources and services for every campus.*

Each campus in a multicampus, two-year college district has its instructional and individual needs met on its campus. Learning Resources needed by off-campus programs are supplied by the campus sponsoring the program. There is no need, however, for duplication of routine technical processes and production facilities where these can be centralized more economically. Organizational structure within the district should facilitate cooperation and exchange of resources.

III. BUDGET

A. *Learning Resources Program budget is a function of program planning. It is designed to implement the realization of institutional and instructional program objectives.*

It is the responsibility of the chief administrator of the Learning Resources Program to see that each unit of a Learning Resources Program receives due attention in the budget and that the allocation of funds is based on appropriate data.

B. *Budget planning for the Learning Resources Program reflects the college-wide institutional and instructional needs, is initiated by the chief administrator, and is changed in consultation with him or her.*

Adequate budget, essential to provide good services, is based upon the needs and functions of the Learning Resources Programs in support of the institutional and instructional process.

C. *Separate categories are maintained in the budget for salaries, student wages, purchase and rental of all types of materials and equipment, production of instructional materials, supplies, external and internal direct costs (computer, fringe benefits, etc.), repairs, replacement and new equipment, travel of staff to professional meetings, and other related items.*

For management purposes, costs relating to the various types of materials and services are separately identifiable. Where specialized facilities and functions are a part of the Learning Resources Program, it is desirable that cost for these be identifiable as well.

D. *Financial records are maintained by, or are accessible to, the Learning Resources Units.*

Costs analyses and financial planning are dependent upon the adequacy of records, with sufficient additional information to enable comprehensive planning and effective utilization of all funds available. These records are not necessarily the same records as are needed in the business office.

E. *All expenditures, other than payroll, are initiated in the Learning Resources Units with payment made only on invoices verified for payment by the staff.*

Purchases are initiated by the staff through preparation of purchase order or requisition. Institutional business operations require approval of all invoices by the operating departments.

F. *To the legal extent possible and within the policies of the Board of Trustees, purchases of materials are exempted from restrictive annual bidding.*

Materials often are unique items obtainable from a single source. Equivalent prices and speedier, service often can be obtained by direct access to the publisher or manufacturer rather than through a single vendor. Satisfactory service requires prompt delivery so that the needs which determined their acquisition might be met; a larger discount might justifiably be rejected if it entails a delay in filling the order. Satisfactory service rendered by a vendor in the past may more than outweigh the confusion and interruption of service inherent in frequent changes of vendors through annual bidding requirements for learning materials.

G. *Purchase of materials is based on curricular requirements and other factors, and thus made throughout the year rather than annually or semiannually.*

Expenditures are based on need, availability and practical considerations such as processing time, rather than through fixed sequences which inhibit the functions of the unit.

H. *Learning Resources Program equipment is purchased through a systems approach.*

The purchase of any Learning Resources Program equipment, like all functions of the Learning Resources Program, should be carried out through a systems approach based on well-defined institutional and instructional objectives.

I. *Development of performance specifications for Learning Resources Program equipment to be purchased for implementation of instruction is based on valid criteria.*

Performance quality, effective design, ease of operation, cost, portability, cost of maintenance and repair, and available service are among the criteria which should be applied to equipment selection.

Most important, however, is how the item or items will fit into planning for maintenance and improvement of curriculum programming as set forth in continuous instructional design plans. Responsibility for evaluating, selecting and recommending purchase of equipment is that of the Learning Resources staff.

J. *Cooperative purchasing of materials, equipment, parts, and services should be effected where possible.*

In an effort to secure the best materials, equipment, parts, and services at the lowest cost, cooperative purchasing should be developed with other area institutions.

Editor's Note: The Guidelines will be concluded in the February issue of *C&RL News*. ■■

Guidelines for Two-Year College Learning Resources Programs (Revised)

PART TWO

Approved by the ACRL Board of Directors on June 30, 1981. These guidelines supersede and replace the previous guidelines which appeared in C&RL News, December 1972. (Part One of the guidelines appeared in C&RL News, January 1982, pp. 5–10).

Association of College and
Research Libraries
Association for Educational Communications
and Technology

IV. INSTRUCTIONAL SYSTEM COMPONENTS

A. *Staff*

1. *The chief administrator of the Learning Resources Program is selected on the basis of acquired competencies which relate to the purposes of the program, educational achievement, administrative ability, community and scholarly interests, professional activities, and service orientation.*

The chief administrator has a management responsibility and is concerned and involved in the entire educational program of the institution as well as with the operation of the Learning Resources Program. The chief administrator is professionally knowledgeable about all types of materials and services and is capable of management of instructional development functions. Because the ultimate success of a Learning Resources Program is to a large extent dependent upon the ability of the chief administrator to perform multiple duties effectively, a comprehensive recruitment and selection process is of paramount importance.

2. *The administrative (or supervisory) heads of the separate Learning Resources Units are selected on the basis of their expertise in and knowledge of the function and role of the particular Learning Resources Unit which they will manage and to which they will give leadership.*

3. *A well-qualified, experienced staff is available in sufficient numbers and areas of specialization to carry out adequately the purposes and objectives of the Learning Resources Program.*

Depending upon the size and programs of the institution, the hours operated, the physical facilities, and the scope and nature of the services performed, the number and specializations of professional and supportive staff will vary from one institution to another.

4. *All personnel are considered for employment following procedures as established by the institution.*

The effectiveness of a Learning Resources Program is determined by the performance of the staff. It is essential, therefore, that all personnel—professional and support staff—be recommended for employment to the chief administrator on the advice of the Learning Resources Unit head who will be involved in the supervision of the new staff member.

5. *Professional staff members should have degrees and/or experience appropriate to the position requirements.*

Professional training is appropriate to assignment in the Learning Resources Program. Additional graduate study or experience in a subject field should be recognized for all personnel as appropriate to such assignments.

Professional staff members are assigned duties. They are accountable for the operational effectiveness of the Learning Resources Program as designated by the chief administrator and heads of units. They may be supervisors as well as professional consultants to the faculty and advisors to students.

6. *Every professional staff member has faculty status, faculty benefits, and obligations.*

Professional staff benefits include such prerogatives as tenure rights, sick leave benefits, sabbatical leaves, vacation benefits, retirement and annuity benefits, provisions for professional development, and compensation at the same level which is in effect for teaching faculty or for those at comparable levels of administration. When Learning Resources personnel work on a regular twelve-month schedule, salary adjustments will be necessary to compensate for additional service days. Where academic ranks are recognized, such are assigned to the professional staff based on the same criteria as for other faculty, and are independent of internal assignments within the Learning Resources Program.

There is the obligation of faculty status to meet all faculty and professional requirements, advanced study, research, promotion, committee assignments, membership in professional organizations, sponsorships, publication in learned journals, etc., which the institution expects of faculty members. It is expected that professional staff will abide by the institutional policy/procedures or contractual arrangements which could include such items as staff evaluation, office hours, work assignments, and other defined working relationships.

7. *Professional development is the responsibility of both the institution and the professional staff member.*

Personal membership and participation in professional activities is expected of all staff members. Further graduate study should be encouraged and rewarded. The institution is expected to encourage and support professional development by providing among other benefits: consultants for staff development sessions; travel funds for regular attendance of some staff members and occasional attendance for every staff member at appropriate state or national meetings, workshops and seminars; and special arrangements for those staff members who serve as officers or committee members or participate on a state or national program.

8. *Teaching assignments by Learning Resources staff members are considered dual appointments in calculating staff work loads.*

When members of Learning Resources staff are assigned regular teaching responsibilities in training technicians or other classroom assignments, the hours scheduled in the Learning Resources Program are reduced by an equivalent time to allow preparation and classroom contact hours.

9. *Support staff members are responsible for assisting the professional staff in providing effective services.*

Responsibility for each level of support staff will be determined by the needs of the institution and the appropriate administrative structure. The number and kind of support staff needed will be determined by the size of the college and the services provided. The educational background and experience of such support staff should be appropriate to the tasks assigned.

In many instances, graduates of four-year degree programs and two-year technical programs will meet the training required; in other cases, one-year programs may be sufficient; or skills may have been learned through extensive work experience in a related position. The support staff may be supervisors as well as technical assistants or aides.

10. *Student assistants are employed to supplement the work of the supportive staff.*

Student assistants are important because of the variety of tasks they can perform effectively. They encourage other students to use the facilities and services, and they serve as significant means of recruitment for supportive and professional positions.

They do not, however, replace provision of

adequate full-time staff, nor can their work be matched on an hour-to-hour basis with that of regular full-time employment.

B. *Facilities*

1. *Planning of new or expanded facilities is accomplished with the participation and concurrence of the chief administrator in all details and with wide' involvement of users and staff.*

The chief administrator and staff work with the architect and the administration in every decision and have prime responsibility in the functional planning of the facility. Employment of a knowledgeable media specialist or library building consultant results in a more functional and useful building operation and should be given serious consideration. In the case of specialized facilities, special technical consultants may be required. As a result of poor design, functions of many buildings fail because those persons who will be working in or using the building have not been involved in planning. Staff, faculty, student representatives, and others who will utilize the facilities should be consulted.

2. *In the design of classrooms and other college facilities where Learning Resources are to be used, Learning Resources specialists should be consulted.*

The effective use of an instructional system is dependent upon the availability of a suitable environment for the use of specified Learning Resources. Frequently, architects and other college staff are not always aware of all of the technical requirements of such an environment.

3. *The physical facilities devoted to Learning Resources and Learning Resources Units are planned to provide appropriate space to meet institutional and instructional objectives and should be sufficient to accommodate the present operation as well as reflect long-range planning to provide for anticipated expansion, educational mission and program and technological change.*

The location and extent of space provided for development, acquisition, design, production, and use of learning resources is the responsibility of the chief administrator of Learning Resources, and should be designed to implement explicit, well-articulated program specifications developed by the Learning Resources and instructional staff of the college. Such a program should include flexible provisions for long-range development and phasing. The alteration, expansion, or consolidation of facilities also should be guided by carefully delineated program objectives which are known and understood by Learning Resources personnel, the instructional and administrative staff of the college, and the Board of Trustees. Factors to be considered when developing facilities requirements from the program specifications include projections of the student enrollment, the extent of community services, growth in the varieties of service, growth of materials collections, support of varying modes of instruction, staff needs, and the impact of curricular development and technological advances.

4. *Facilities of Learning Resources Units should be located conveniently for use by both students and instructional staff.*

Flexibility is essential to meet advances in technology and changes in instructional requirements. Service areas within the Learning Resources Unit are grouped to aid the user and to permit the staff to perform duties effectively and efficiently.

Learning Resources services for administration, acquisition, and cataloging should be centralized for more efficient operation. Planning should provide for convenient locations of facilities for storing and using equipment and materials close to the learning spaces or central to student traffic flow in which they are to be used. Where existing facilities will not permit this arrangement, an effort should be made to reduce confusion and frustration by making clear to the user the specific function of each facility.

The number of users varies in all units from peak periods when crowded conditions make service difficult to times when few students are present. Physical arrangements should make continued service with minimal staff possible during quiet times and at the same time provide for augmented service at other periods.

Services provided are dependent upon staff, whose efficiency is in turn dependent upon adequate office, workroom and storage space. The production facility should provide for consultation and demonstration space. It should be equipped to permit the demonstrating and previewing of all components of an instructional system. A staff conference room, apart from the administrative head's office, is desirable in all but the smallest institutions.

5. *The physical facilities provide a wide variety of learning and study situations.*

Students require various types of facilities for learning and study. Some require programmed learning equipment; others learn best by use of isolated individual study areas. In some circumstances they need to study together as a group or relax in comfortable lounge chairs. Proper arrangement and sufficient space for utilization of instructional equipment and materials should be provided for individualized instruction, browsing, and media production.

6. *The physical facilities are attractive, comfortable, and designed to encourage use by students.*

Attractive and well-planned areas encourage student utilization. Air conditioning and comfortable heating, proper lighting, acoustical treatment, regular custodial care, prompt maintenance of equipment, and regular and systematic repair of damages are necessary. Attention to the needs of the handicapped must be met in accordance with legal requirements.

7. *Space requirements, physical arrangements, and construction provide for full utilization of specialized equipment.*

Specialized facilities are necessary for certain types of equipment. For example, computer services, listening and viewing equipment, media production, and use of other types of electronic equipment require special consideration in terms of electrical connections, cables, conduits, lights, fire protection, security, and other factors which affect service.

C. *Instructional Equipment*

1. *Necessary instructional equipment is available at the proper time and place to meet institutional and instructional objectives.*

Centralized control of inventory and distribution of all equipment is necessary. A thorough and continual evaluation is desirable to ensure that enough of the appropriate equipment is available.

2. *Classroom and Learning Resources Program use of equipment is managed in the most effective manner to minimize operational mishaps and insure effective utilization.*

Assistance from Learning Resources staff is available as a regular service when needed and for the maintenance of equipment. Except for more complex equipment, the instructor and student should be responsible for the operation of the equipment.

3. *Learning Resources and instructional equipment are selected and purchased on the basis of specific criteria. (See Section III.)*

D. *Materials*

1. *Materials are selected, acquired, designed, or produced on the basis of institutional and instructional objectives, developed by the faculty, students, and administration in cooperation with Learning Resources.*

A written statement regarding acquisition and production of learning materials has such an important and pervasive effect upon the instructional program and the services of the Learning Resources Program that all segments of the academic community should be involved in its development. The statement should be readily available in an official publication.

Learning Resources Programs provide materials presenting all sides of controversial issues. The position of the American Library Association, and comparable associations, on the subject of censorship is firmly adhered to.

2. *Materials may be acquired and made available from a variety of sources.*

In an effort to meet the needs of the instructional process and cultural enrichment, it will be necessary to acquire materials through:

a. purchase of commercially available materials;
b. lease or rental of materials where purchase is neither possible or practical in terms of cost,

utilization, or type;

    c. loan through free loan agencies;

    d. acquisition of materials as gifts;

    e. design and production of materials not readily available.

    3. *Materials must be accessible to authorized individuals.*

Although there is no uniformly accepted system to make all resources available, the materials must be properly organized and the necessary staff, facilities, and hardware provided. Highly sophisticated systems for retrieving, manipulating and displaying information might be necessary.

    4. *Final management decision as to the order in which materials are to be purchased or produced is the responsibility of the chief administrator or delegated subordinate.*

Within the established framework of the written statement on acquisition and production, and the budgetary restraints, the final management decision and priority judgment must be the responsibility of the chief administrator and duly designated subordinates.

    5. *Representative works of high caliber which might arouse intellectual curiosity, counteract parochialism, help to develop critical thinking and cultural appreciation, or stimulate use of the resources for continuing education and personal development are included in the collection even though they do not presently meet direct curricular needs.*

One function of higher education is to develop adult citizens intellectually capable of taking their places in a changing society. Provision of materials beyond curricular needs is essential for this goal.

    6. *Materials reflect ages, cultural backgrounds, intellectual levels, developmental needs, and career goals represented in the student body.*

Two-year college students represent all strata of community and national life. To meet their needs, the collection must contain materials of all kinds and at all levels. Those students who require basic remedial materials, those who seek vocational and technical training or retraining, those who seek an understanding of their culture, and those who are utilizing their retirement years for personal stimulation should each find the materials which can serve their interests and solve their problems. Special care is taken to include representative materials related to the needs of minorities as well as materials reflecting divergent social, religious, or political viewpoints.

    7. *A broad policy is developed concerning gifts to a Learning Resources Program.*

Generally, gifts are accepted only when they add strength to the collection and impose no significant limitations on housing, handling, or disposition of duplicate, damaged, or undesirable items. It is recognized that gifts frequently require more time to screen, organize, catalog, and process than new materials. Storage space and staff time requirements must be considered in accepting gift materials. In acknowledgment of gifts, attention should be called to government recognition of such contributions for tax purposes, as well as to the impropriety of any appraisal by the recipient of a donation.

    8. *In local reproduction of materials for instructional use, care is taken to comply with copyright regulations.*

Laws restrict the copying of many items without permission. Procedures and guidelines must be established regarding reproduction of copyrighted materials and made easily accessible.

    9. *The reference collection includes a wide selection of significant subject and general bibliographies, authoritative lists, periodical indexes, and standard reference works in all fields of knowledge.*

Every two-year college requires extensive bibliographical materials for use in locating and verifying items for purchase, rental, or borrowing, for providing for subject needs of users, and for evaluating the collection.

    10. *Newspapers with various geographical, political, and social points of view on national and state issues are represented in the collection.*

Newspapers should reflect community, national, and worldwide points of view. Back files of several newspapers are retained in print or microform.

    11. *Government documents are required as significant sources of information.*

Some two-year colleges which are document depositories receive government publications as a matter of course. All Learning Resources Programs should acquire regularly such publications.

    12. *Files of pamphlets and other ephemeral materials are maintained.*

An effective and up-to-date pamphlet file is a strong resource in any college. Included are vocational and ephemeral materials developed through systematic acquisition of new materials, including subscriptions to pamphlet services and requests for free materials. References in the catalog to subjects contained in pamphlet files are desirable in providing the fullest access to the materials. Periodic weeding of the collection is essential.

Manufacturers' and publishers' catalogs and brochures which describe new materials and equipment are needed to supplement published lists and to provide up-to-date information.

    13. *A collection of recorded and other materials should be available for individual use as well as for meeting instructional needs.*

    14. *Policy or procedures for the conservation of materials, deletion, and weeding the collection of obsolete materials should be developed as part of an ongoing procedure.*

The materials in the collection should be examined regularly to eliminate obsolete items, unnecessary duplicates, and worn-out materials. Procedures regarding deletion need to be explicit for weeding and disposing of such materials. Prompt attention must be given to damaged materials so that repairs and replacement (including rebinding of printed materials or replacement of portions of projected or recorded materials) are handled systematically, along with prompt action to replace important items, including those discovered to be missing.

15. *The Learning Resources Unit functions as an archive for historical information and documents concerning the college itself.*

An effort should be made to locate, organize, and house institutional archives to the extent defined by the administration.

V. SERVICES

A. *Users of Learning Resources have the right to expect:*

1. That facilities, materials, and services are available and accessible to meet demonstrated instructional needs for their use regardless of location;
2. That an atmosphere be provided which allows sensitive and responsive attention to their requirements;
3. That professional staff be readily available for interpretation of materials and services and for consultation on instructional development;
4. That physical facilities be properly maintained to make use comfortable and orderly;
5. That requests for scheduling, circulation, distribution, and utilization of materials and related equipment be handled expeditiously;
6. That acquisition, production, and organization of materials meet educational, cultural, and personal needs.

7. If an institution is conducting classes in off-campus locations, careful planning and funding must be provided to ensure that equal services are available to those programs.

VI. INTERAGENCY COOPERATIVE ACTIVITIES

A. *Cooperative arrangements for sharing of resources are developed with other institutions and agencies in the community, region, state, and nation.*

To provide the best possible service to the students and faculty in the two-year college, close relationships with other local institutions and agencies and with institutions of higher education in the area are essential. Through consortia, media cooperatives, and loan arrangements, institutions can share resources. The college may need to make arrangements so that its students may use the area facilities and resources. When an undue burden is placed on a neighboring institution, financial subsidy may be appropriate.

B. *The institution is willing to consider participation in cooperative projects, such as shared cataloging, computer use, and other services which may be mutually beneficial to all participants.*

By cooperative planning much expense and wasteful duplication can be avoided in the community and region. Learning Resources personnel and institutional administrators need to be alert to cooperative activities of all kinds and to be willing to explore the possibilities of participation for their own institution.

C. *Responsibility for the collection and preservation of community history and for the accumulation of other local and statistical data is shared with other institutions and is coordinated with them.* ■■

Statement on
Quantitative Standards for
Two-Year Learning Resources Programs

FOREWORD

The following statement on quantitative standards for two-year college learning resources programs has been prepared by the Ad Hoc Sub-committee to Develop Quantitative Standards for the "Guidelines for Two-Year College Learning Resources Programs." The statement is a draft copy presented for reaction and comment. At the ALA Dallas Conference in June 1979, the Community and Junior College Libraries Section will hold a hearing on the draft statement. In the meantime, comments may be sent to James O. Wallace, Director of Learning Resources, San Antonio College, 1001 Howard Street, San Antonio, TX 78284; (512) 734–7311, ext. 257.

INTRODUCTION

When the "Guidelines for Two-Year College Learning Resources Programs"* was completed in 1972, it was planned that a supplementary statement of quantitative standards should be developed. This document is the intended supplement, designed to meet the recurring requests for suggested quantitative figures for help in planning and evaluating programs. No absolutes are presented here; too many variables must be considered for this to be possible. In addition, although extensive use has been made of existing statistics when these were appropriate,† no conclusive research provides quantitative measurements of some factors. In such cases the professional judgment and extensive experience of the members of the committee have been the basis for the recommendations.

*American Association of Community and Junior Colleges—Association for Educational Communications and Technology—American Library Association, "Guidelines for Two-Year College Learning Resources Programs," *Audiovisual Instruction*, XVIII, p.50–61 (Jan. 1973); *College & Research Libraries News*, XXXIII, p.305–15 (Dec. 1972).

†For example, extensive computer analysis was made of the 1975 HEGIS statistics, which had the only comprehensive coverage of audiovisual holdings. These statistics were analyzed by FTE, by types of materials, and by other factors. The quartiles developed have been used extensively by the committee. Stanley V. Smith, *Library Statistics of Colleges and Universities: Fall 1975 Institutional Data* (U.S. Dept. of Health, Education and Welfare, National Center for Education Statistics, 1977).

Adherence to every single element in the Learning Resources Program (as defined in the "Guidelines") is not considered essential in this document. For example, collection size is viewed as relating not to book holdings alone or to audiovisual holdings alone but rather to total bibliographical unit equivalents (as defined in section on collections).

The significant variable accepted for most elements is enrollment expressed as full-time equivalent (FTE) students. The tables reflect from under 1,000 FTE to the largest enrollments for a single Learning Resources Program. Should the total enrollment be more than twice the FTE, collection, staff, and space requirements will exceed the quantities in the tables. Levels of attainment of Learning Resources Programs will vary. Two levels are addressed in this document in each enrollment bracket: "minimal" (indicated in the tables by M) and "good" (indicated by the M by G). A program consistently below the M level for its size is probably not able to provide services needed. A program consistently above the upper, or G level, will usually be found to have the capability of providing outstanding services.

It cannot be expected that these quantitative standards will remain constant. To reflect changes in two-year colleges, results of additional research, new technological and professional developments, experience in the use of this statement, and changes in the economic and educational conditions in the nation, it is recommended that a review committee be appointed three years from the date of initial adoption and at three-year intervals thereafter.

STAFF

Staff components are defined in the "Guidelines." The positions in table 1, which include the director, are full-time equivalents for staff working thirty-five to forty hours a week for twelve months a year, including vacations and holidays, in a Learning Resources Unit in which most processing occurs on campus. Staff in a central unit, such as a processing center for a multicampus district, should be in proportion to the services rendered each campus.

Staffing of branches, extension centers, commercial level production facilities, computer operations, printing services, extensive learning or developmental laboratories, bookstore operations, or on-the-air broadcasting are not included in the table. Most institutions will need to modify the

TABLE 1

STAFF

Full-Time Equivalent Enrollment	Level	Profes-sional	Support
Under 1,000	M	2	4
	G	4	6
1,000–3,000	M	2.5	5
	G	4	10
3,000–5,000	M	3.5	9
	G	6	18
5,000–7,000	M	6	15
	G	8	24
Additional for each 1,000 FTE over 7,000	M	.5	1
	G	1	3

staffing pattern to include such factors as longer or shorter workweeks and annual contracts.

BUDGET

Budget formulas in a true sense are not possible in two-year colleges because of wide variances in practice from institution to institution. For example, film rentals may be charged to departmental budgets, and staff fringe benefits may or may not be included in the budget for Learning Resources Programs. In addition to these, various other services, such as learning or developmental laboratories, which are definitely part of such programs, will not always be so charged in the institutional budgets.

The formulas are further complicated where there are centralized services, satellite operations, and continuing education responsibilities, so that an absolute formula is not possible without examining all elements of staff, materials, services, and the delineations listed in IIIC of the "Guidelines" at each campus.

Experience indicates, however, that a fully developed Learning Resources Program will usually require from 7 to 12 percent of the educational and general budget of the institution, whether these are separately identified as learning resources or diffused in a multiple number of accounts.

COLLECTION SIZE

Size of the collection available on any two-year college campus is best expressed as "bibliographical unit equivalents." Where a multicampus district maintains some materials centrally, these holdings should be distributed for statistical purposes proportional to use by the various campuses.

Bibliographical unit equivalents (BUE) consist of written, recorded, or other materials. Each item in the following three groups is one BUE.

Written Materials

1. One cataloged bound volume.
2. One periodical volume.

3. One cataloged document.
4. One reel of microfilm.
5. One cataloged microfiche.
6. Five uncataloged microfiche.
7. Five microcards.
8. One cataloged musical work.
9. One periodical currently received.

Recorded Materials

10. One videocassette or videotape reel.
11. One reel of 16mm motion picture film.
12. One cataloged 8mm loop film.
13. One cataloged 35mm slide program.
14. One cataloged set of transparencies.
15. One cataloged slide set.
16. Fifty cataloged 2 x 2 slides, not in sets.
17. One cataloged sound recording (disc, reel, or cassette).
18. Five films rented or borrowed during an academic year.

Other Materials

19. One cataloged map, chart, art print, or photograph.
20. One cataloged kit.
21. One cataloged item of realia, model, or art object.
22. Any other comparable cataloged item(s).

Table 2 shows the total number of BUEs used to measure the collection. Normally, written materials should constitute at least 70 percent of the BUEs. All other proportions of the totals may be adapted to the Learning Resources Program of the institution. Flexibility in determining the informational needs of the program then makes it possible to choose to purchase either a book or an audiovisual item, a periodical subscription, or any other materials. No two-year college should be without some BUEs in each of the five categories used in table 2. Technical institutes with extremely specialized programs may reduce the total BUE requirements as much as 40 percent.

ANNUAL ACCESSIONS

If the materials are to meet the instructional needs of the institution served, continued acquisitions accompanied by continued weeding are needed even where holdings exceed recommendations. New materials are needed for presentation of new information and new interpretations or the collection becomes dated and decreases in educational value. New courses added to the curriculum and new instructional programs require new materials to meet classroom and individual needs of students. As enrollment increases there is need for more duplication and for broader approaches to topics already represented in the collection.

Five percent of the collection size should be the minimum annual acquisition for each Learning Resources Program. This percentage does not include replacements of lost or stolen items or materials to support new courses or curricula, which should be additional.

TABLE 2
COLLECTION SIZE

FTE Enrollment	Level	Written Materials Periodical Subscriptions	Written Materials Other Written Materials	Recorded Materials Motion Pictures & Videotapes	Recorded Materials Other Recorded Materials	Other Materials	Collection Size Totals
Under	M	200	20,000	15	350	50	20,615
1,000	G	300	30,000	125	1,350	350	32,125
1,000–	M	300	30,000	125	1,350	350	32,125
3,000	G	500	50,000	350	3,200	1,200	55,250
3,000–	M	500	50,000	350	3,200	1,200	55,250
5,000	G	700	70,000	700	5,350	2,350	79,100
5,000–	M	700	70,000	700	5,350	2,350	79,100
7,000	G	800	85,000	1,250	8,500	4,500	100,100
Additional	M	5	6,000	13	10	5	6,133
each 1,000 FTE over 7,000	G	30	12,000	150	405	305	12,890

TABLE 3
SPACE REQUIREMENTS

Full-Time Enrollment	Print Materials and Services Minimum	Print Materials and Services Maximum	Audiovisual Materials and Services Minimum	Audiovisual Materials and Services Maximum	Related Instructional Services	Total Assignable Square Feet
1,667	7,500	9,250	5,000	6,750	750	15,000
2,500	9,503	13,055	5,000	8,552	950	19,005
5,000	15,495	21,693	7,748	13,946	1,550	30,990
8,333	23,000	32,200	11,500	20,700	2,300	46,000
10,834	28,503	39,904	14,251	25,652	2,850	57,005
14,167	35,488	49,683	17,744	31,939	3,549	70,975
16,667	40,650	56,910	20,325	36,585	4,065	81,000

SPACE REQUIREMENTS

Space standards for two-year colleges have already been developed by the Learning Resources Associaton of California Community Colleges and should be utilized for permanent facilities to be in use for ten or more years. Their *Facilities Guidelines*,‡ if adjusted to FTE by use of the formula provided, will serve as a satisfactory standard.

Table 3 has been adapted from the *Facilities Guidelines* using absolute FTE to allow easy comparison when that publicaton is not available. The premises upon which the original was based deserve more attention than is possible in these standards.

To be added to the total square feet in table 3 is any additional space needed for related instructional services for individualized instruction, such as learning laboratories, study skills center, language laboratories, etc. Also to be added are internal offices, office service areas (file rooms,

‡Learning Resources Association of the California Community Colleges, *Facilities Guidelines for Learning Resources Centers: Print, Non-print, Related Instructional Services* (P.O. Box 246, Suisun City, CA 94585, 1978), $25.

vaults, duplicating rooms, internal corridors, office supply rooms, etc.), office-related conference rooms and conference room services (kitchenettes, sound equipment storage, etc.), internal classrooms and laboratories, and nonassignable space (janitor's closets, stairways, public corridors, elevators, toilets, and building utility and operational facilities).

EQUIPMENT FOR DISTRIBUTION

There is need for sufficient equipment for distribution to classrooms beyond equipment necessary for individual utilization of audiovisuals in the learning centers. Recommendations are limited to major types of equipment. Opaque projectors should be available even in minimal programs; quantity will depend upon utilization. Overhead projectors should be available in all classrooms. Recommendations in table 4 are for classroom equipment distribution only and assume a replacement schedule not longer than five years.

Quantitative formulas for some equipment are inherent in use. In a laboratory situation, type and quantity of equipment will depend upon what the course or program is. Permanent sound and projection equipment will be installed in large lecture halls. All classrooms will have per-

TABLE 4

EQUIPMENT FOR DISTRIBUTION

Uses per Year	16mm Projector	Super 8mm Projector	Video-cassette Player	Slide Projector	Audio-cassette Player	Record Player
1–100	2–9	2–9	2–9	2–24	2–49	2–9
101–1,000	10–24	10–24	10–24	25–49	50–99	10–24
1,001–3,000	25–44	15–19	25–32	50–64	100–174	25–35
3,001–5,000	45–49	20–24	33–49	65–99	175–249	36–49
5,000+	50+	25+	50+	100+	250+	50+

manently installed projection screens and room-darkening drapes or shades and will have connections and outlets for closed-circuit television where it exists.

In determining the number of pieces of equipment, a reasonable distribution of demand is assumed, i.e., that all use will not be concentrated on a peak period of either the days or the academic year. Random access or broadcast delivery systems will also affect the needs for equipment.

PRODUCTION

All Learning Resources Programs should provide some production capability according to the needs and requirements of the curricula, the availability of commercial materials, and the capability of the delivery system. Production, except where part of an instructional program or meeting a specific institutional need, is not an end in itself. Neither is it related to institutional size.

Basic production capability for all campuses consists of minimal equipment items for:

Still photography (1 35mm camera and arrangements for developing film elsewhere).

Ability to make and duplicate sound recordings.

Sign production.

Graphics layout and lettering.

Laminating and dry-mounting.

Ability to make overhead transparencies.

Simple illustrations.

Videoplaying and duplication.

One camera videotaping and videodubbing.

Intermediate production capability consists of all elements above and in addition equipment items for:

Photographic black-and-white printing and processing.

Ability to edit sound recordings.

Two-camera video production.

Advanced production when justified consists of all above and in addition equipment items for:

Simple studio videoproduction in color.

Simple studio for sound recording and editing.

Optional production (justifiable only when needed for programs for cooperative distribution

or highly sophisticated institutional needs) in addition consists of:

Color television directing, production, and editing.

16mm motion picture directing, production, and editing.

Color photographic developing and processing.

USER SERVICES

The most important aspect to measure in standards for Learning Resources Programs may well be the services to the user. No data now exist on which to base standards of use except for a few isolated elements. In lieu of such standards a checklist (which attempts to identify those elements for which user statistics might be collected) has been developed, including some of those elements already recognized as significant. Others, which have not been collected, are suggested along with these for institutional use and experimentation in the Appendix.

APPENDIX
CHECKLIST OF USER SERVICES
STATISTICS TO BE COLLECTED

A. Circulation to students for out-of-building personal use (number of items)

B. Circulation to faculty for personal use (number of items)

C. Interlibrary loans (i.e., through mail or delivery systems)
 1. Requests to borrow (number of items).
 2. Items received (number of items).
 3. Photocopies received (number of items).
 4. Requests to loan (number of items).
 5. Loans made (number of items).
 6. Photocopies sent (number of items).

D. Use of materials in-house
 1. Periodicals (number of volumes or issues).
 2. Other printed materials (number of items used by count of materials on tables, reserve use, etc.).
 3. Microforms (number of items).
 4. Audiovisuals (number of items by type).

E. Group use in-house
 1. Audiovisuals seen or heard (number of students served).

2. Audiovisuals used in learning laboratories (number of students served).

F. Direct instruction
   1. Directed learning sessions (number of students served).
   2. Instructional sessions (number of students served).
   3. Classroom instruction for other faculty (number of students served).
   4. Taped individual programs used (number of students served).
   5. Workshops and seminars conducted (number of students served).

G. Community service
   1. Direct loans to nonstudents (number of items).
   2. Direct loans to students and faculty of other institutions (number of items).
   3. Tour groups of campus visitors (number of individuals served).
   4. Groups attending meetings in facilities (number of individuals served).
   5. Telephone reference questions (number of requests received).
   6. Research projects assisted (number of projects).

H. Reference services to students, faculty, and staff
   1. Directional reference questions (number of questions).
   2. Brief ready reference (number of questions).
   3. Extensive assistance (by number of questions and item descriptions).
   4. Assistance to physically handicapped (number assisted).
   5. Referrals to outside agencies (by number).
   6. Reference questions not answered (by number and item descriptions).

I. Bibliographical services
   1. Telephone verification of ownership (number of items).
   2. On-line reference services utilized (number of queries handled).
   3. Preparation of brief (i.e., less than ten items) bibliographies (number of bibliographies).
   4. Preparation of longer bibliographies (number of bibliographies and descriptions).

J. Consultative services
   1. Informational and current awareness services (number of contacts).
   2. Individual assistance to faculty for instructional problems (number of contacts).
   3. Team involvement in instructional projects (number of projects).
   4. New faculty orientation (number of faculty served).

K. Distribution and delivery services
   1. Short-time (less than one week) use of equipment (number of items).
   2. Long-time use of equipment (number of items).
   3. Off-campus use of equipment (number of items).

L. Classroom and other group use of materials
   1. Short-term (less than one week) use (number of items).
   2. Long-term use (number of items by type).
   3. Off-campus use (number of items by type).

M. Viewing audience
   1. Classroom (number of students viewing or listening to materials).
   2. Special events (number of individuals viewing or listening to materials).
   3. Off-campus audience (number of individuals viewing or listening).

N. Television closed-circuit use
   1. Programs owned locally (number of showings).
   2. Programs rented or borrowed (number of showings).
   3. Viewing audience (number of individuals).

O. Production
   1. Recording and duplication (number of items and number of staff hours).
   2. Videotape recording and duplication (number of items and number of staff hours).
   3. Graphics production (number of items and number of staff hours).
   4. Transparency production (number of items and number of staff hours).
   5. Slide production (number of items and number of staff hours).
   6. Other photography (number of items and number of staff hours).
   7. Dry-mounting and laminating (number of items and number of staff hours).
   8. Duplicating/copying services (number of items and number of staff hours).

P. Maintenance
   1. Bench repair of equipment (number of items and number of staff hours).
   2. On-site repair of equipment (number of items and number of staff hours).
   3. Contractual maintenance (number of items repaired).

Q. Projectionist services
   1. Classroom projection (number of occasions).
   2. Recreational and community projection (number of occasions).
   3. Other projection (number of occasions).

R. Display and public relations
   1. Bulletin board displays (number prepared).
   2. Exhibits provided (number prepared).
   3. Informational publications (number prepared). ▪▪

Index